Day Hikes
from
Oregon
Campgrounds

Rhonda and George
Ostertag

The Mountaineers/Seattle

THE MOUNTAINEERS: Organized in 1906"...to explore, study, preserve and enjoy the natural beauty of the Northwest."

4 3 2 1
5 4 3 2 1

Published by The Mountaineers
1011 SW Klickitat Way, Seattle, Washington 98134

Published simultaneously in Canada by Douglas & McIntyre, Ltd., 1615 Venables Street, Vancouver, B.C. V5L 2H1

Published simultaneously in Great Britain by Cordee, 3a DeMontfort Street, Leicester, England, LE1 7HD

Manufactured in the United States of America

Edited by Bob Wanetick
Maps by George Ostertag
Cover photographs: *left panel*, Confluence of the Imnaha and Snake Wild and Scenic Rivers, from the Imnaha River Trail, Hells Canyon National Recreation Area; *right panel*, Ancient Douglas fir forest along the Riverside National Recreation Trail, Clackamas Wild and Scenic River corridor, Mount Hood National Forest; *inset*, The breakfast ritual starts the day at this Cascade Mountain campsite. *Title page*, Pacific tree frog in shore pine, Oregon Dunes National Recreation Area.
All photographs by George Ostertag
Cover design by Elizabeth Watson. Book design and layout by Barbara Bash

Library of Congress Cataloging-in-Publication Data

Ostertag, Rhonda, 1957-
    Day hikes from Oregon campgrounds / Rhonda and George Ostertag.
        p.   cm.
    Includes index.
    ISBN 0-89886-310-4
    1. Hiking—Oregon—Guide-books.   2. Camp sites, facilities, etc.–
–Oregon—Directories.   3. Oregon—Description and travel—1981- -
–Guide-books.   I. Ostertag, George, 1957- . II. Title.
GV199.42.07085   1991
917.95—dc20   91-22622
                                                           CIP

CONTENTS

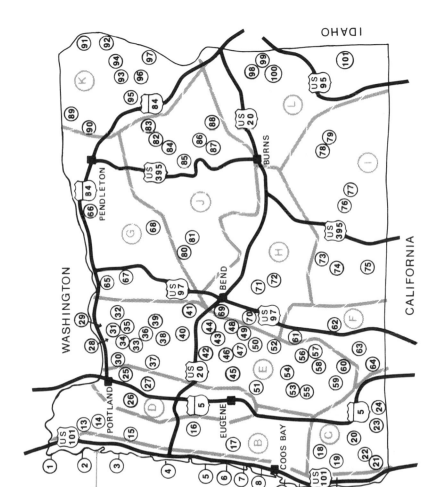

LEGEND

A. Coast
B. Coast Range
C. Siskiyous
D. Willamette Valley
E. Cascade Mountains
F. Klamath Basin
G. Deschutes–Umatilla
   Plateau
H. High Lava Plains
I. Basin and Range
J. Blue Mountains
K. Wallowas and
   Northeast Mountains
L. Southeast Canyonlands

A Note About Safety

Safety is an important concern in all outdoor activities. No guidebook can alert you to every hazard or anticipate the limitations of every reader. Therefore, the descriptions of roads, trails, routes, and natural features in this book are not representations that a particular place or excursion will be safe for your party. When you follow any of the routes described in this book, you assume responsibility for your own safety. Under normal conditions, such excursions require the usual attention to traffic, road and trail conditions, weather, terrain, the capabilities of your party, and other factors. Keeping informed on current conditions and exercising common sense are the keys to a safe, enjoyable outing.

The Mountaineers

PREFACE

As we traced the tangled web of trails and roads across the face of the state, we learned that Oregon has a lot for which it can be proud. For many of the areas, this was our first peek in the door, and what we found delighted us. This large western state holds a variety of textures, moods, and outdoor experiences, with ample space for solitude, recreation, and discovering nature's handiwork. While our time was limited, the sampling guarantees our return again and again.

But there were some disturbing discoveries as well. Meeting the formula of the book—pairing campgrounds with nearby outdoor attractions, a seemingly simple task—often proved a trial. In some areas, we discovered great expanses of public land with virtually no recreation. In others, recreational opportunities were little publicized or difficult to access, and in still others, former campgrounds and trails had been abandoned.

We appreciate the work of individuals (both private citizens and agency personnel) who carried the banner for recreation and the protection of natural resources in the past. Now, our own ranks must rise to the challenge to ensure that the state's natural and recreational treasures prosper for generations to come. The need is great for cooperation and support among recreationists and managing agencies.

While lobbying for adequate budgets to maintain, improve, and add to our recreational facilities is important, greater volunteerism is needed. It's a system that works, and in our travels, we've benefited from its effectiveness. A hike down Round Mountain Trail, in Central Oregon, after the local riding club had cleared it of winter downfalls brought relief to one author's knees. The twice-yearly volunteer beach cleanup has made tidepool viewing more productive and barefoot strolling once again a carefree enjoyment. Boy Scout–built footbridges over swollen creeks have allowed the toes to stay snug in the boot.

Volunteer-constructed trails have opened up new avenues of discovery. The all-ability trail at Susan Creek Campground offers North Umpqua River overlooks to individuals otherwise denied, and the Little North Fork Santiam Trail brings an additional 4.5 miles to the Oregon trail system that otherwise might have been long delayed or might not have been built at all.

Today, more than ever, with restricted budgets and the cry for "no new taxes," all of us, as users, must give support to the land and recreation system—whether it be through writing letters, repairing a collapsed cairn along a trail, adopting a trail, or leaving a camp a little cleaner than it was found. After all, it's a small investment for the return of the great outdoors.

We would like to acknowledge the many people who helped bring this book to its conclusion: the staff at The Mountaineers Books, the personnel at the managing agencies who fielded our many inquiries and checked our drafts for accuracy, and the people we met along the way who shared their favorite haunts and experiences, patched a tire at quitting time, or suffered our requests for photos. Our thanks.

Rhonda and George Ostertag

INTRODUCTION

Oregon abounds with natural splendor and diversity. From west to east, the state exhibits rocky headlands and sandy strands; coastal temperate rain forests; valley grasslands and foothills; snowcapped volcanoes; plateaus, lava lands, and desert plains; and the split-character eastern section, with Oregon's "Little Switzerland," the Wallowas, in the north and a canyon country emulating Utah in the south.

Rivers—natural routes and playgrounds—thread the state. To date, Oregon has more miles of protected waterway than any state outside Alaska, and it boasts a bonanza of major waterfalls. What's more, Oregon has some fine campgrounds from which to explore this amazing abundance.

This campground getaway guide is not intended to be a full treatise on Oregon's natural legacy or a complete coverage of all of Oregon's camping opportunities. Instead, it should serve as an adequate sampling to whet an interest for discovery.

Assembled within these pages is information for the camping enthusiast and outdoor generalist. The focus is on family outings, with both new haunts and time-proven favorites featured.

The book is not a how-to guide but rather a what-to and where-to guide, with suggestions for camping, hiking, beachcombing, caving, nature study, photography, berry picking, and sightseeing. Short hikes radiating from camp provide intimate looks at each area. Drives and special-interest attractions complete the story. ■

Oregon grape, Tillamook State Forest

USE OF THE BOOK

This book is designed as a trip-planning tool, whether for plotting a weekend outing or planning an "explore Oregon" vacation. It also may be used as a glove-compartment companion, highlighting area side trips and attractions for the traveler.

Maps. Twelve geographical regions defined by terrain and natural history give structure to the book (see the introductory map, page 5). Numbers identify campgrounds within those regions. The introductory map and the

Camping at the Elkhorn Valley Recreation Site

individual campground-area maps are intended for use in conjunction with state, United States Forest Service (USFS), Bureau of Land Management (BLM), and other recreational maps to speed the traveler to the destination and to pinpoint area highlights. They are not intended to replace the more detailed maps.

Campgrounds. The majority of the campgrounds were selected because they offered the most comfortable, convenient, and scenic bases from which to get to know an area. Where clusters of campgrounds serve the same area, we feature what we considered the best base, referencing the other facilities as alternative or back-up sites.

Campground information includes a "services at a glance" section, access information, and a description. We classify campgrounds as "full service" (a service mix that may include restrooms, showers, hookups, dump stations, and garbage dumpsters), "standard service" (tables, grills, some form of bathroom facility, and often water), and "primitive" (minimal or no facilities). Our labels may differ from those given to facilities by the managing agencies, as we evaluated the services relative to the other campgrounds represented in the book. We avoided listing primitive campgrounds unless an area holds exceptional merit and the campground is the sole accommodation.

Campsites are available on a first-come–first-served basis, unless otherwise noted. "Water" indicates that a campground has a formal potable source. The indicated season represents a typical schedule for opening, which may vary because of budget cuts, weather, or other reasons. For early- or late-season visits, campers may wish to call ahead to confirm that a facility is open.

Fees, too, are changeable. We've noticed a trend in the eastern part of the state for the elimination of fees and the dropping of maintenance services or the frequency of those services. When visiting new sites, make a practice of carrying water, bathroom tissue, and other necessities.

Activities. Each campground section includes suggestions for walks, short hikes, or vista routes that explore the campground neighborhood. Each activity listing carries a summary information table (including distance, difficulty, and special conditions) for evaluating the trip as well as access information and a description of what you'll find. Generally, the selected activities address users with beginning to moderate skills and abilities.

The hikes feature nature walks and trails with a round-trip distance of 6.0 miles or less. Included trails of greater length possess one or more of the following qualities: exceptional merit, easy walking, or interesting attractions along the early miles of the trail. Informal trails are clearly specified.

Hikes and trail lengths should be personalized for individual interest and physical ability. Because a trail continues does not mean the hiker must. Much of the enjoyment comes in passing along the way.

We avoided estimates of hiking times. As Harvey Manning stated in *Backpacking, One Step at at Time,* "How fast a hiker *can* go is one thing; how fast he *wants* to go is another." Personal health and physical condition, party size, the attraction of special features along the way, and weather and trail conditions all influence hiking time.

Access. The campsites, trailheads, and sights named in this book are almost all accessible with conventional vehicles via either paved or good, improved-surface roads. Exceptions are clearly noted. Routes that have long stretches of gravel or dirt surface are specified. Most activities are reachable within a 30-minute drive from campgrounds.

OUTDOOR PRIMER

Using the outdoors and campground and trail facilities responsibly is the best way to protect and preserve the privilege of a quality outdoor experience. The following "basics" are cornerstones to responsible outdoor behavior and participation:

Ten Essentials. The following ten items have been judged by outdoor experts to be critical to the safe outdoor experience: extra clothing, extra food, sunglasses, a knife, fire. starter, a first-aid kit, matches (in a waterproof container), a flashlight (with extra bulb and batteries), the appropriate maps for the trip, and a compass (with the knowledge of its use and the proper declination). Armed with these items, the outdoor user will be able to meet and survive most unforeseen events that may occur in the back country.

Notification Safeguard. As being stranded or injured in the wild poses greater problems than similar situations at home, prior to leaving on any outdoor adventure, you should notify a responsible party of your intended destination and time of return. Contact that individual upon your return to complete this safety procedure.

Water. Drinking water taken from lakes and streams should be treated. Even clear, pulsing streams in remote reaches may contain *Giardia*, a bacteria that causes stomach and intestinal discomfort. Boiling the water for 10 minutes remains the best protection. Water-purification systems that remove both debris and harmful organisms offer a satisfactory alternative to boiling.

Hypothermia. The best protection against hypothermia, the dramatic cooling of the body that occurs when heat loss surpasses body-heat generation, is heeding the "ten essentials," along with dressing or packing for the unpredictability of weather. If a party member appears sluggish, incoherent, or clumsy, immediately get the individual warm and dry. Drinking hot beverages helps restore body heat.

Heat Exhaustion. Guards against overtaxing the body's cooling system include wearing a hat, drinking plenty of water, eating properly (including salty snacks), and avoiding fatigue.

Poison Oak and Ivy. To avoid the evils of these plants, learn what they look like and in what environments they grow. Scientists are working toward creating creams or vaccines that will inhibit the plants' poison. Meanwhile, should these plants come in contact with the skin, rinse the skin in cold water, avoid heat, and do not cover or scratch the skin.

Stings and Bites. The best protection against stings and bites is, again, knowledge. It's important to become aware of any personal allergies and sensitivities and to become knowledgeable about the habits and habitats of snakes, bees, ticks, and other "menaces" of the wild and how to deal with the injuries they cause. After removal of a tick, watch for signs of redness and swelling, which could be an early indication of Lyme disease. Consult a physician whenever any wound shows sign of infection.

Sanitation Procedures. In washing yourself or utensils, use small amounts of biodegradable soap, well away from lakes and waterways, preferably in a rocky area removed from vegetation. In campgrounds, dispose of waste water in the provided sites. When bathroom facilities are inaccessible, human waste should be buried 6 to 8 inches deep, 300 feet away from any watercourse and well removed from any trails. Garbage generated while hiking along the trail should be packed out. This includes all cores, peelings, peanut shells, disposable diapers, cigarette butts, wrappers, and cans. Burying or drowning litter is not a suitable alternative.

Wilderness Courtesy. Guests in the wild should minimize the signs of their having passed by staying on trails, keeping campsites in their natural state, preserving nature's silence, and leaving the area cleaner than it was found.

Camping. Pitch camps in established sites to minimize harm to the natural setting. Any new sites should be well removed from trails and water and should leave no clue to their presence when camp is broken. Food should be stored in closed containers when not in use. Fires should be kept small and contained in a barbecue, grill, or fire pit. Outdoor stoves are a responsible substitute for open fires in informal camps. Wood collection, where permitted, should be limited to downed wood; never cut snags or live trees. Unless garbage containers are provided, the rule for litter is pack it in, pack it out.

Trailhead Safety. Unattended vehicles are vulnerable to "car-clouting" thieves. To smooth the way to a carefree outing, park away from designated trailheads when possible, and take all valuables with you. Be sure that items left behind advertise that they have no value, be suspicious of loiterers, and be cautious of revealing the details of your outing to strangers.

Hiking. Good boots protect feet and ankles, reducing the likelihood of an injury from an ill-planted foot or a stubbed toe. Being familiar with maps and compass use will enhance a trip and promote safety. Off-trail excursions introduce additional risks. Cross-country hiking requires good physical health and sound wilderness and map-reading skills. Eating properly, drinking plenty of water, and avoiding fatigue all guard against injury.

Cliffs above Wildcat Basin

Beachcombing. Familiarize yourself with the rules for tidepooling and collecting along the beach; rules vary among areas. Before taking a long hike, study the tide tables to learn the times of high and low tides and avoid the danger of becoming stranded. Make sure you have adequate time and adequate beach property to complete the hike or reach safety before the incoming tide reaches you. "Sneaker" waves—unexpected, irregular-sized waves that can knock you off your feet—occur along the Oregon coast. Drift logs do not provide a safe haven from incoming waves. They can roll and shift in the surf, tumbling and perhaps even striking or crushing the rider.

Caving. Sturdy shoes, three sources of light, a jacket, gloves, and a "bump" cap are the gear of the caver. Uneven ground, boulder jumbles, and low, jagged ceilings are common encounters, especially in primitive caves. Most caves have nearly constant year-round temperatures of 40 to 50 degrees Fahrenheit, while ice caves maintain subfreezing temperatures even in summer.

Driving. Back-country roads demand greater respect than city roads, where services and assistance are readily available. For safe back-country travel, keep the vehicle in good repair, top off the gas tank before entering the back country, and carry vehicle emergency gear: a jack, a useable spare, a tire inflator, jumper cables, and chains (if foul weather). Take along basic survival gear for the unexpected—water, a survival blanket, food, matches, a first-aid kit, and a flashlight—and carry maps for the area you are visiting.

Outdoor Awareness. With any trip into the back country, hikers should be aware of the possibility of risk. Nature is everchanging; the maintenance of roads, camps, and trails (all dependent on available funding) may change from year to year. In addition, each user brings to the outdoors a different set of skills and physical abilities—skills and abilities that can change with time. Because a trip is represented within these pages does not mean it will be safe for you.

Common sense and independent judgment, paired with good preparation and a knowledge of one's own skills and abilities, are the best armor against the uncertainty of the wilds and the best insurance for achieving a safe, fun, and fulfilling outdoor adventure.

For detailed information on outdoor preparedness, there are many good instructional books and classes on outdoor etiquette, procedures, and safety. Even the outdoor veteran can benefit from a refresher, as field experts are constantly finding better approaches to safely enjoying the outdoors while minimizing the effects of human presence.

COAST

By all appearances, at the beginning of time the varied ingredients of drama, beauty, and grace were tossed in a bag, liberally mixed, and spilled out on the Oregon coast. Rolling dunes, sandy strands, rocky shores, rugged headlands, secluded coves, a surging surf, sea stacks, and pastoral inland settings were the result. All that is missing is warm tropical waters, but most beachgoers forgive the oversight.

What has not been overlooked is the safe-keeping of this treasury: Oregon has adopted a management policy of preserving the beach for the public. This policy has resulted in what many call the most wisely developed stretch of shoreline in America. Some ninety state parks and waysides provide access to coast offerings. Despite great

Cape Blanco

Wood violets, Cape Perpetua

visitor numbers and brimming campgrounds, one can always find an open stretch of Oregon beach to tour—a tribute to the state's planning. To make a good thing better, Oregon is developing a coastal trail system, which will one day travel its some 350 miles of shoreline.

When exploring, one discovers that history clings to the Oregon coast like the ocean spray. The coast legacy traces back to the early explorations of the British, Americans, and Spanish, with such names as Captain James Cook, Captain Robert Gray, Lewis and Clark, and Don Bruno de Heceta. Gold discoveries, Prohibition rumrunning, Japanese strikes to the mainland, and Indian encounters provide subplots to the story. But perhaps shipwrecks carry the greatest romance; nearly every coastal locale carries the tale of some ill-fated voyage.

Lighthouses dot the Oregon coast. Heceta Head has the most powerful beacon, in one of Oregon's six remaining operational lighthouses. Others still stand and invite photographs or tours.

The coast, with its offshore rocks, sea cliffs, tidepools, estuaries, and coves, holds untold discovery for the naturalist. Binoculars earn their transport. Beachcombers find driftwood and agate prizes in their rambles.

The Oregon coast offers year-round recreation. Fall and spring often hold the finest weather at the coast, while the temperature inversions of summer bring morning fog and afternoon winds. Winter is ideal for the storm watcher, with pleasing sun breaks occurring between foul-weather systems. ■

1   FORT STEVENS STATE PARK

605 tent/trailer units (summer reservations by mail)
Full service fee campground
Flush toilets; showers
Water
Open year-round

For information: State Parks, Tillamook Regional Office
Map: state park brochure
Access: The park is located 13.0 miles west of Astoria, off US 101.

As their number suggests, campsites are closely spaced. Natural vegetation threads between sites and forms borders for campground loops. Units have service, rather than scenic, value, but a wealth of park activities—hiking and

The Peter Iredale *wreck, Fort Stevens State Park*

bicycle trails, ocean and Columbia River beach walking, surf and freshwater fishing, and sightseeing—draw visitors away from camp. A shipwrecked hull, a historic museum, and fort and artillery batteries tell park-area tales. From mid-December to mid-May, bald eagles feed on fish runs and perch on pilings along the Lower Columbia River between Astoria and Knappa.

COFFENBURY LAKE LOOP TRAIL

2.2-mile loop
Elevation change: none
Trail condition: good, forested path
Easy
Year-round

Access: From the campground entrance road, go west to Coffenbury Lake. Find the trailhead at the far end of the swimming beach in day-use area A.

Encircling a long, narrow lake, the loop travels the west shoreline, crosses a causeway, and returns via the east shore, stringing together beaches, boat docks, and picnic areas. The trail travels through planted pine and native Sitka spruce forests, alder woodlands, and tall-grass shores and skirts the estuary at the lake's south end. Ducks, herons, kingfishers, and even a bald eagle may be sighted.

A longer loop encircles the lake's isolated south end, but side trails lead to private property; to avoid confusion, take the causeway route.

BATTERY RUSSELL LOOP TRAIL

2.3-mile loop
Elevation change: minimal
Trail condition: foot trail and
paved bicycle path
Easy

Year-round
Access: Find the trailhead near the
entrance to the northern campground loops, just west of the four-
way junction.

Paralleling a narrow, mucky creek draining to Swash Lake, the trail passes between camp loops to meet a bike path at 0.6 mile. Alders and a few large Sitka spruce border the route. Continuing 0.2 mile on the paved bike and foot trail, a left followed by a quick right leads to Battery Russell, a coastal artillery fort from the time of the Spanish-American War to World War II. Japanese planes fired upon it in 1942. Housed within the stark concrete battery is a maze of rooms, halls, stairways, and dark recesses.

From the battery, the trail passes through a gate and continues up a slope, rounding the hill-embedded Battery Commander Station. The loop proceeds through an area of grasses, Scotch broom, Sitka spruce, and planted shore pine. The foot trail parallels a bike path secluded below to the east. Where they meet, a right followed in 50 feet by a left leads to the campground and the end of the loop hike.

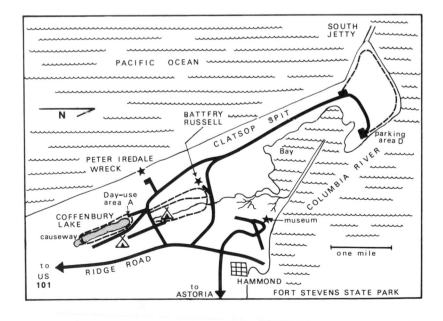

COLUMBIA RIVER MOUTH BEACH HIKE

2.4 miles one way (to South Jetty) Easy
Elevation change: none   Year-round
Trail condition: compacted sand Access: Find trailheads at parking
of river and ocean beach; beach areas along Clatsop Spit.
driving allowed beyond jetty

From parking area D, this hike along the Columbia River to its mouth finds a fringe of dunes with lush grass giving way to lower dunes scattered with driftwood. Views of Cape Disappointment, its lighthouse, and the low coastal mountains of the Washington shore combine with river views. Ships and small pleasure craft navigate this major Northwest transportation route.

By 1.2 miles, as the beach curves south toward South Jetty, ocean forces play in the Columbia River mouth. Gulls are everywhere, fog banks build over the ocean, and waves crash against the jetty. Because beach driving is allowed south of the jetty, off-hour and off-season touring prove best when extending the hike along that stretch.

2 OSWALD WEST STATE PARK

36 walk-in tent sites   For information: State Parks,
Standard service fee campground Tillamook Regional Office
Flush toilets   Map: Siuslaw National Forest
Water   Access: From Cannon Beach, go
Open seasonally: mid-April to late 10.0 miles south on US 101.
October

A 0.25-mile paved path leads to these scenic sites occupying a forested flat of ancient Sitka spruce, cedar, and fir just inland from the ocean. On-site wheelbarrows aid campers in shuttling gear between car and camp. Old-growth rain forest, coastal bluff meadows, Cape Falcon, and a Coast Range peak bearing tales of buried treasure are nearby attractions.

A full-service facility south of here, at Nehalem Bay State Park, provides trailer campers with similar, convenient access to these attractions, along with a 2.0-mile spit for ocean beach or bay-shore walking. Harbor seals bob in the bay.

NEAHKAHNIE MOUNTAIN TRAIL

3.0 miles round trip   Access: From Oswald West Camp-
Elevation change: 1,100 feet   ground, go south 2.2 miles on US
Trail condition: good,   101. Turn east on a gravel road
steady-climbing   marked for the trailhead, which is
Moderate   on the left in 0.4 mile; parking is
Year-round   on the right. For a longer hike,
                                begin at Oswald West Camp.

According to Indian legend, in the early 1700s a Spanish galleon was shipwrecked near the mountain base, and there the marooned sailors buried the

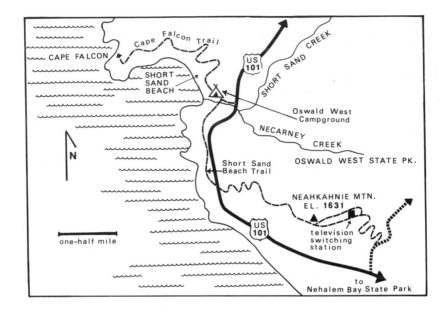

ship's treasure. But the true treasure of Neahkahnie Mountain is the summit vista of the Nehalem River flood plain, Nehalem Bay, the beach and coastal communities to the south, and the ridges of the Coast Range.

After a 1.0-mile switchback course up the mountain flank, the trail meets the dirt track leading up to the television switching station. Either follow the track to the station and a footpath beyond or cross it to follow a trail just below the ridge to reach the summit in 0.5 mile.

A longer hike (6.0 miles round trip; 1,400 feet elevation change) begins directly from the south end of Oswald West Campground, following Short Sand Beach Trail to the summit. This route travels through a wonderful ancient forest of impressive Sitka spruce and standing snags, a corridor of adult-high salal, and the dense grasses and salmonberry thickets of the open coastal headland. After crossing US 101 at 1.0 mile, the trail rises in long switchbacks up the mostly forested northern slope of Neahkahnie Mountain before reaching the ridge just east of the summit.

CAPE FALCON TRAIL
4.0 miles round trip
Elevation change: 300 feet
Trail condition: good,
steady-climbing
Moderate

Year-round
Access: Find the trailhead on the west side of US 101, north of the Oswald West Campground parking area.

This hike begins as a wooded walk along Short Sand Creek and quickly ventures into one of the state's most accessible, premier ancient coastal forest strips. Stout Sitka spruce reigns over bountiful salal, which grows to 7 feet high.

The trail offers a look at a "rehabilitated forest"—an area of choked, younger trees—before eventually leading into the open. Ocean sound and mist dominate where the trail drifts out of the forest.

En route to Cape Falcon, the trail offers views of Neahkahnie Mountain, Short Sand Beach, and the headland cliffs to the south. Atop the headland, side trails weave through salal and brushy thicket to a vista of jutting cliffs, blow spouts, pounding surf, and pulsing waves. Seals, sea lions, and gulls are common passersby.

3 CAPE LOOKOUT STATE PARK

250 tent/trailer units (summer reservations by mail)
Full service fee campground
Flush toilets; showers
Water
Open year-round

For information: State Parks, Tillamook Regional Office
Map: state park brochure
Access: The park is located 12.0 miles south of Tillamook, off US 101.

Tightly packaged sites rest in a second-growth coastal rain forest and cedar wetland, protected from ocean winds by a long dune. Borders of coastal thicket provide privacy between sites. Sandy beaches, dunes, a bay, and forested headlands invite investigation. Hiking, sightseeing, birdwatching, and beachcombing are among the favorite pastimes.

A 0.25-mile all-ability interpretive loop trail tours a forest grove near the registration booth, where trail brochures may be borrowed. Along the trail, visitors will discover some quirks of nature, such as the twice-anchored red cedar and natural grafting.

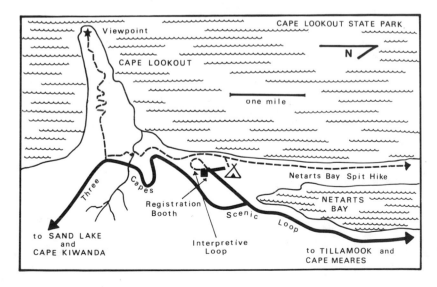

Sitka spruce forest, Cape Lookout Trail

CAPE LOOKOUT TRAIL

5.0 miles round trip
Elevation change: 400 feet
Trail condition: wide forest path,
with steep-dropping sides in places
Moderate

Year-round
Access: Leaving camp, turn right
(south) and drive uphill to the
Cape Lookout Trailhead.

The trail tours the coastal rain forest atop this weather- and surf-beaten basalt headland. Stands of Sitka spruce, western hemlock, and western red cedar rise above a thick mat of fern, salal, waxmyrtle, and salmonberry. The trail passes a commemorative plaque to a flier who died here in a B-17 crash in 1943 and then opens up to spectacular views. Nesting sea birds, gray whales (in winter and spring), and sea lions can be seen.

NETARTS BAY SPIT HIKE

10.0 miles round trip
Elevation change: none
Trail condition: tide-washed,
compacted sand, with some s
cattered cobbles

Easy
Year-round
Access: Find beach access at the
day-use area or the campground.

This hike journeys north along a broad beach, with Cape Meares and Three Arches National Wildlife Refuge in view the entire way. Vegetated dunes with eroded faces and a protective rock base border the beach for 1.25 miles. There, the rock corridor dies, leaving drift log litter at the base of a more natural dune.

The rolling dunes invite exploration and provide views of the bay when dense fog is absent. Gulls, cormorants, and shorebirds; sand fleas and sand shrimp; shell fragments and sand dollars; and crab pots and buoys await discovery.

Travel quietly when approaching the mouth of Netarts Bay and the end of the spit: On the bay side of the spit, harbor seals frequently haul out to sun. They're particularly wary of approaches from the beach, so bring binoculars and maintain a cautious distance.

THREE CAPES SCENIC LOOP DRIVE

20.0-mile drive
Road quality: paved circuit
connecting to US 101
Estimated speed: 35 to 40 mph

Access: With Cape Lookout
centrally located on the loop, leave
the park in either direction.

To the north, Netarts Public Access overlooks the bay and the end of the spit, where harbor seals commonly haul out. At Cape Meares, visitors discover an offshore migratory-bird and sea lion refuge (Three Arches National Wildlife Refuge), a lighthouse, and an amazing "Octopus Tree." Reached via a short trail heading south from the day-use parking area, this unusual Sitka spruce lacks a central trunk. Instead, it sports six limbs up to 12 feet around and 3 to 5 feet thick, branching close to the ground.

To the south is Anderson's Viewpoint, with a tripod memorial and a panoramic view of Netarts Bay and Cape Meares. Then comes Cape Kiwanda, with its sandstone cliffs, dunes, crashing waves, and beach. The dramatic setting, bounded by Cape Lookout to the north and Cascade Head to the south, is a favorite of photographers.

4 BEVERLY BEACH STATE PARK

279 tent/trailer units (summer reservations by mail)
Full service fee campground
Flush toilets; showers
Water
Open year-round

For information: State Parks, Tillamook Regional Office
Map: state park brochure
Access: Turn east off US 101 about 7.0 miles north of Newport.

The campground provides access to one of Oregon's most popular stretches of beach, boasting marine gardens, views of coastal wildlife, geologic points of interest, a historic lighthouse, and sandy strands. Campsites nearest the beach suffer greatest intrusion from US 101 and lack natural forest shelter; those farthest from the beach, while still closely spaced, enjoy greater quiet amid a setting of Sitka spruce, rhododendron, and waxmyrtle.

SPENCER CREEK NATURE TRAIL

0.75 miles round trip
Elevation change: minimal
Trail condition: riparian and forest path, sometimes muddy

Easy
Year-round
Access: Find the trailhead in loop C or near the program area.

The trail tours the riparian habitat of Spencer Creek, a clear-water stream with a silted bottom. *Maianthemum*, nettles, salmonberry, grasses, and sword and lady fern crowd the alder- and ash-lined bank. Marshes of skunk cabbages, ancient stumps bearing marks of old-time springboard logging, and some scenic, twisted Sitka spruce are among the trail highlights.

BEVERLY BEACH HIKE

4.0 miles one way (more during low tide)
Elevation change: none
Trail condition: tide-washed, compacted sand, with a few cobbles
Easy (small drainages to cross; tidal concern rounding a rocky point along Moolack Beach, to the south)

Year-round
Access: Find the trailhead at the west end of the campground, at t he US 101 underpass. The path arrives at the beach on the south bank of Spencer Creek.

Hiking north requires wading or rock-hopping across Spencer Creek. The hike follows a broad, sandy avenue below eroding cliffs topped by wind-sculpted shore pine and Sitka spruce. The coastal headland with its arch point and offshore Otter Rock occupy the northern view. Boulders sporting shell fossils litter the drainage crossing at 0.6 mile.

Stairs to the cliff top (at 1.2 miles) lead to Marine Gardens and an overlook of Devils Punchbowl, where the roof of two interconnected sea caves collapsed. Water surging into the formation during high seas creates a churning caldron. A 0.1-mile trail off the dead-end road north of the Marine Gardens day-use parking leads to the protected tidal pools holding sea lettuce, barnacles, coral-line algae, fish, crabs, eel grass, rock weed, and more. Beachcombers may find agates amid the sands. Both Devils Punchbowl and Marine Gardens are drive-to destinations via Otter Crest Loop, north of the campground off US 101.

Yaquina Head Lighthouse

Alternatively, the first 0.6 mile of a southbound hike follows the base of a reinforced cliff, with residences and US 101 visible above. Later in the trek, natural, eroding sea cliffs nudge the beach. Yaquina Head Lighthouse and Colony Rock are prominent in the view to the south. Bedrock unveiled at low tide sports fossilized shells and intertidal life. At 1.8 miles, the hike crosses Moolack Beach (parking above on US 101 allows car shuttles for one-way hiking).

At 2.8 miles, a rocky point marks the end of the hike during high tide. Located here is a geologic feature similar to Devils Punchbowl: an arch tightly placed against a cliff. Apparently, the roof of this former shallow sea cave collapsed, creating the arch. Seams of shell fossils riddle the rock of both the arch and the cliff.

YAQUINA HEAD LIGHTHOUSE

Outstanding Natural Area, open to the public dawn to dusk
For information: BLM, Salem District

Access: From the campground, go south 3.6 miles on US 101. At the sign, turn west to arrive at the lighthouse in 0.75 mile.

The Civil War–era Yaquina Head Lighthouse stands sentinel to a natural area providing the closest mainland views of a seabird nesting colony anywhere in the United States. Binoculars, scopes, and telephoto lenses are in order.

In spring and summer, murres, cormorants, and pigeon guillemots stand shoulder to shoulder atop offshore Colony Rock. Tufted puffins nest in burrows deep in the rock. Cormorants display aqua-blue throat pouches to potential mates and vie with gulls over prized grasses for nesting material. Later, plump gray gull chicks eagerly await feedings. Winter and spring activity at the observation deck centers around watching gray whale migrations.

A stairway to a marine gardens area introduces the intertidal community and provides easy viewing of the offshore rocks, where harbor seals and sea lions haul out to sun. Their slick heads and sleek bodies can often be seen in the cove waters.

5 CAPE PERPETUA CAMPGROUND

38 tent/trailer units
Standard service fee campground
Flush toilets
Water
Open seasonally: May 15 through September 30

For information: Cape Perpetua Visitor Center; Waldport Ranger District
Map: Siuslaw National Forest
Access: On US 101, go 2.5 miles south of Yachats.

This campground along Cape Creek provides access to rocky shores, coastal headlands, ancient Sitka spruce forest, a record-sized tree, and history. On March 7, 1778, Cape Perpetua received its name from Captain James Cook. At the time of Cook's visit, Indians occupied the area, subsisting on shellfish. With films and exhibits, the visitor center, next door to the campground, is a good place to launch a cape expedition or to duck a raindrop.

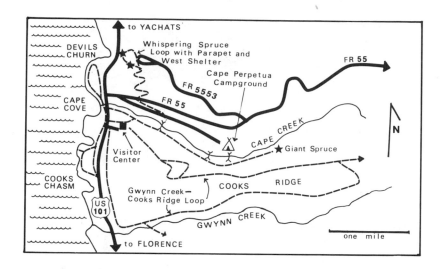

GIANT SPRUCE TRAIL

1.0 mile round trip (from
southwesternmost footbridge)
Elevation change: 100 feet
Trail condition: good forest path
Easy

Year-round
Access: From any campground
footbridge, turn left after the Cape
Creek crossing.

The quiet beauty of Cape Creek complements this trail to a 500-year-old Sitka spruce standing 190 feet high. Salal, thimbleberry, huckleberry, and salmonberry rim the trail, along with ferns, bleeding heart, trillium, oxalis, and wild lily of the valley. Skunk cabbages crowd the moist hollows of side creeks. Large Sitka spruces characterize the forest as the trail draws toward Giant Spruce, where one finds a viewing bench and a stairway encircling the star attraction.

ST. PERPETUA–WHISPERING SPRUCE LOOP TRAIL

2.8 miles round trip
Elevation change: 600 feet
Trail condition: good, steady-
climbing

Moderate
Year-round
Access: Find the trailhead near the
campground pay station.

From the camp, the trail crosses FR 55, passes through open Sitka spruce forest, and zigzags up Cape Perpetua's grassy south face to reach Whispering Spruce Loop, which boasts a view spanning some 150 miles between Capes Foulweather and Blanco. Its 1938 stone structures, Parapet and West Shelter, serve as scenic outposts for whalewatching from late fall to early spring.

The 0.3-mile Whispering Spruce Loop passes Parapet, overlooking the visitor center and Heceta Head. It then travels through headland forest, passes West Shelter, and tours an alder thicket (formerly cleared for a World War II artillery position) before ending at the viewpoint parking lot. Reenter the loop to find the St. Perpetua Trail for the return trek.

The Giant Spruce, Cape Perpetua

GWYNN CREEK–COOKS RIDGE LOOP

5.4-mile loop
Elevation change: 1,100 feet
Trail condition: good forest path, comfortable grade
Moderate

Year-round
Access: Find the trailhead on the south side of the visitor center driveway, just above US 101.

A counterclockwise tour begins tracing a length of the original 1895 wagon road that ran between Yachats and Florence, a corridor now rimmed with tightly bunched Sitka spruce. It then turns inland, exchanging ocean vistas for coastal old-growth habitat. After bypassing the connector spur to the Cummins Creek Trail, the loop assumes an elevated course along Gwynn Creek's north bank.

At the crest of the ridge is the Cooks Ridge junction; a left continues the loop. Parts of the ridge reveal the blowdown-salvage story of the 1962 Columbus Day Storm. Leaving the ridge, the trail tours a stand of giant Sitka spruce and hemlock, crowded with fern and offering limited views of Cape Perpetua to the north. In another 0.8 mile, the loop concludes at the visitor center.

COAST HIKING

1.3 miles of trail
Elevation change: minimal
Trail condition: rocky shore,
tidepools, beach

Easy (beware sneaker waves and
slippery tidepool rocks)
Year-round
Access: Start at US 101 across from
the campground and visitor center.

The Restless Waters, Cape Cove, and Captain Cook trails tour this rugged, scenic shoreline, revealing Indian shell mounds, blow holes, crashing waves, and some of Oregon's finest tidal pools, protected against harvesting and disturbance. Urchin, starfish, limpets, sea anemone, mussels, crabs, and camouflaged fish draw the curious to these mini-windows to the sea. At Devils Churn, along the Restless Waters Trail, tides roar and tumble into a deep rock chasm, churning foam and shooting spray.

6 SUTTON CAMPGROUND

93 tent/trailer units
Standard service fee campground
Flush toilets
Water
Open year-round (one loop)

For information: Mapleton Ranger
District
Map: Siuslaw National Forest
Access: Turn west off US 101 2.5
miles north of Florence.

The campground lies alongside Sutton Creek, amid a dune forest of alder, cedar, and salmonberry. Campers find easy access to dunes, a coastal estuary, darlingtonia (cobra lily) bogs, coastal lakes, the beach, and Sutton Creek for hiking, fishing, and nature study. Twelve habitats comprise the Sutton Creek area, with a wildlife diversity of some 300 species, including river otter, heron, rough-skinned newt, and alligator lizard.

DARLINGTONIA WALKWAY

0.1 mile one way
Elevation change: none
Trail condition: all-ability
boardwalk

Easy
Year-round
Access: Find the trailheads in
loop B.

A wooden walkway offers a brief tour of a darlingtonia bog. Explanatory signs describe this insect-eating cobra lily. Cedar, waxmyrtle, deer fern, salal, and Labrador tea crowd the isolated darlingtonia patches. Red-yellow blooms hang from the lily during May and June. A premier bog, the Darlingtonia Wayside, is found 0.1 mile north on US 101.

SUTTON TRAIL SYSTEM

6.0 miles of interconnecting loops
and spurs
Elevation change: 100 feet
Trail condition: compacted and
loose sand
Moderate

Year-round
Access: Find trailheads at camp
loops A, B, and C and at Holman
Vista, 1.4 miles west via Sutton
Beach Road.

From the Holman Vista parking lot, the 300-foot Holman Vista Trail
travels a paved and boardwalk path, framed by wind-sculpted Sitka spruce and
a waxmyrtle–salal hedge, to an observation deck overlooking the braided
Sutton Creek estuary. Low, vegetated dunes edge the estuary. Herons, ducks,
and geese are among the birds that can be sighted.

A clockwise tour of the 1.25-mile Lower Loop journeys north from
Holman Vista parking lot, along the estuary bank. At the parking area, a short,
paved spur leads to the estuary shore. Hikers may wade its waters (when levels
permit) and cross a 30-foot-high foredune to reach the beach. The lower-loop
hike travels the estuary bank, soon turning inland to tour the upstream coastal
thicket–shore pine forest of Sutton Creek. The trail offers limited creek views
and features patches of tall rhododendron. At a bench at 0.9 mile, a right turn
closes the loop.

The 2.4-mile Middle Loop begins to the left of the trail kiosk near the loop
A group camp and travels the coastal thicket along Sutton Creek, mirroring its
course downstream. Sitka spruce alternates with shore pine as the dominant
canopy species. At 1.2 miles, the trail crosses the westernmost footbridge to
climb a ridge and travel the forested rim of a bowl-like parabola dune. Loose
sand now defines the trail. At the bench at 2.0 miles, a left turn leads to a

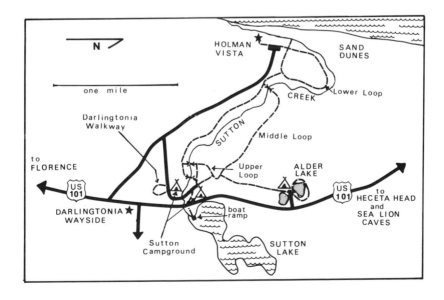

campground at Alder Lake in 0.6 mile while touring habitats of dune, reclaimed-dune, and transition forest. The loop continues straight ahead. At the bench at the base of a dune (at 2.3 miles), a right turn leads to a footbridge crossing to loop A and the end of the hike.

The 0.75-mile Upper Loop crosses the footbridge in loop B and travels upstream above Sutton Creek, touring a mixed evergreen forest with black huckleberry, salal, and rhododendron. At 0.2 mile, it turns inland, mounting the steps to a junction, where the loop turns left. The trail then travels the ridge between the forested Sutton Creek canyon and an open transition forest with Scotch broom and dune grass. At 0.5 mile, near a bench at the bottom of a dune, the trail descends to Sutton Creek. Crossing a footbridge at either loop A or B completes the tour.

From loop C, the 0.25-mile Boat Ramp Trail follows Sutton Creek upstream to Sutton Lake, a fairly large, residential, coastal lake that's attractive to anglers. An underpass avoids the traffic of US 101.

SEA LION CAVES

Private, open year-round except Christmas; winter hours 9:00 A.M. to one hour before dark; summer hours 8:00 A.M. to one hour before dark; fee

For information: Sea Lion Caves
Access: From the campground, go about 9.0 miles north on US 101.

An elevator descends 208 feet to a gallery floor, where the public views this rare mainland Steller's sea lion rookery, located in one of the largest sea caves ever discovered. Pigeon guillemot squawks and sea lion roaring and barking unite in audio chaos. In June, the pups are born. Heceta Head lighthouse stands sentry to this popular coastal attraction.

7 LAGOON & WAXMYRTLE CAMPGROUNDS

96 tent/trailer units
Standard service fee campgrounds
Flush toilets
Water
Open year-round (Waxmyrtle) and seasonally (Lagoon: May through October)

For information: Oregon Dunes National Recreation Area
Map: Oregon Dunes National Recreation Area
Access: On US 101, go 13.3 miles north of Reedsport or 7.7 miles south of Florence, and turn west.

Occupying opposite sides of Siltcoos Road, these lagoon and riverside sites provide access to Siltcoos River and Lake, an oxbow lake, the dunes, the beach, and a salt marsh, serving hiker, birdwatcher, and angler. At both campgrounds, sites are set amid coastal thicket with shore pine plantings; Lagoon Campground has the more scenic layout. A separate campground 0.5 mile west serves off-road vehicle (ORV) riders.

SILTCOOS LAKE TRAIL

4.1 miles round trip
Elevation change: 300 feet
Trail condition: forest path, with
gradual dips and rises
Easy

Year-round
Access: From camp, go east on
Siltcoos Road, crossing over US
101 to the trailhead access road.

A single-story changeless forest of second-growth Sitka spruce and
Douglas fir envelops much of this trail. Giant stumps from the 1920 harvest
punctuate the stand. Salal, sword fern, and huckleberry provide patchy accents.
The moist bottomlands brim with giant ferns and rich mosses. At 0.7 mile, the
trail branches to form a loop, visiting five lakeside campsites to the north and
one to the south. Siltcoos Lake sports a varied habitat: Willow, alder, slough
sedge, and salmonberry thrive along the marshy shore; reeds and cattails edge
the water; and the shallows house water lilies and duckweed mats. Such
diversity supports deer, rabbits, cormorants, ducks, and newts, virtually guaranteeing a wildlife sighting.

WAXMYRTLE TO THE SEA TRAIL

2.6 miles round trip
Elevation change: minimal
Trail condition: good earthen and
sandy path
Easy

Year-round
Access: Find the trailhead at the
south end of the bridge on the
Waxmyrtle Campground road.

The trail travels downstream between the Siltcoos River and the campground perimeter. Beginning at 0.3 mile, it runs opposite a salt marsh estuary,
a rarity on the Pacific coast. Birders can spy ducks, grebes, geese, cormorants,
osprey, kingfishers, and herons from the river bench and a reclaimed dune. Stay
right, rounding a bank and traveling along the edge of the salt marsh, to reach
the hard-packed sand of the river mouth and, beyond it at 1.0 mile, the beach.
Storm-washed logs litter the river mouth. A 0.3-mile river buffer offers a brief
vehicle-free beach stroll; beyond that there may be beach traffic.

RIVER OF NO RETURN LOOP TRAIL

0.6-mile loop
Elevation change: none
Trail condition: good coastal
thicket path
Easy

Year-round
Access: Find trailheads opposite
Waxmyrtle Campground on
Siltcoos Road and near site 4 at
Lagoon Campground.

From the Siltcoos Road trailhead, the loop travels along a boardwalk
between black-mirror lagoon waters rimmed by marsh grass, shore pine, and
lichen-burdened willows. Ducks paddle in the lagoon, while towees and varied
thrush flit through the thickets. A left at the junction begins a clockwise tour
along the land-locked river that gives the trail its name. The access trail from
Lagoon Campground enters from the right. Red and green aquatic plants often
color the still, oxbow river surface. At 0.4 mile, a bench overlooks a setting with
cattails. The loop continues, entering Lagoon Campground. To return to

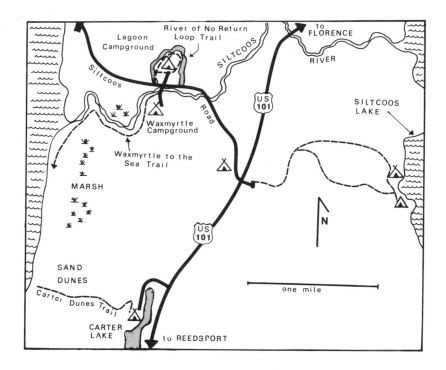

Siltcoos Road, take the Lagoon Trail from campsite 4 to the junction, and go left for the boardwalk.

CARTER DUNES TRAIL

1.6 miles round trip	**Easy**
Elevation change: 100 feet	**Year-round**
Trail condition: reclaimed dune and	**Access: Find the trailhead at Carter**
loose sand; in winter and spring,	**Lake Campground, 1.0 mile south**
the dune bottoms hold water,	**off US 101.**
requiring wading	

The trail travels through coastal scrub, offering access to open dunes, free from ORV travel, in 0.2 mile. A dune overlook at 0.1 mile provides a destination for anyone unable to explore the loose sand. From the dunes, blue-banded cedar posts, spaced at 0.1-mile intervals, point the way to the beach, where ORVs are allowed. Stay at the dunes to view nature's tracks instead of tire tracks. During the night, insects and mice inscribe lacy signatures in the sand.

Carter Lake Campground has a small, sandy beach and swimming access. The lake is a good size for canoes and rafts, but its proximity to US 101 steals from the tranquility and setting.

8 EEL CREEK CAMPGROUNDS

78 tent/trailer units
Standard service fee campgrounds
Flush toilets
Water
Open year-round (one loop of
North Eel only)

For information: Oregon Dunes
National Recreation Area
Map: Oregon Dunes National
Recreation Area
Access: Turn west off US 101 about
10.0 miles south of Reedsport.

North Eel Campground is the larger and quieter of these two campgrounds set amid coastal thicket and reclaimed-dune forest. Adjacent to the
Umpqua Scenic Dunes and within easy access of Eel Lake, the campgrounds
provide opportunities for hiking, beachcombing, dune play, water recreation,
and birdwatching. A 0.25-mile nature trail links the loops of North Eel
Campground, touring the dune-field perimeter amid a corridor of waxmyrtle,
black huckleberry, shore pine, and salal. Along the way, spur trails lead to the
dunes. Tree frogs and hummingbirds are seasonal visitors.

UMPQUA DUNES TRAIL

4.0 to 5.0 miles round trip
(depending on the course over the
dunes)
Elevation change: 200 feet
Trail condition: loose sand and
reclaimed dune; in winter and
spring, the wet bottom of the
deflation dune requires wading

Moderate
Year-round
Access: Find the trailhead in
the south loop of North Eel
Campground.

The trail travels through coastal thicket before reaching a magnificent
dune field at 0.2 mile. Offering the finest undisturbed playground in the dunes
recreation area, some dunes rise 400 feet. While hikers can select their own
course to the beach, the most direct route mounts the large east–west dune
ridge immediately to the left and travels a high road across the dune tops,
passing to the right of a central tree island (visible from atop the dune). Blue-
banded cedar posts guide the way to the beach from the deflation plain (the
low, vegetated area behind the beach foredune).

The dunes (along with a 5.0-mile stretch of beach between Tenmile Creek
and Ziolkowski Beach) are closed to ORVs, allowing undisturbed roaming.
Before exploring the beach, however, make a visual note of the dune-access
point for the return trek, as it is not well marked. In spring, seasonal ponds form
at the base of the dunes, and a chorus of tree frogs can be heard near camp and
along the deflation plain.

An alternate route crossing the dunes to the beach, Eel Dune Trail, is
found along the 0.25-mile tie trail between North and Middle Eel campgrounds. It climbs to the dunes at the Eel Creek footbridge below Middle Eel
Campground and merges with Umpqua Dunes Trail at or before the deflation
plain. Follow the cedar posts north to reach the beach.

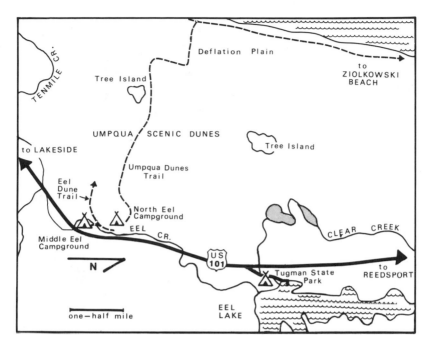

EEL LAKE, TUGMAN STATE PARK

No fee day-use area; fee campground

For information: State Parks, Coos Bay Regional Office

Access: Turn off US 101 about 1.0 mile north of North Eel Campground.

Eel Lake, a large, coastal lake with mostly undeveloped shore, offers water recreation, with a boat ramp (10-mph boat speed) and a swimming area. A large, pine-shaded lawn provides picnic spots. Loons, herons, osprey, vultures, grebes, and ducks will keep the binoculars moving.

9 SUNSET BAY STATE PARK

138 tent/trailer units (summer reservations by mail)
Full service fee campground
Flush toilets; showers
Water
Open year-round

For information: State Parks, Coos Bay Regional Office
Map: state park brochure
Access: Go about 12.0 miles southwest of Coos Bay via the Cape Arago Highway.

These compactly spaced, landscaped sites provide access to coastal trails, exciting shorelines, and sculptured gardens. Across the highway is a large day-use area and scenic Sunset Bay, with its 0.25-mile beach crescent, eroding cliffs,

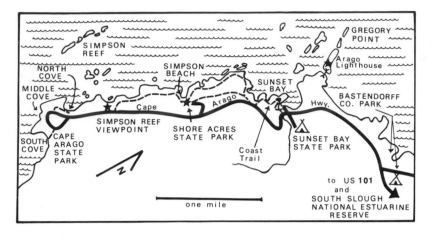

and a tree-topped rock island just offshore. Harbor seals occasionally bob in the cove, while gulls congregate at the mouth of the stream near the cove's south end. Nearby Bastendorff County Park offers additional camping and a 1.0-mile stretch of beach, bounded by the south jetty and Yoakam Point.

COAST TRAIL

3.25 miles one way (to Simpson Reef Viewpoint)
Elevation change: 100 feet
Trail condition: forest and paved path, with connecting road segments

Easy to moderate
Year-round
Access: Find the trailhead at the south end of Sunset Bay Beach.

The trail crosses a footbridge and makes a quick, hardy climb to the top of the sea cliffs in 0.1 mile. Second-growth Sitka spruce and shore pine shade the trail. Salal, black huckleberry, waxmyrtle, and bracken fern comprise the understory. Along the route, side paths lead to cliff overlooks of the rugged shore. At 1.0 mile, after a brief road segment, the trail splits; take either fork to Shore Acres State Park. Opting for the Coast Trail route to the right provides views of Arago Lighthouse, rugged cliffs, and offshore rocks along the first leg, followed by views of Cape Arago and Simpson Reef.

At 2.0 miles, the Observation Building at Shore Acres offers an enclosed shelter for watching both weather and whales. Photographs and plaques depict the early-day lumber-shipping magnates, the Simpsons, who owned the estate. The 7.0-acre formal gardens feature ponds, statues, lawns, walkways, benches, and native and exotic trees, flowers, and shrubs.

The hike continues on a paved path to Simpson Beach, passing through salal and rhododendron thickets to arrive in 0.2 mile at a small but broad driftwood-littered beach framed by picturesque cliffs. Crossing a small creek, the trail climbs away from the beach to a cliff top, where barks from the sea lion colony on Simpson Reef can be heard. The trail passes through open meadow and thick coastal forest to a reef overlook. Morning is the best time to see sea lions hauled out on the rocks. For those with limited time, both Shore Acres and Simpson Reef Viewpoint are accessible via the road.

CAPE ARAGO STATE PARK

Day-use picnic area, beach access
For information: see page 35

Access: Continue south from Sunset Bay on Cape Arago Highway.

This state park has two steep, 0.25-mile descents to the beach. North Cove has the larger beach, with a rocky, log-littered corner and a 0.3-mile sandy strip that is inaccessible at high tide. At South Cove, tidepools hold starfish, algae, fish, hermit crabs, and more. The park also has ocean viewpoints and a marker noting Sir Francis Drake's sighting of the North American coastline in 1579. Blown off course, his vessel took shelter in South Cove.

SOUTH SLOUGH NATIONAL ESTUARINE RESERVE

Research sanctuary open to the public; visitor center hours 8:30 A.M. to 4:30 P.M. Monday through Friday (daily in summer)
For information: South Slough National Estuarine Reserve

Access: From camp, go 2.5 miles northeast on the Cape Arago Highway, and take Seven Devils Road south about 4.0 miles to the reserve.

At this nation's first estuarine reserve, films, displays, self-guided nature trails, canoe trails, and a 3.0-mile study trail introduce this vital habitat, where fresh water and saltwater merge. Binoculars enhance birdwatching.

10 BULLARDS BEACH STATE PARK

192 tent/trailer units
Full service fee campground
Flush toilets; showers
Water
Open year-round

For information: State Parks, Coos Bay Regional Office
Map: state park brochure
Access: Turn west off US 101 about 2.0 miles north of Bandon.

These sites, landscaped with grass and shore pine and rimmed by coastal tangle, offer access to the beach, a bay, and a historic lighthouse. Located across the Coquille River from Bandon Marsh National Wildlife Refuge, the park also boasts excellent birdwatching. A paved trail ties together the campground, a day-use area, an equestrian camp, and the beach.

BULLARDS BEACH HIKE

8.0 miles one way (to Seven Devils Wayside)
Elevation change: none
Trail condition: water-washed, compacted sand, with looser sand above the high-tide line
Moderate to difficult (long-distance hiking requires crossings of Cut

and Whiskey Run creek drainages and, at high tide, a scramble over Five Mile Point)
Year-round (creeks may suggest shorter hikes during winter and spring)
Access: Begin at the end of the spit near the lighthouse.

This long, wide, sandy strand bordered by a low, grass-reclaimed foredune and dune field, with a backdune area of small shore pine, offers an irresistible invitation to beachcombers and joggers. Farther north, vegetated coastal cliffs bump against the avenue of sand. Drift logs litter reaches above the high-tide line.

The beach retains a wild flavor, escaping intrusions of development and US 101 despite its proximity to populated areas. Isolated strolling is possible beyond the lighthouse and campground area, with only the mesmerizing, rhythmic sights and sounds of the ocean, small discoveries washed to shore, a passing cormorant or seal, and weather changes for companions.

COQUILLE RIVER BAY HIKE

4.0 miles round trip
Elevation change: none
Trail conditions: soft, sometimes
swamp sand; low-tide hiking only
(may need to travel the river bank
in places; old sneakers are
recommended)

Easy
Year-round
Access: Find the trailhead at the
lighthouse.

Coquille River Lighthouse

Following the old road east from the lighthouse and North Jetty, the trail travels along riprap, pairing manmade views of old-town Bandon, pilings, boat docks, and warehouses with natural views of roosting cormorants and harbor seals. Seals are particularly abundant during steelhead runs (November through March). From the end of the old road, hikers may travel along the bay via the higher reaches of the low-tide shore or via the dune-grass bench. Opposite the horse camp, riprap again rims the river, marking the turnaround point for the hike.

COQUILLE RIVER LIGHTHOUSE

National Historic Place, open to the public; jetty access
For information: see page 37

Access: Go to the southwest end of the park road.

Built in 1896, this lighthouse (no longer in operation) warned approaching vessels of the treacherous Coquille River mouth, where bar swells and freshwater currents created a ship graveyard. In 1902, the schooner *Advance* ran aground here. The 47-foot light tower is closed to visitors, but the house portion is open, offering an ideal post for storm watching and ocean viewing.

During calm seas, hikers can stroll the 0.1-mile concrete walk atop North Jetty to the point of its fracture, near the jetty end. The jetty affords ocean anglers a casting edge. While gulls await the results, surf scoters rise and dip with the waves. Evening finds photographers lined up on the jetty to capture the lighthouse in the sunset glow.

---

11 CAPE BLANCO STATE PARK

58 tent/trailer units
Full service fee campground
Flush toilets; showers
Water
Open seasonally: mid-April to late October

For information: State Parks, Coos Bay Regional Office
Map: state park brochure
Access: Turn west off US 101 about 9.0 miles north of Port Orford.

Dense coastal thicket and shore pines provide privacy between these inland sites. A 0.2-mile connecting trail leads to a horse camp with corrals and water. The park holds the most westerly lighthouse in the contiguous United States. Other attractions include beach and headland hiking, agate and shell collecting, offshore fishing, and a historic house and pioneer cemetery.

COAST TRAIL

7.0 miles round trip (south to Elk River)
Elevation change: 200 feet
Trail condition: earthen path and beach sand, with fording of a side river channel

Moderate
Year-round
Access: Find trailheads in the campground, opposite site A-40, and on the south side of the park road, near the lighthouse.

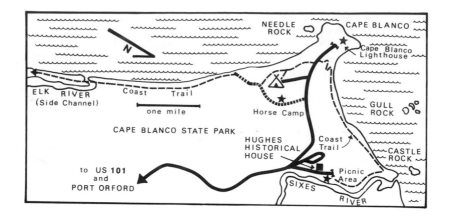

From the campground, a thick coastal-scrub corridor ushers hikers to the Coast Trail. To the south, the trail briefly visits a grassy headland bluff before following a paved access road to the beach. A thick border of drift logs lines the base of the bluff. A vehicle clearing at 0.7 mile gives hikers easy access to the 2.8-mile beach ending at the Elk River. Ocean rocks with shells embedded in them, clams cemented shut from the action of sand and water over time, and gravel bars littered with agates draw beachcombers to their knees.

At 2.25 miles, a side channel from the Elk River requires wading to continue the hike. Beyond it is a wonderful wilderness beach below low dunes. In the distance, one can see sheep grazing on green bluffs, the lighthouse, and small fishing craft. The beach itself is isolated and untouched.

COAST TRAIL

4.2 miles round trip (north to the Sixes River mouth)
Elevation change: 200 feet
Trail condition: improved path and beach sand; consult a tide table
Easy

Year-round
Access: Find trailheads alongside the campground entrance road, near site A-40, and on the north side of the park road, near the lighthouse.

Campground spur trails pass through coastal scrub to meet the Coast Trail and follow it north. The trail crosses a meadow headland overlooking the rocky coast before meeting the park road. Go briefly west along the road to find the next segment of the trail, a gravel path snaking down the rolling coastal meadow slope. Just north of the cape, the trail meets the sandy shore with a few rock outcrops and scattered stones. Spectacular weather—fog, cloud, mist, rainbows, and sunny brilliance—occurs here. Thundering waves crash and roll to shore, stirring the sand and rocks.

At 1.5 miles, hills give way to low, vegetated dunes. Elk tracks may be seen along the beach in early morning, and sea palms and tangles of kelp litter the shore in winter. The spit at 2.1 miles pairs ocean and river-mouth views. Castle Rock stands sentinel; harbor seals, cormorants, grebes, and ducks congregate at the river mouth.

An extended hike follows the estuary upstream, where the bay shore gives way to a pastureland bench with logs and stumps deposited by spring floods. At 3.0 miles, the hike ends at a gate at the picnic area and boat launch below the historic Hughes House, built in 1898. With sheep grazing on the park pasture, be sure to secure gates.

CAPE BLANCO LIGHTHOUSE

Photo subject; closed to the public   **Access: Go west from the camp-**
For information: see page 39   **ground to the end of the park road.**

This historic, functional lighthouse, which dates from 1870, sits atop the park's deeply furrowed westernmost point. Wind-sculpted spruce accent the slope. Utility lines alone intrude upon the scene, challenging photographers. North–south views span from the Sixes River to Humbug Mountain, with offshore rocks dotting the ocean expanse.

12 HUMBUG MOUNTAIN STATE PARK

108 tent/trailer units   **For information: State Parks, Coos**
Full service fee campground   **Bay Regional Office**
Flush toilets; showers   **Map: state park brochure**
Water   **Access: Take US 101 about 6.0**
Open seasonally: mid-April to late   **miles south of Port Orford.**
October

Sites set amid landscaped lawns and shore pines at the foot of a forested ridge and alongside a creek provide access to Humbug Mountain. A 0.5-mile-long gray-black sandy beach, cut by Brush Creek and reached via a highway underpass, features the jagged-rock north base of Humbug Mountain, off-shore rocks, and gravel bars sprinkled with small agates. The campground's proximity to US 101 is convenient for travelers but steals from the tranquility of the camp setting.

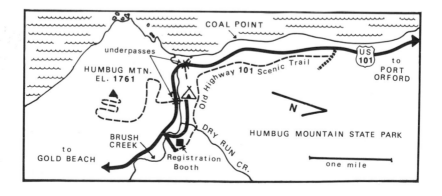

The rugged base of Humbug Mountain, near Brush Creek

HUMBUG MOUNTAIN TRAIL

6.0 miles round trip
Elevation change: 1,700 feet
Trail condition: wide forest path,
with steady climbing
Difficult

Year-round, except during brief
periods of snow
Access: Find the trailhead on the
campground road, near site B-53.

A footbridge over Brush Creek and a tunnel under US 101 lead to the
trailhead of this coastal mountain hike (summit elevation 1,748 feet). The trail
passes through alders and sword fern to an impressive grove of giant myrtles in
a small creek canyon. Higher up, smaller myrtles remain amid the old-growth
forest complex of grand fir, Douglas fir, and western hemlock. Toward the
southern end of Humbug Mountain, tanoak woodlands appear. Along the way
are showings of rhododendron and beargrass.

Ocean vistas are few on this trail, which for the most part travels the flank
above US 101. At 0.5 mile, a "window" through the trees offers a limited view
of the offshore rocks to the north. Atop Humbug, a grassy spot ringed by trees
offers views of the ocean, the jagged shoreline to the south, and the rugged
ridges of the southern Oregon Siskiyous.

OLD HIGHWAY 101 SCENIC TRAIL

2.0 or 5.0 miles round trip
Elevation change: 200 feet
Trail condition: old pavement, with
steady grade
Easy to moderate

Year-round
Access: Find the trailhead off the
campground entrance road, just
before the registration booth.

Part of the Oregon Coast trail system, this trail is ideal for joggers and exercise walkers, with the wide, paved surface remaining unbroken and free from obstruction. Moss paints the roadbed green, and a mat of leaves and needles softens its appearance. A mixed forest crowds its edge, providing a shady canopy for much of the first leg of the hike. As the trail tops out and begins to descend, its course is more open, passing below arid, planted slopes of manzanita and tanoak.

At the 0.25-mile guardrail, a footbridge crosses below a tiered cascade on Dry Run Creek; it is particularly pretty following rains in winter and spring. Beyond a water tower at 1.0 mile, the trail affords ocean vistas of Humbug Mountain, the park's beach cove, and offshore rocks. This is the turnaround point for the shorter tour.

The road peaks out at 1.5 miles. Its descent offers frequent additional coastal views reaching as far north as Port Orford. The route ends at a trailhead east off US 101 3.0 miles north of the campground.

COAST RANGE

Oregon's most overlooked recreation area is the Coast Range. For many residents and visitors, views through a windshield of a twisted, tree-lined pass between Oregon's metro corridor (Interstate 5) and the coast are the sole exposure to these mountains. Venturing off the primary routes onto the back roads or simply taking advantage of the turnouts is the first step to discovering their wealth.

Although an apparent lack of interest led to the closure of a number of campgrounds and trails over the years, in recent years, the Forest Service has shown a renewed interest in developing the recreation potential of this range.

The Coast Range houses vital wildlife habitat for species as diverse as the Roosevelt elk, the northern spotted owl, and the rare silver-spot butterfly. The mountain range, laced by churning rivers and quiet waters, contains secluded pockets of old-growth Douglas fir and Sitka spruce; towering waterfalls; record-sized trees; coastal, mountain, and valley vistas; summit meadows; and quiet wilderness retreats.

In 1805 and 1806, the Corps of Discovery, responsible for exploring and charting the land west of the Mississippi, under the leadership of Meriwether Lewis and William Clark, wintered in the Coast Range. "Altho' we have not lived sumptuously this winter and spring at Fort Clatsop, we have lived quite as comfortably as we had any reason to expect," wrote Meriwether Lewis. In Indian legend, prominent Coast Range features embody events and figures from the spiritual world. The mountains themselves tell stories of homestead efforts, mining attempts, old-time logging practices with springboards and sleds, and the precedent-setting forest-rehabilitation effort in what is now Tillamook State Forest.

But the true wonder of the Coast Range is the temperate rain forest: the lush undergrowth of salal, sword fern, huckleberry, oxalis, and Oregon grape; the moss-draped alders and maples; the

Noble firs, Marys Peak

prized waterways; and the sensory richness found under the old-growth canopy.

With a moderate climate, the Coast Range is accessible year-round, although snow caps the highest peaks and occasionally brushes the passes. The frequent heavy rains of winter and early spring reveal the waterfalls in their full glory.   ■

Jewell Meadows Wildlife Area

13 SPRUCE RUN COUNTY PARK

40 tent/trailer units (accom-
modates spill-over traffic)
Standard service fee campground
Flush and nonflush toilets
Water
Open seasonally: Memorial Day
through Labor Day
For information: Clatsop County
Parks Department

Map: Oregon State
Access: West of the Jewell Junction
and east of the Saddle Mountain
turnoff on US 26, turn south onto
Nehalem River Road at the sign
for Spruce Run County Park.
Continue 7.0 miles to the
campground.

Nehalem River Road and a small creek divide into quadrants this 128-acre campground alongside the Nehalem River. Bigleaf maple, alder, Douglas fir, and spruce shade the well-spaced sites. The lower river attracts canoeists and anglers. Wildlife-study, photography, and sightseeing opportunities draw visitors away from camp. The park is open year-round for day use.

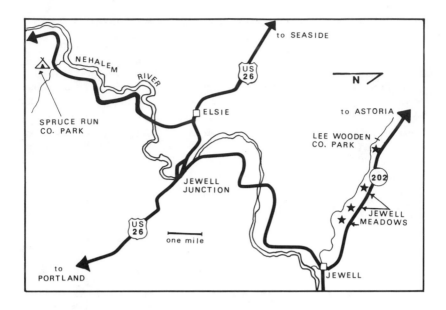

LOWER NEHALEM RIVER ROAD DRIVE

28.0 miles one way (linking US 26 and OR 53)
Road quality: winding; mostly paved, with gravel segments; not recommended for trailers or large RVs

Estimated speed: 25 mph
Access: Continue south from camp on Nehalem River Road.

The road offers exceptional views of the Nehalem River as it twists and bends with the river's course. Periodic turnouts provide safe spots for stopping. Alders dominate the canyon slopes, while only a few old-growth Sitka spruce and Douglas fir provide contrast. Nehalem Falls, a 5- to 10-foot water slide on the river, can be viewed from the angler path at Nehalem Falls Park. The unmarked turn for this park (with its primitive campground and river access), angles back upstream 0.5 mile north of the Nehalem River crossing. Respect private lands along the route.

JEWELL MEADOWS WILDLIFE AREA

Public viewing area, no fee
For information: Oregon Department of Fish and Wildlife

Access: From the campground, return to US 26, and go east to the Jewell Junction. Travel north to Jewell. The viewing areas lie just west of Jewell off OR 202.

At this 1,200-acre viewing area in the northern Coast Range, large open meadows, sedge marsh, brush thickets, and an abandoned orchard provide a vital habitat for wintering Roosevelt elk and other native wildlife. The site's forest rim further benefits the animals, offering protection, shelter, and privacy.

Roosevelt elk are most visible from November through April, with best viewing in the early morning or late afternoon. Rutting season is from mid-September to mid-October; the calves arrive in mid-June.

FISHHAWK FALLS VISTA

Public-access photo-interest point, picnicking
For information: Clatsop County Parks Department
Access: From camp, go east on US 26, and turn north at Jewell

Junction. The falls lies 4.4 miles northwest of Jewell, on the south side of OR 202. A small "public access" sign near milepost 25 indicates the steep downhill turn.

Next door to the Jewell Meadows Wildlife Area, Lee Wooden County Park houses a 100-foot falls reached via a short informal footpath. In winter, the swollen creek falls in watery chaos, while summer finds fine silver threads spilling over the terraced rock. A beautiful old Sitka spruce spreads its arms over a picnic site next to the falls. Moss-draped maples add to the setting.

14 GALES CREEK FOREST PARK

30 tent/trailer units
Standard service no fee campground
Nonflush toilets
Well water (bring water for drinking and cooking)
Open year-round

For information: Oregon Department of Forestry, Forest Grove
Map: Oregon State, "Tillamook Forest Trails" brochure
Access: Exit north off OR 6 about 15.0 miles west of Forest Grove and 3.6 miles west of the Timber junction.

These alder-shaded sites above Gales Creek lie in historic Tillamook State Forest. In 1933, 1939, 1945, and 1951, fires swept this area in one of the great disasters of the Pacific Northwest. Today, a thriving second-growth forest invites exploration. Tillamook Forest is a popular destination for ORV enthusiasts as well as hikers. Along OR 6, five campgrounds with some 100 sites in all serve travelers.

GALES CREEK TRAIL

1.8 miles one way (ending prior to the OR 6 ascent)
Elevation change: 100 feet
Trail condition: good forest path
Easy

Year-round
Access: Find the trailhead on the west side of the road 40 yards south of the campground.

The trail switchbacks up a slope, enters a second-growth forest, and traces an abandoned railroad grade of mossy planks to parallel Low Divide Creek. Tall stumps, green with lichen and moss, record the forest history: centuries of

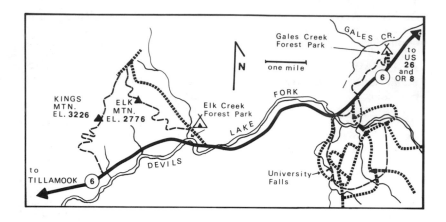

undisturbed growth, followed by old-time logging with springboards, followed by fire. At 1.8 miles, the trail abandons the creek and charges 0.2 mile
uphill to the OR 6 summit and the University Falls trailhead.

For those seeking an all-day outing, the 8.0-mile University Falls Loop
Trail strings together a recovering forest, a 65-foot falls, old trestles, and
segments of the old Wilson Wagon Road.

RIPPLING WATERS NATURE TRAIL

0.5-mile loop
Elevation change: none
Trail condition: wood-shaving path;
floods in winter
Easy

Late spring through fall
Access: Go 10.0 miles east of the
campground via OR 6 and OR 8.
Find the signed trailhead on the
south side of OR 8.

This interpretive loop trail tours the bank of Gales Creek, shaded by alder
and maple. Blackberry, snowberry, wild rose, and fern grow wildly in the
understory. Nesting boxes along the creek house wood duck pairs. A guidebook by the local branch of the Izaak Walton League gives children a first-rate
introduction to wildlife habitats and riparian environments. The guidebook is
available at the Oregon Department of Fish and Wildlife in Forest Grove.

KINGS MOUNTAIN TRAIL

5.0 miles round trip
Elevation change: 2,400 feet
Trail condition: rugged and steep;
not recommended for the young or
health-impaired
Difficult

Spring through fall
Access: Go 10.0 miles west of the
campground on OR 6. Find the
signed trailhead on the north side
of the highway.

The trail immediately ducks into a red alder–maple woodland and zigzags
up the south flank of Kings Mountain, making frequent use of old skid roads.
Second-growth firs gradually replace the deciduous woodland. At 1.2 miles,
the trail travels across an open slope of bracken fern and foxglove, offering views
of Tillamook State Forest, the Wilson River Valley, and the Coast Range.

University Falls, Tillamook State Forest

As the trail grows steeper, silver snags pierce the sky. The primary summit is at 2.4 miles, with a second summit beyond. In the high meadows, Columbia lily, gentian, daisy, thistle, yarrow, and Indian paintbrush parade their colors. Views of Elk Mountain and Mounts St. Helens, Adams, and Hood invite hikers to stay.

The Elk Mountain Trail is only slightly less rugged and steep (4.0 miles round trip; 1,900 feet elevation change), while offering similar vistas. The trailhead is at Elk Creek Forest Park east of the Kings Mountain trailhead.

15 HEBO LAKE CAMPGROUND

10 tent/trailer units
Standard service fee campground
Nonflush toilets
Water
Open seasonally: mid-April
through October

For information: Hebo Ranger
District
Map: Siuslaw National Forest
Access: At Hebo, turn east off OR
22 onto FR 14, near the Hebo
Ranger Station. Travel 4.5 miles
east on FR 14, to the campground.

The campground offers both tree-shaded and open-meadow sites ringing scenic little Hebo Lake, the centerpiece of an area healed from the ravages of forest fires in 1845 and 1910. Attractions include the surrounding lush second-growth forest, tree plantations, bracken fern meadows, and broad summit meadows, which are home to the endangered silver-spot butterfly.

PIONEER INDIAN TRAIL

7.0 miles round trip
Elevation change: 1,200 feet
Trail condition: well-maintained
forest trail

Moderate
Year-round
Access: Begin at the south side of
Hebo Lake Campground.

Traveling a restored segment of the historic Grande Ronde Indian Trail, this trail ties together Hebo, North, and South lakes. These mountain lakes are a Coast Range oddity. Interpretive signs describing the vegetation, the burn, and the reforestation dot the first mile of the trail. Woodland and meadow alternately frame the path.

At 1.25 miles, the trail passes through an old homestead meadow, where twenty to twenty-five elk may be seen on some mornings. Posts mark the trail's course through the meadow. At 3.5 miles, the trail reaches the open ridge and mountain meadow of Mount Hebo, providing vistas of Tillamook and Nestucca valleys.

The homestead and the ridge meadow are good turnaround destinations; for the hardy, the trail continues to South Lake (for an 8.0-mile one-way hike). A high-clearance shuttle vehicle is required for the one-way tour, as FR 14 becomes rough and narrow en route to the South Lake trailhead.

HEBO LAKE TRAIL

0.5-mile loop
Elevation change: none
Trail condition: all-ability,
crushed-slate surface

Easy
Year-round
Access: Find trailheads at campsites
1 and 6.

This all-ability trail rings three-fourths of Hebo Lake, with a road section completing the loop. Two fishing platforms provide handicapped visitors with unobstructed access to the water. Water lilies create colorful mats along the

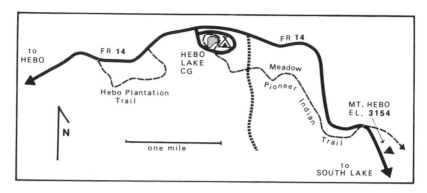

water's edge, and tall alders shade the banks. Newts bubble the lake surface. Planted with trout, Hebo Lake often sports one or two trolling inflatable rafts.

HEBO PLANTATION TRAIL

2.0 miles round trip
Elevation change: 500 feet
Trail condition: marshy or
overgrown in places
Easy

Year-round
Access: From the campground, go
0.9 or 1.4 miles west on FR 14.
The trail travels between the two
trailheads.

This trail tours the reforestation that followed the fire of 1910. Beautifully carved wooden signs introduce the features of the trail and the tree-planting schemes. Despite the sometimes-obvious pattern of row planting, the lush undergrowth of sword and bracken fern, salmonberry, vanilla leaf, and false Solomon's seal gives a feeling of wildness to the setting. Return as you came, or walk along FR 14 for a 1.5-mile loop.

16 MARYS PEAK CAMPGROUND

6 tent/trailer units (18-foot
maximum trailer size)
Standard service fee campground
Nonflush toilets
Water
Open seasonally: June through
September

For information: Alsea Ranger
District
Map: Siuslaw National Forest
Access: Turn north off OR 34 onto
Marys Peak Road 10.0 miles west
of Philomath. Reach the camp-
ground in 9.0 miles.

Small noble firs thread between the sites of this near-summit camp-ground, offering shelter from the wind. Parker Creek, summit meadows, and noble-fir forest create a rich botanical neighborhood. Sweeping mountain and valley vistas, hiking trails, a spring wildflower showcase, and wildlife sightings are among the area's attractions.

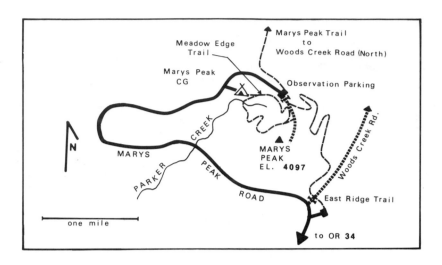

EAST RIDGE TRAIL

2.3 miles one way
Elevation change: 1,100 feet
Trail condition: good, steady-
climbing trail
Moderate
Year-round (in winter, call about
road conditions)

Access: Find the trailhead 3.5 miles
south of the campground, on
Marys Peak Road. The parking area
is on the left past gated Woods
Creek Road.

The trail first passes through a recovering clearcut with red currant, thimbleberry, salal, Oregon grape, and young Douglas fir. As the trail pulls up and away from Woods Creek Road, it leads to a mature forest of tall Douglas fir, intermixed with noble fir near the crest of Marys Peak. In summit meadows, mountain-meadow plant species raise their heads. The crest vista encompasses the Cascades, the Willamette Valley, and the Coast Range. At 2.3 miles, the trail intersects the Summit Trail, a closed service road.

SUMMIT TRAIL

1.2 miles round trip
Elevation change: 400 feet
Trail condition: gravel road
Easy

Spring through fall
Access: From the parking lot northeast of camp, follow the closed
gravel road (foot traffic only).

The Marys Peak summit beckons with a 360-degree vista. Views of the Willamette Valley extend north to Salem and south to Eugene. In the east looms the Cascade Range with its key features: Mount Hood, Mount Jefferson, Mount Washington, Three Fingered Jack, the Three Sisters, and Mount Bachelor. On clear days, Mounts Adams, St. Helens, and Rainier, all in Washington, can be seen. The western horizon holds ridges of the Coast Range and the Alsea River Valley. Hikers should remain on the road and the footpath, as Marys Peak houses many sensitive plants.

MEADOW EDGE TRAIL

2.0-mile loop
Elevation change: 200 feet
Trail condition: well-marked, good
forest and meadow path
Easy

Spring through fall
Access: Begin at the day-use area of
the campground, or take the Summit Trail (see below) for 0.3 mile
and turn right at the loop.

Where the campground spur meets the meadow loop, turn left to begin a clockwise tour. After entering the summit meadow, the loop ducks into a noble-fir stand, part of the Marys Peak Scenic Botanical Area (a Forest Service designation recognizing and protecting the area's botanical value). Leaving the forest, the trail snakes through a meadow of wind-tossed, waist-high grasses laced with bracken fern, lupine, and yarrow. As the trail twists down to Parker Creek, the forest becomes decorated with oxalis, bleeding heart, twisted stalk, and vanilla leaf. The trail returns to camp via a left spur.

MARYS PEAK AUTO TOUR

9.6 miles one way
Road quality: paved, climbing
Estimated speed: 25 to 30 mph

Access: Turn onto Marys Peak
Road off OR 34.

The route winds to within 0.6 mile of the summit of the highest peak in Oregon's Coast Range (elevation 4,097 feet). The observation parking area offers a sampling of the summit vista, overlooking the Cascades, the Willamette Valley, and the Coast Range. Tour pamphlets (available at the road-entrance wayside) identify geology, natural features, and vistas along the way to the campground and the end of the road.

---

17 WHITTAKER CREEK RECREATION AREA

31 tent/trailer units
Standard service fee campground
Nonflush toilets
Water
Open seasonally: June through
October
For information: BLM, Eugene
District

Map: Siuslaw National Forest
Access: Turn south off OR 126
12.5 miles east of Mapleton.
Follow signs to reach the camp-
ground in 2.0 miles via Siuslaw
River and Whittaker Creek roads.

Located along Whittaker Creek where it feeds into the Siuslaw River, this large recreation site has camping and picnic facilities and offers swimming, a boat launch, horseshoe pits, and sport areas. Excursions away from camp lead to both river fun and old-growth serenity. To the west, off OR 126, is Archie Knowles USFS Campground, which offers facilities with running water but has more road noise and is farther removed from the trailhead and old-growth splendor.

Rafters and canoeists find Lake Creek and Siuslaw River accesses at nearby Lane County Parks, including Indiola, Tide, and west Brickerville, along OR

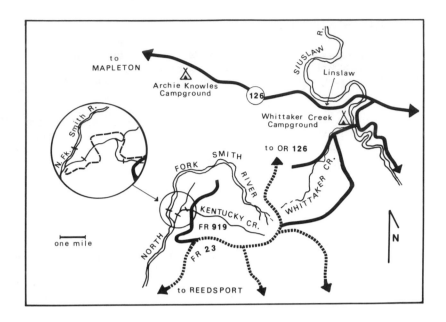

36, and Linslaw, on OR 126. Linslaw offers a particularly pleasant riverside stay. Launch sites have restrooms and picnic tables. Anglers find ample challenge in these parts.

KENTUCKY FALLS TRAIL
4.0 miles round trip
Elevation change: 1,000 feet
Trail condition: good forest path
Moderate
Year-round (in winter, call about road conditions: Mapleton Ranger District)
Access: From the Whittaker Creek Recreation Area, go southwest 1.0 mile on BLM 18-8-21 (Whittaker Creek Road), and bear left on Dunn Ridge Road (paved). In 6.9 miles, turn left on the gravel road to Reedsport. Go another 2.7 miles, and turn right onto FR 23. In 1.6 miles, a right turn onto paved FR 2300.919 leads to the trailhead in 2.7 miles. (The total distance from the campground is about 15.0 miles. Signs mark the route.) The trailhead is on the left, with parking for up to five cars on the right.

The beginning of the trail parallels Kentucky Creek and plunges into old-growth abundance. Alder and salmonberry line the creek, while salal, deer and sword fern, and Oregon grape fill the understory. The trail wanders through beautiful old-growth forest and second-growth Douglas fir to three spectacular waterfalls, each approximately 80 to 90 feet high. Fed by winter rains, thick veils of chilling mist peel off the falls. Along the trail, deer and elk, woodpeckers and varied thrushes, and giant salamanders provide surprise encounters. The falls are the centerpiece of this designated USFS Special Interest Area.

SISKIYOUS

The Siskiyous are a fiercely rugged mountain range, in which ecosystems found amid the Coast and Cascade mountain ranges blend with those of arid reaches. Within this transition-zone habitat, visitors discover uncommon diversity and rare plants. The greater area of the Kalmiopsis Wilderness has been proposed for preservation as Siskiyou National Park, which would be the first botanical preserve in our national park system.

Diversity in this southwest corner of the state includes the northernmost grove of Pacific redwood, Brewer's spruce (weeping spruce), pitcher plant, knobcone pine, *Kalmiopsis leuchiana*, myrtle, and more. Wet and dry plant species mingle in unexpected arrays. The uncompromising terrain creates a variety of microclimates, producing this floral magic show. Unstable soils and noncom-

Redwood Nature Trail

Candysticks, Panther Ridge Trail

mercial timber delayed forest harvest in this range, indirectly ensuring temporary preservation of many rare plant species.

The region boasts a history rich with tales of trappers, prospectors, Indian raids, and military mismanagement. Active claims still pepper streams, with some waters open to recreational panning. Before dipping for color, it is best to consult with the managing ranger district regarding regulations, techniques, and acceptable locales.

The coastal rivers of the Siskiyous are noted for their exceptional wild salmon runs. The Rogue River was popularized by noted Western author Zane Grey, who had a cabin here and often tested his angling prowess against the region's salmon.

Rugged trails and winding forest roads lead to exciting old-growth galleries, waterfalls, and wild beauty. Wildlife viewing, fishing, and river rafting (both guided and self-guided tours) number among the other enticements of the region.

The Siskiyous have a climate of extremes, marked by cold winter temperatures, snow in the high country, and sun-baked summer and fall days. The range's proximity to the coast is often evident as the coastal fog seeps into the river valleys and sweeps up through the mountain draws.

In these wild reaches, visitors should be alert to the menace of poison oak and the potential for snakes, but these should not deter visitors from enjoying this region's splendor. ■

18 SQUAW LAKE CAMPGROUND

6 tent/trailer units
Standard service no fee campground
Nonflush toilets
Water
Open seasonally: June through September
For information: Powers Ranger District

Map: Siskiyou National Forest
Access: From Powers, go south on County 219/FR 33 for 16.5 miles, and turn east onto FR 3348. In 3.8 miles, turn right onto FR 3348.080 (gravel) to reach the campground in 0.8 mile.

Set amid a second-growth fir forest near a small alder-rimmed lake (suitable for inflatable rafts but small for canoes), these campsites offer an ideal base from which to explore old-growth transition forest, wilderness vistas, and waterfalls. A 0.3-mile trail rings the lake, where a small grove of virgin fir cloaks

Coquille River Falls Trail

the slope opposite the campground. Single-site campgrounds lie east along FR 3348. Daphne Grove Campground on FR 33 holds seventeen sites alongside the South Fork of the Coquille River, with similar access to area offerings.

PANTHER RIDGE TRAIL

1.0 mile one way (Bald Knob Lookout to FR 5520.026)
Elevation change: 400 feet
Trail condition: good forest path
Easy
Spring through fall

Access: From the campground, go west 1.8 miles on FR 3348, and turn south onto gravel FR 5520, following signs to the lookout. The trailhead lies on the left side of FR 5520.020, about 0.3 mile before the lookout

Panther Ridge Trail travels 11.2 miles, linking Bald Knob Lookout and Buck Point—landmarks of the Rogue River Valley skyline. Much of the trail leads through the Wild Rogue Wilderness. This 1.0-mile sampling visits a

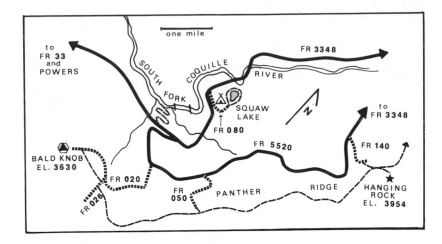

cedar–Douglas fir forest rich with rhododendron. The Panther Ridge Trail boasts perhaps the finest rhododendron showcase in Oregon's coastal mountains. Elsewhere, tanoak, knobcone pine, manzanita, and chinquapin provide texture. Late spring to early summer marks the favorite time to tour.

Mount the Bald Knob lookout tower at own risk. It offers expansive views of the Rogue River Corridor, Big Bend, Panther Ridge, Mount Bolivar, and the Wild Rogue Wilderness. Wildlife sightings may include elk, deer, and bear.

HANGING ROCK TRAIL

1.5 miles round trip
Elevation change: 700 feet
Trail condition: steady-climbing
Easy
Spring through fall

Access: From the campground, go west 1.8 miles on FR 3348, and turn left onto FR 5520. Go 7.0 miles on FR 5520 and turn right onto FR 5520.140. The trailhead is 1.0 mile farther.

The trail tours a fir forest, turning left on the Panther Ridge Trail in 0.25 mile. In another 0.25 mile, it turns right, traveling across an open manzanita shrubland to southwest Oregon's geologic prize—Hanging Rock. The area offers spectacular views of the Rogue River Valley, with an impressive skyline of Mount Bolivar, Diamond Peak, and Saddle Peaks. Hanging Rock is a spectacle, with vertical-dropping walls and violet-green swallows darting from nooks below the dome. Binoculars and camera gear prove to be worth their weight.

COQUILLE RIVER FALLS TRAIL

1.1 miles round trip
Elevation change: 600 feet
Trail condition: switchbacking forest trail; the segment approaching the falls can be slippery when wet or frosty—supervise children near the falls and on the rocks

Easy
Year-round
Access: From the campground, go west 2.2 miles on FR 3348. Find the trailhead on the north side of the road, just before Squaw Creek Bridge.

The outstanding feature here is Coquille River Falls, with its upper, triple set of falls feeding the lower, double set, all arranged in a moss-mantled rock bowl. Coquille River Falls Natural Area houses this spectacle and showcases a beautiful old-growth forest of cedar, fir, hemlock, and myrtle. The understory bursts with Oregon grape, oxalis, blackberry, and black huckleberry. Riverside, alder and bigleaf maple reign. During dry season, a rocky scramble to the upper falls is possible, although the rocks command respect.

19 ILLAHE CAMPGROUND

22 tent/trailer units
Standard service fee campground
Nonflush toilets
Water
Open seasonally: mid-May through September
For information: Gold Beach Ranger District
Map: Siskiyou National Forest

Access: From Gold Beach, go east 30.0 miles on South Bank Road (FR 33). At the junction just beyond the Rogue River bridge near Agness, turn north (right) onto County 375 (a one-lane paved road with turnouts) for the campground in 2.4 miles.

Located on a bench above the Rogue River, this campground offers excursions to two Wild and Scenic Rivers, the Rogue and the Illinois. Camp offers only limited river access: Follow a path downhill from the former camp loop to a rocky river bar (beware of poison oak). Second-growth fir, myrtle, madrone, alder, and chinquapin accent the well-spaced sites.

Foster Bar, 1.0 mile north of the campground, offers a boat launch and better river access. Large trailers and RVs may be better served by the private campgrounds in the area or USFS campgrounds farther west on FR 33 (all boast riverside sites).

LOWER ROGUE TRAIL

5.2 miles round trip (Agness to Copper Canyon overlook)
Elevation change: 200 feet
Trail condition: good, rolling trail
Easy
Year-round (in winter, call about road conditions)

Access: From the campground, return to the junction with FR 33, and follow signs to Agness. Near the Agness Store, go west on a "dead end" road to find the trailhead across from the post office. Park at the Community Library, just before it.

The trail tours the "scenic" segment of the Rogue Wild and Scenic River. After the Rilea Creek crossing, a left on the dirt road leads to a right-of-way passage through farm property. Be sure to leave all gates as you find them, pass quickly and quietly, and respect private lands.

In 0.1 mile, the trail proper begins on the right. After Briar Creek, the trail works back toward the river through a myrtle–tanoak woodland. In the early morning, river otters sometimes frolic along the shore. At 1.4 miles, the trail charges uphill to a dirt road, passing an osprey nest atop a snag. Turn left to

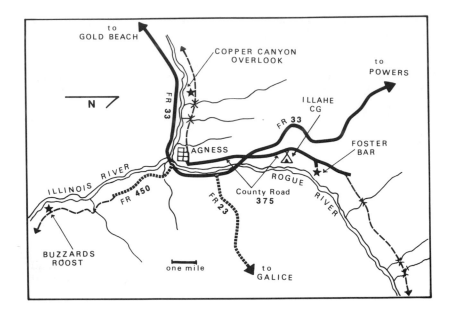

cross Blue Jay Creek on a bridge, after which the trail bears to the right.

The trail remains fairly well marked, but one trouble spot occurs just after Smithers Creek. Here, the Lower Rogue Trail branches to the right. A rock cairn and a semi-hidden trail sign indicate the turn. The well-trampled path ahead is private.

At 2.6 miles, Copper Canyon's rocky outpost offers a grand Rogue River vantage and an inviting place for a rest and a snack. The trail continues west another 9.6 miles, if you wish to explore. Otherwise, return as you came.

ILLINOIS RIVER NATIONAL RECREATION TRAIL

4.5 miles round trip (to Buzzards Roost)
Elevation change: 800 feet
Trail condition: good forest trail
Moderate
Spring through fall

Access: From the campground, return to the junction with FR 33, and go south for 3.6 miles. Turn left onto FR 450 (unpaved) at the sign for the Illinois River Trail, Oak Flat, and the Game Lake Trail. Find the trailhead on the left in 3.2 miles.

This hike samples a portion of 27.0-mile Illinois River National Recreation Trail, traveling a transition-forest bench above the Wild and Scenic River. The trail offers only teasing river views. Side creeks enter with cascades swirling over moss-capped rocks. Old fence posts mark homestead efforts. A vegetated rock outcrop, Buzzards Roost (elevation 1,146 feet), affords prized vistas. A fairly easy climb to its saddle provides views of the Illinois River and its broad, sweeping valley to the west. A more difficult climb to the top leads to views of the upstream waters.

UPPER ROGUE NATIONAL RECREATION TRAIL

9.0 miles round trip (Foster Bar to
Flora Dell Creek)
Elevation change: 500 feet
Trail condition: good, rolling trail
Moderate

Year-round (in winter, call about
road conditions)
Access: From the campground, go
1.1 miles north on County 375 to
the trailhead, on FR 3700.300.

The hike samples the west end of the 47.0-mile National Recreation Trail, which tours 40.0 miles of the beautiful, churning Rogue River, unveiling its many moods. Traveling upstream well above the river, this section follows a right-of-way snaking around and through the open ranchland property of Big Bend Pasture. River accesses are few.

Between Dan's and Hicks creeks, old-growth forest claims the trail sides, with fern, tanoak, dogwood, maple, madrone, and some majestic fir parading their splendor. Flora Dell Creek houses an inviting swimming hole, fed by a 30-foot waterfall. A lower falls spills to the river. The occasional roar of a jet boat alone shatters the river calm.

20 BIG PINE CAMPGROUND

14 tent/trailer units
Standard service fee campground
Nonflush toilets
Water
Open seasonally: mid-May through
September
For information: Galice Ranger
District

Map: Siskiyou National Forest
Access: From the I-5 Merlin exit,
north of Grants Pass, go west 14.5
miles on Merlin–Galice Road. Turn
south onto Taylor Creek Road (FR
25), which arrives at the campground in 12.0 miles.

This scenic campground and day-use area, set amid a grove of ancient ponderosa pine and Douglas fir, offers access to a Siskiyou "neighborhood" that traces its beginnings to the placer gold strikes in the early 1850s. Makeshift

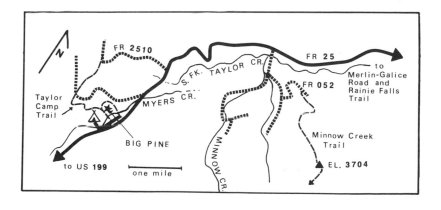

Big Pine

markers warn would-be trespassers of present-day claims, but unclaimed waters where novice panners can dip for color still exist (contact the ranger district). The nation's record-setting ponderosa pine is the centerpiece of the grove.

BIG PINE NATURE TRAIL

0.5-mile loop (outer circuit)
Elevation change: minimal
Trail condition: all-ability, crushed-slate path
Easy

Year-round (except during low-elevation snows)
Access: Find the trailhead at the day-use end of the recreation site.

Three hundred years old, Big Pine stands 250 feet high and measures more than 5.5 feet in diameter. It presides over a rich old-growth grove of Douglas fir and ponderosa pine. Tanoak, sword and bracken fern, and Oregon grape ornament the otherwise open understory. Gentle Myers Creek nurtures a riparian area at the start of the trail. At 1.0 mile, Taylor Camp Trail departs from nature loop D, touring the forested flat inland from Myers Creek before climbing steeply through younger mixed forest to a forest road and logging area.

MINNOW CREEK TRAIL

4.4 miles round trip
Elevation change: 1,400 feet
Trail condition: climbing, sometimes steep; heavy leaf mat obscures
the trail in places. (In 1991, the
Forest Service was making plans to
upgrade and extend this trail,
utilizing sections of the historic
Minnow Creek Trail.)

Difficult
Year-round (except during low-
elevation snows)
Access: From camp, go north on
FR 25, and turn east (right) in 5.6
miles. Find the trailhead at the end
of FR 2500.052.

The trail travels a ridgeline above Taylor Creek, barely disturbing the naturalness of the habitats it strings together. Beginning up an old road cut between jeep trails, the trail soon becomes a footpath, climbing through a forest of fir, live and white oak, madrone, mixed pines, and chinquapin. At a fir- and madrone-forested saddle in 1.0 mile, the trail loses definition. After streaking up the slope ahead in the same general direction for 0.1 mile, the path returns, wrapping around to tour a dry, forested ridge.

At 1.5 miles, a rugged outcrop of glassy serpentine overlooks the Taylor and Burned Timber creek drainages and the distant ridges and deep-cut valleys of the Siskiyous. At the second rocky slope, be alert for yellow ribbons that flag the switchback course up and over the saddle. Manzanita crowds the trailbed. At 2.0 miles, the trail charges to the summit, where hikers find wildflowers and views of Taylor, Burned Timber, and Pickett creek drainages. Manzanita, beargrass, and pine hug the ridge.

RAINIE FALLS TRAIL

4.0 miles round trip
Elevation change: 100 feet
Trail condition: rocky in places,
with a few rises and dips
Moderate
Year-round (except during low-
elevation snows)

Access: From the campground, go
12.0 miles north on FR 25, and
turn west on Merlin–Galice Road.
Continue about 10.0 miles to find
the trailhead on the southwest side
of the Grave Creek Bridge, on what
is now Almeda Road.

The trail travels downstream, tracing a cliff and the steep slope of the south canyon wall above the Wild Rogue River. Wildflowers adorn the cliff. Oak, live oak, myrtle, and madrone form the canopy, accented by flowering dogwood in the spring. With spur trails leading to the riverside, the trail passes rapids, islands, and remnants from the past. It also offers looks at the national recreation trail, which tours the north wall.

During spawning season, salmon jump up Rainie Falls, a scenic 3- to 5-foot river cascade. A portage trail continues 0.2 mile beyond the falls.

21 ALFRED A. LOEB STATE PARK

53 tent/trailer units
Full service fee campground
Flush toilets; showers
Water
Open year-round

For information: State Parks, Coos Bay Regional Office
Map: Siskiyou National Forest
Access: From Brookings, drive 8.0 miles east on County 784.

The campground, which has a wonderful myrtle–evergreen forest setting alongside the Chetco River, offers convenient access to the river, the beach, and a redwood forest. The state park also has day-use facilities, a boat launch, and a trailhead.

RIVERSIDE TRAIL TO REDWOOD NATURE TRAIL LOOP

2.5 miles round trip
Elevation change: 200 feet
Trail condition: rolling forest path, with some steep places

Easy
Year-round
Access: Find the trailhead parking area near the picnic area entrance.

The trail skirts picnic sites to travel a bench above the Chetco River, touring a rich myrtle stand. Farther upstream, a mixed forest of Douglas fir, hemlock, alder, and maple frames the path. A rush of greenery colors the floor. The trail offers river overlooks, with more open views in winter. In fall and winter, gulls feed on spawned-out salmon.

After the first 0.25 mile, the trail travels below the road, with some noise intruding. At 0.75 mile, a crosswalk leads to the Redwood Nature Trail. This 1.0-mile interpretive loop tours the world's northernmost grove of coastal redwoods, threaded by Elk Creek (trail brochures are usually available in the information box at the start of the loop). Along the trail are monarchs 300 to 800 years old boasting diameters of 5 to 13 feet. Douglas fir are the skyline rivals. Rhododendron bushes, blooming in late spring and early summer, riddle the grove with color. A small fish hatchery and the rotting remnants of a log-cage bear trap are points of interest along the way.

HARRIS BEACH STATE PARK

Campground, day-use area, picnic area, and beach access
For information: see page 64

Access: Take US 101 to the turnoff 2.0 miles north of Brookings.

The park occupies a scenic stretch of the Oregon coastline. Cliffs, offshore rocks, and sea stacks are part of the vista, with Goat Island holding a place of prominence. Viewpoint Trail, near the campground entrance, offers ocean overlooks featuring a natural bridge to the south, through which waves surge. Scoters, gulls, oystercatchers, and turnstones are among the birds that can be sighted.

SAMUEL BOARDMAN STATE PARK

10.0-mile protected coastal strip
with trails, beaches, sea cliffs,
viewpoints, and day-use areas

For information: see page 64
Access: From Brookings, go 4.0
miles north on US 101.

This state park houses some of the most impressive coastline in Oregon. Lone Ranch Beach, a day-use and picnic area below rolling coastal-meadow hills, claims a 0.5-mile beach featuring water-soaked drift logs and rugged offshore rocks. The 0.5-mile Cape Ferrelo Viewpoint Trail traces the grassy summit to the cape's west point for an extensive north–south vista: a scenic oceanscape of coves, beach parcels, headlands, offshore rocks, and ceaseless blue water.

A 1.3-mile segment of the extensive Coast Trail system ties the Cape Ferrelo and House Rock viewpoints, touring through coastal meadow, alder woodland, Sitka spruce forest, and salal thicket. During the winter and spring migrations, spouts signal offshore whale pods, adding to an already dramatic view. Whalehead Beach has picnicking and beach access, with the often photographed Whalehead Island occupying center stage.

22 RED PRAIRIE CAMP

1 tent unit
Primitive no fee campground
Nonflush toilet
No water
Open seasonally (depending on snow)
For information: Chetco Ranger District
Map: Siskiyou National Forest

Access: From Brookings, go east on North Bank Chetco River Road (County 784/FR 1376), a paved route becoming gravel. In 15.7 miles, turn right onto FR 1909. Stay on FR 1909, following the signs to the Kalmiopsis Wilderness, to find the campground on the left in 12.3 miles. The route is not recommended for trailers or RVs.

Set amid the evergreen–deciduous diversity that is characteristic of the Siskiyou transition forest, this quiet site provides a base for short treks into the Kalmiopsis Wilderness, exploring its skyline, lakes, mining history, and unique flora. Campgrounds along FR 1376 offer alternative base sites for those with trailers or RVs or desiring a Chetco River setting.

VULCAN PEAK TRAIL

3.0 miles round trip
Elevation change: 900 feet
Trail condition: rocky, steady climb; loose summit rock
Moderate
Spring through fall

Access: From the campground, go east 0.7 mile, and turn right onto FR 1909.260. Find the trailhead parking in 0.3 mile or a low-clearance-vehicle pullout in 0.1 mile.

The trail ascends the west-facing slope for early views of the coastal ridges, Red Mountain Prairie, and Mount Emily. Pine, tanoak, myrtle, and low brush

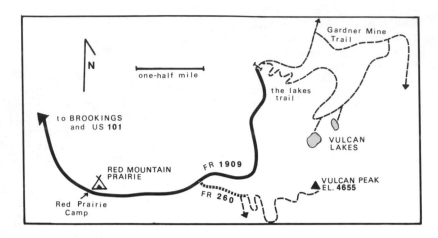

define the trail, while gnarled pines hug the summit. Vulcan Peak (elevation 4,655 feet), the site of a former lookout, provides lofty overviews of the rugged Kalmiopsis Wilderness terrain. The red rock of the mountain suggests the name "Vulcan," for the Roman god of fire. The summit vista includes Chetco Peak and Divide, the Fresno Creek drainage, Whetstone Butte, Eagle Mountain, and Pearsoll Peak, with the Chetco River Valley and the Pacific Ocean to the west.

VULCAN AND LITTLE VULCAN LAKES TRAIL

3.6 miles round trip
Elevation change: 400 feet
Trail condition: rocky; steep in places
Moderate

Spring through fall
Access: From the campground, go 0.7 mile, bearing left and staying on FR 1909. Find the trailhead in 1.7 miles.

In 100 feet, the lakes trail heads uphill to the right, with Jeffrey pine and cedar defining its corridor. Western azalea, red huckleberry, and beargrass embroider its flanks. After rounding a ridge, the trail makes a no-nonsense descent to the lakes. At 1.25 miles, Gardner Mine Loop departs to the left, and the lakes trail heads right. Beginning a loop hike here is possible, but it's easier to hike the Gardner Mine leg first (see below).

Classic mountain pools, Vulcan and Little Vulcan lakes, shimmer at the base of a forested ridge and provide spots for quiet repose, a picnic lunch, and nature study. Cedars, western azaleas, and pitcher plants dot the shore of Little Vulcan Lake.

GARDNER MINE TRAIL

1.8 miles one way (to Vulcan lakes junction)
Elevation change: 400 feet
Trail condition: rocky path and road, with rises and drops

Moderate to difficult
Spring through fall
Access: Same as Vulcan and Little Vulcan Lakes Trail (see above)

Mining adit, Gardner Mine Trail

At the first junction, continue straight along the old, rocky mining road. (Boots are a necessity in the Kalmiopsis Wilderness.) At the ridge saddle, in 0.7 mile, bear right, staying on the road. The trail passes through open, mixed pine–cedar–fir forest with kinnikinick and manzanita, bypassing an old shaft and a tumbledown cabin.

At the 1.0-mile junction, turn right, toward the Vulcan lakes. Where the road broadens near an old catchment basin, follow the rock cairns, leaving the road and tracing the left side of the basin to a trail sign on a tree. Well-spaced cairns now indicate the slow, rocky ascent to a ridge and the slow, rocky descent to the lakes basin. Runty pines, myrtle, and beargrass frame the trail. At 1.7 miles, a downhill spur leads to Little Vulcan Lake. A cut through the trees straight ahead leads to the Vulcan lakes trail junction for the loop-hike option and to Vulcan Lake.

Toad

23 CAVE CREEK CAMPGROUND

18 tent/RV units
Standard service fee campground
Nonflush toilets
Water
Open seasonally: end of May
through mid-September

For information: Illinois Valley
Ranger District
Map: Siskiyou National Forest
Access: From Cave Junction, go
east 15.3 miles on OR 46.

These open-forest sites fill a long, narrow flat alongside Cave Creek and provide access to the above- and below-ground offerings of Oregon Caves National Monument, old-growth and second-growth forests, record-sized trees, and flowering rhododendron and dogwood in late May and early June. Grayback Campground, 4.0 miles west on OR 46, has 35 tent/trailer units.

CAVE CREEK TRAIL

4.6 miles round trip
Elevation change: 1,000 feet
Trail condition: good forest trail
Moderate

Spring through fall
Access: Find the trailhead at the
end of the campground's one-way
loop.

This trail connects the campground to Oregon Caves National Monument. It begins along the south bank of Cave Creek, touring a forest of tanoak, rhododendron, young cedar, and fir. Growing beneath the tree branches are

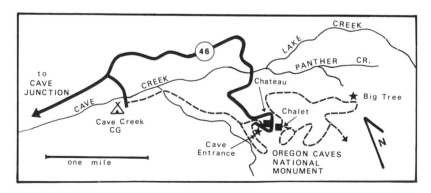

salal, Oregon grape, bracken fern, and moss. Crossing to the north bank, the trail quickly settles into a steady ascent, offering frequent views of Cave Creek. Horsetail reeds, maidenhair ferns, and other water-loving plants thrive along the creek. At the junction of No Name Loop, a left turn provides the shortest route to the visitor area at Oregon Caves National Monument.

BIG TREE LOOP TRAIL

3.3-mile loop
Elevation change: 1,000 feet
Trail condition: paved, becoming forest trail
Moderate

Spring through fall
Access: From camp, go east 4.0 miles on OR 46 to the monument. The trailhead is located behind the chalet, accessed via the archway.

This small national monument boasts a quality nature-trail system, which interlocks with the major trail systems of the region. Turn left to begin a clockwise loop tour through a mixed forest of live oak, madrone, and manzanita. This gives way to a tall fir forest above a varied floor of vanilla leaf, Oregon grape, wild rose, and Indian pipe.

At 1.3 miles stands "Big Tree," a Douglas fir measuring more than 41 feet in circumference and standing 160 feet high—the chief aboveground attraction at the monument. An estimated 1,200 to 1,500 years old, it's one of the oldest trees in Oregon.

At the 1.7-mile junction, a left onto Lake Mountain Trail leads uphill to such destinations as Mount Elijah (named for the cave's discoverer), Lake Mountain, and Bigelow lakes. The loop trail continues downhill to the right, passing through a meadow of thigh-high cow parsnip, false hellebore, Indian paintbrush, and asters. Go either way on the Cliff Nature Trail (a 0.75-mile loop) to return to the chalet.

OREGON CAVES TOUR

Guided tour; open year-round, fee
0.6-mile cave passage, plus 0.3-mile trail
Floor surface: smooth, sometimes slippery
Physical requirements: 550 stairs, some bending

Easy to moderate (children under six are not allowed in the caves; babysitting is available at the chalet)
Access: Purchase tickets at the chalet before joining tour groups at the cave entrance.

More than 100 years ago, Elijah Davidson discovered this marble cave. The tour reveals the wondrous formations created by water over time and hints at their future splendor, as formations continue to grow. Flowstone, stalactites, stalagmites, columns, draperies, and soda straws are just some of the features adorning rooms with such descriptive names as Neptune's Grotto, Niagara Falls, and Banana Grove. Joaquin Miller's Chapel, one of the most ornate galleries in the cave, is named for the "Poet of the Sierra," who helped popularize and protect this cave.

24 FLUMET FLAT CAMPGROUND

27 tent/trailer units
Standard service fee campground
Flush toilets
Water
Open seasonally: May through
September
For information: Star Ranger
Station

Map: Rogue River National Forest
Access: From Jacksonville, go south
16.0 miles via OR 238 and
Applegate Road. Turn right onto
Palmer Creek Road for the
campground.

The campground, in a mixed forest setting of ponderosa pine, fir, and oak with open, parklike grounds, lies across the road from the Applegate River. It provides access to the gold legacy of the past, as well as to hiking, fishing, and birdwatching opportunities. Beaver–Sulphur Campground, to the southeast off FR 20, offers additional camping and a recreational panning area (permit required). Nearby day-use areas offer picnicking, fishing, and swimming, with many having placer tailings from a bygone era. McKee Bridge Picnic Area, to the northeast, houses a covered bridge.

GIN LIN NATIONAL RECREATION TRAIL
0.75-mile loop
Elevation change: 100 feet
Trail condition: rocky, rolling
terrain

Easy
Spring through fall
Access: Find the trailhead adjacent
to the campground.

This interpretive trail tells the story of hydraulic mining, touring the 1881 claim of Gin Lin, a Chinese miner who coaxed more than a million dollars in gold dust from these rugged Siskiyou hillsides. Manzanita, fir, madrone, and

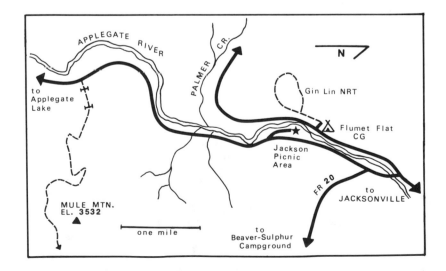

pine have reestablished themselves here, with mosses reclaiming the piles of cobble (placer tailings). Benches along the route allow a leisurely appreciation of the site's habitat and history. Beware of poison oak in off-trail travels.

MULE MOUNTAIN TRAIL

4.2 miles round trip (to the ridge)
Elevation change: 1,700 feet
Trail condition: well-marked,
steady-climbing trail
Moderate to difficult
Spring through fall
Access: From camp, go south on

Applegate Road to find the
trailhead, on the east side of the
road, 2.1 miles south of the Jackson Picnic Area. Park alongside the
road 600 feet south of the trailhead
(don't block driveways or mailboxes).

The trail travels on a right-of-way through an oak woodland on private property for 0.2 mile before reaching public forest lands. (Stay on the trail, respect private ownership, and close all gates.) Small ponderosa pine intermix with the oak woodland as the trail climbs alongside a narrow, dry gulch. In spring, dwarf star tulip, lilies, shooting stars, larkspur, and buttercup adorn a floor of needle-leaf mat and grass. Poison oak is also present; beware of it in off-trail explorations. Lizards rustle in the leaf mat, and grouse drum in the distance.

Along the way, look for views of the California–Oregon Siskiyous, Applegate Valley, Kinney and Billy mountains, Mule Mountain, Little Grayback, and Baldy. Vegetation alters with changes in slope exposure and elevation.

Where the trail crosses over a ridge at 2.1 miles, hikers can scramble to the top of Mule Mountain (a 0.5-mile side trip). The faint lines of animal trails hint at routes. The trek can be hot, so carry water.

APPLEGATE–SQUAW LAKES AREA

Reservoir and natural lakes offering
water sport, camping, and hiking
opportunities
For information: see page 70

Access: Continue south on
Applegate Road, following signs to
the reservoir and lakes. (The Squaw
Lakes road is not suitable for
trailer/RV travel.)

Set amid the pine-, fir-, and madrone-forested slopes of the Siskiyous, this is one of southwest Oregon's prized playgrounds. The often snowcapped, higher peaks to the south accent the skyline. Extensive, interlocking trails tour lake shores, ridgelines, and the surrounding forest. Trailheads are well marked, with mapboards at parking areas for trip planning.

The 2.5-mile Grouse Loop Trail, opposite Hart-tish Picnic Area, is a restful forest tour along a rugged slope above Applegate Reservoir. It offers brief views of the reservoir and the California–Oregon Siskiyous. The trail is easier than its rugged terrain might suggest.

WILLAMETTE VALLEY

Cradled between the Coast and Cascade mountain ranges, the Willamette Valley is the state's heartland, breadbasket, and metro pulse. Its fertile bottomland threaded by the mighty Willamette River extended an invitation rivaling gold, bringing pioneering homesteaders west on a grueling, 1,900-mile overland journey. Oregon City, along the I-5 corridor, is one of two Oregon cities claiming to be the terminus to the historic Oregon Trail (the other is The Dalles, along the Columbia Gorge). Newcomers tamed the flooding river waters, cultivated the land, and established communities. Because of the attractiveness of this productive land, little escaped private ownership. But a few pockets remain that capture both the mood and the habitat of the Willamette Valley.

Located along the Pacific Flyway, the valley is a historic wintering ground for the Canada goose. As mass cultivation threatened the goose, the government moved, in the mid-1960s, to set aside some traditional wildlife lands for the bird's protection. Wetland habitats have likewise been saved in city and county parks along the I-5 corridor. Trails touring these wildlife lands offer excursions from camp. Osprey, geese, heron, hawks, kingfishers, beaver (the state animal), river otter, and muskrat number among the wildlife sightings. When touring the trails, be alert to poison oak, which is well represented along the valley floor.

Bicyclist trail, Champoeg State Park

The broad, quiet-flowing Willamette River offers lengthy float trips perfect for the novice and just the solution to those hot, lazy, summer afternoons. Like many of the nation's rivers troubled by citizen excess, the Willamette was once spoiled. Today, the recovered river again carries chinook salmon runs—a testament to the success of the cleanup effort.

Farmlands, covered bridges, and valley harvests highlight backroad touring. "U-pick" farms and fruit stands bring sweet tastes to a country outing. Roadside blackberry brambles are a valley standard.

Equestrian trail, Milo McIver State Park

The region's mild climate welcomes year-round activity—if you have good rainwear. This is the land of the intermittent windshield wipers, although heavier rains do occur. Morning fog can lay in the valley almost any time of the year. The valley, a leader in grass-seed production, also holds claim to the dubious distinction of "hay fever capital of the world." ∎

25 MILO McIVER STATE PARK

45 tent/trailer units
Full service fee campground
Flush toilets; showers
Water
Open seasonally: mid-April to late October

For information: State Parks, Portland Regional Office
Map: state park brochure
Access: Take OR 211 south of Estacada. Turn west at a sign for the park, and then turn north onto South Springwater Road.

Well-spaced wooded sites above the Clackamas River provide access to the park's ample riverfront, hiking and equestrian trails, boat launch, day-use picnic sites, sweeping lawns, and fish hatchery. Rafters putting in here use Barton County Park (off OR 224 southwest of Barton) as a take-out site. Raptors, woodpeckers, shore birds, and songbirds signal birders to raise binoculars.

LOOP TRAIL

4.3-mile loop
Elevation change: 400 feet
Trail condition: equestrian/hiking;
various surfaces
Moderate

Year-round (except during periods
of heavy rain)
Access: Find trailheads opposite the
entrance road to the campground
and via spurs near sites A-18, A-20,
and A-22.

Beginning at the trailhead opposite the camp entrance, a scrub-bordered grassy path leads away from the park road. At a junction in 100 yards, the branch to the right leads to the forested, riverside segment of the loop. At the base of the hill, a left onto the service road leads to the Clackamas Fish Hatchery, where visitors can view the holding ponds and daily operation.

The loop continues to the left along the hatchery border, crossing side creeks where large fish may be seen during spawning season. Past the hatchery creek footbridge, two paths lead to a riverside picnic area and the continuation of the loop. Beaver activity is visible along the river.

Leaving the picnic area, the path resumes 200 feet up the road from the boat ramp. Here begins the most scenic leg of the journey, traveling through a rich cedar forest dotted by Pacific yew and painted green with ferns and moss. Side paths break away toward the river. The trail next turns inland, touring a second-growth Douglas fir forest.

A web of trails in this area and the absence of signs can produce confusion. Where the trail draws into the open at a multiple junction, the more central path heading inland, prior to the gate, continues the loop. In 0.1 mile, spurs to the right enter the campground near sites A-18, A-20, and A-22 for a shorter loop (1.3 miles).

After rounding the campground, the trail heads up, passing through a corridor of young Douglas fir and tall Oregon grape and scotch broom. Soon the trail skirts a meadow reclaimed by brushy scrub and new forest. Grouse stir

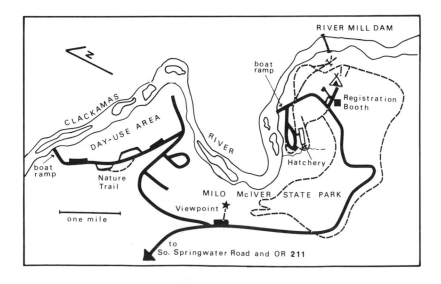

in the thickets. By 1.6 miles, the trail starts to climb amid a forest of mature alder and bigleaf maple. Heavy rains can turn this stretch to mire. Wetlands below the trail host beaver, while hawks patrol the sky.

At 2.1 miles, the trail levels out to travel the boundary between the park and neighboring farmland. After crossing a farm-access road, the loop arrives at the park road at 2.6 miles, turns left, and follows the road shoulder. In 0.1 mile, the trail crosses over the road, passes beneath an ancient oak, and travels along the alder border of a sweeping lawn. Hikers gain limited river views before switchbacking down a woodland slope above the Clackamas River. The loop tour bears right at the 4.25-mile junction to end near the camp entrance.

NATURE TRAIL

1.0 mile round trip
Elevation change: minimal
Trail condition: wide forest trail
Easy

Year-round
Access: Find the trailhead opposite the entrance to picnic area C.

The trail travels a bench below a second-growth cedar slope and above a marshy drainage with alder and bigleaf maple. Rich moss and fern drape the trunks, while sword and maidenhair fern and plentiful salmonberry riddle the drainage and line the trail. Benches dot the route. The trail ends near the picnic shelter in parking area D.

MEMORIAL VIEWPOINT

Vista point at the end of a paved, all-ability path

Access: From the campground, follow the park road to the memorial turnoff and parking area.

A short walk leads to a vista of a scenic Clackamas River bend, its deciduous–evergreen border, valley farmland, and the community of Estacada. Colorful rafts and boats often ply the river.

---

26 CHAMPOEG STATE PARK

48 tent/trailer units
Full service fee campground
Flush toilets; showers
Water
Open year-round
For information: State Parks, Portland Regional Office

Map: state park brochure
Access: From either I-5 or OR 99W, follow the signs marking the exits and the route to the park, located 7.0 miles east of Newberg.

On a flat above the Willamette River, these tightly spaced sites intersperse a grove of tall mature oaks. Landscaped bushes provide privacy, while the surrounding open lawns dispel the sense of close community. The park offers access to bicycle and foot trails, river sport, wildlife study, and discovery of Oregon's early-day history. A summer pageant tells the story of the first organized government in the Northwest.

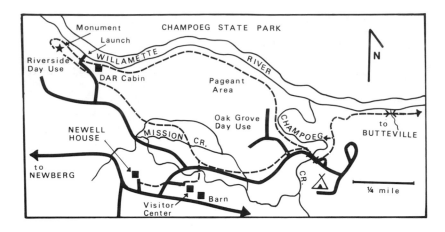

BUTTEVILLE TRAIL

2.0 miles round trip	Easy
Elevation change: 100 feet	Year-round
Trail condition: wide, paved bicycle and foot trail	Access: Find the trailhead off the campground dump-station road.

Turning right, the trail first travels through a woodland corridor of cedar and oaks, bypassing the lawns and horseshoe pits along the campground perimeter. The 0.25-mile dirt Champoeg Creek Trail soon branches left to travel a wild bracken fern field, visit the gravesite of an early-day leader's child, and arrive at the bank of slow-moving Champoeg Creek.

The Butteville Trail continues straight from the junction to tour a narrow riparian strip framed by the Willamette River and private farms. Oaks, alders, maples, and an occasional fir tower above the tangle of blackberry, ivy, and fern. Side trails dip to the river, while clearings offer river views from the main path.

At 0.4 mile, the trail crosses a scenic bridge with a lichen-etched fence (the bridge crossing is slippery following rains). Leaving the bridge, the trail travels a richly forested area, with mixed conifers and cottonwood and a lush fern and moss floor. Skirting an area of private residences, the trail meets the road at 1.0 mile. Cyclists may continue to Butteville via the road.

WILLAMETTE RIVER LOOP TRAIL

3.0 miles round trip (with Newell house detour)	Year-round
	Access: Find the trailhead off the
Elevation change: 100 feet	bike trail 100 feet west of the
Trail condition: paved bicycle and	Champoeg Creek bridge, 0.1 mile
foot trail, dirt footpath	from the campground entrance (it
Moderate	is a footpath only here).

Markers along this counterclockwise loop unravel Champoeg's past as an Indian village, a French-Canadian trading post, a shipping point, the center of Northwestern government, and a flood-devastated site. Journeying toward the Willamette River, the route passes the Oak Grove day-use area, travels along a bench above Champoeg Creek, and skirts the pageant grounds. It then travels upriver via the edge of a field sometimes grazed by sheep.

Touring a riverside forest–riparian habitat with cottonwoods, the trail affords occasional views of the Willamette, an important transportation and recreation waterway. After passing the rustic Daughters of the American Revolution (DAR) cabin, the loop resumes upstream from the paved boat launch, traveling closer to the shore. Woodpeckers are commonly seen and heard in the woodland along this river segment. The loop then swings uphill and passes through the Riverside day-use area to return to the DAR cabin.

From the parking area south of the cabin, a right on the paved bike path continues the hike, traveling along the edges of fields and bypassing the visitor center, the Newell house, and the Manson barn. The Robert Newell House Museum, the restored 1850s house of Champoeg's town planner, has varied exhibits. Its grounds house the old Butteville jail and schoolhouse. (The museum is open afternoons Wednesday through Sunday; closed December and January.) The loop concludes at the campground.

27 SILVER FALLS STATE PARK

104 tent/trailer units
Full service fee campground
Flush toilets; showers
Water
Open seasonally: mid-April to late October

For information: State Parks, Portland Regional Office
Map: state park brochure
Access: The park is located 26.0 miles east of Salem, off OR 214.

Country roads wrap around orchards, tree farms, and fields on the way to this surprising destination: a pocket of old-growth forest along Silver Creek Canyon, which houses ten major waterfalls. A campground with both open and mature-evergreen–shaded sites, a day-use area with sweeping lawns, and hiking, bicycle, and equestrian trails help make this park a Willamette Valley treat. Deer are commonly seen grazing on lawns or bounding for wooded shelter. Some enormous ant mounds dot the woodland of the park's canyon rim—interesting discoveries from a distance.

SILVER CREEK CANYON TRAIL

9.0-mile circuit, with spurs and interlocking shorter loops
Elevation change: 400 feet
Trail condition: good paved or forest path, with some stairs
Easy to moderate (depending on length)

Year-round
Access: Find trailheads at day-use areas and at turnouts along the park road. Map boards are well placed for identifying routes and access points.

South Falls, the most visited and photographed falls in the park, can be examined from the top, sides, back, and face via a 0.5-mile loop beginning at South Falls day-use area A. The 177-foot veiling falls spills over a beautiful hollowed cliff, allowing hikers to pass behind the spray for an unusual perspective. Waterleaf, miner's lettuce, salmonberry, and grasses adorn the

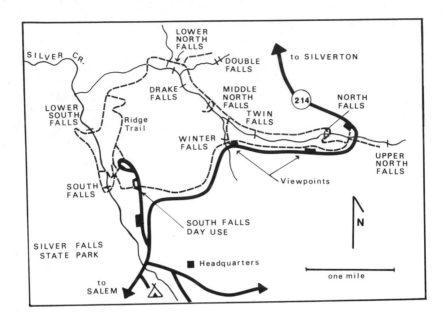

cliff, while bigleaf maples accent the canyon.

From the bridge crossing below South Falls, another 0.8 mile of path extends the outing, providing views from behind the 93-foot watery curtain of Lower South Falls. Along the way to the falls, the path travels through a canyon rich with cascading greenery and offers views of the South Fork of Silver Creek.

From the northernmost parking area (where OR 214 leaves the park en route to Silverton), a 0.3-mile upstream trail probes the moist canyon of the North Fork of Silver Creek, ushering hikers to the Upper North Falls vista. This broad falls enters its canyon slipping over a rocky bowl for a 65-foot drop into a circular pool. The force of the water fans the boughs of nearby cedars, with the roar of the falls amplified by the canyon. A chilly spray peeling from the falls discourages lengthy close-up viewing.

A hike downstream from this parking turnout provides multiple perspectives on the 136-foot North Falls in 0.5 mile. The beginning of the trail offers overlooks of the scenic pools and swirling cascades of the North Fork of Silver Creek as the trail and the creek descend into the canyon. Moss and fern adorn the canyon's steep rock walls. (Beware: The trail's stone steps may be slippery when wet, especially when temperatures drop.) As with South and Lower South falls, hikers may pass into the gaping mouth of the cliff to stand behind the falls and peer out through the thick droplet veil.

From North Falls, a longer loop hike tours the canyon floor and rim before returning to the parking area. This 3.0-mile loop ties together North, Twin, and Winter falls. A 0.2-mile downstream detour at the bridge below Twin Falls leads to one of the prettiest falls in this gallery, Middle North Falls (106 feet).

With long summer days, an all-day leisurely completion of the 9.0-mile circuit is possible, allowing time both for detours and for appreciation of the many falls. Cameras and plenty of film are recommended.

Middle North Falls, Silver Falls State Park

CASCADE MOUNTAINS

Prince's pine, Sky Lakes Wilderness

With their proximity to the I-5 metropolitan corridor and their outstanding scenic and recreational values, the Oregon Cascades are the premier playground of the state. The mountains host year-round recreation, with Nordic and downhill skiing filling the short days of winter and with an array of fair-weather activities. Whether visitors tuck a picnic basket under the arm or sling on a heavy backpack, the mountains supply the desired mix of adventure, beauty, and physical challenge.

In 1792, the Vancouver Expedition noted the Cascade Mountain Range, which separates moist coastal and valley areas from the semi-arid inland. In 1805, Lewis and Clark sighted and charted this range from Hat Rock, and by the mid-1800s, Barlow Road represented the final obstacle to the 1,900-mile overland route of the Oregon Trail.

It was David Douglas, the noted botanist, who first called the range "Cascade." Acclaimed for its string of snowcapped volcanoes, the entire range has been proposed for national park status. While passage of such broad-sweeping protection remains unlikely, the motivation for the proposal is obvious. Two stages of volcanic activity shaped this range; the older volcanoes are in the west, and the younger ones are in the east. Although Oregon volcanoes have been silent in recent years, the westward migration of the North American plate over the sea floor continues to create a reserve of magma, which geologists say will fuel future activity.

Vegetation varies with elevation, latitude, and longitude. Generally, Douglas fir, western red cedar, and western hemlock dominate the western slopes, while ponderosa and lodgepole pine and western larch abound on the eastern slopes. Regional differences introduce other varieties. Rhododendron, huckleberry, bigleaf and vine maple, sword fern, Oregon grape, and vanilla leaf are common understory plants on the western slopes, while bunchgrass and sagebrush are abundant on the drier eastern slopes.

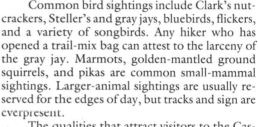

*Ancient forest, Oxbow
County Park*

*White Canyon and
Mount Hood*

Common bird sightings include Clark's nutcrackers, Steller's and gray jays, bluebirds, flickers, and a variety of songbirds. Any hiker who has opened a trail-mix bag can attest to the larceny of the gray jay. Marmots, golden-mantled ground squirrels, and pikas are common small-mammal sightings. Larger-animal sightings are usually reserved for the edges of day, but tracks and sign are everpresent.

The qualities that attract visitors to the Cascades are now threatened by the very popularity they inspire. Too many boots, too many campsites, and too much civilization brought to the wilds have degraded the wilderness experience in prized areas. Beginning in 1991, day hikers and backpackers must secure permits prior to entering three wilderness areas: Mount Jefferson, Mount Washington, and the Three Sisters. As the Forest Service is still ironing out the procedure for securing these permits and deciding whether to limit numbers or days and perhaps charge fees, contact the appropriate managing ranger district prior to going into these areas.

For outings into the Oregon wilds, clearly the time has come to put the well-being of the land before the comfort and ease of the outing. Just because you can go somewhere doesn't mean you should.

Limit the stays and frequency of your visits to sensitive areas. Consider the possibility of off-season visits. Lobby for new wild areas, camps, and trails to spread visitor use. Become a steward, not just a user.

The time has come to bring back the concept of "roughing it." If you cannot live without the comforts of home, then stay there or at least leave them at the campground. Let's not compromise the sacred separation of wilderness and home. ■

28 AINSWORTH STATE PARK

45 tent/trailer units
Full service fee campground
Flush toilets
Water
Open seasonally: mid-April through
October
For information: State Parks,
Portland Regional Office

Map: Mount Hood National Forest
Access: Take exit 35 off I-84, and
head for the campground at the
east end of the Columbia Gorge
Scenic Highway (US 30).

The park offers both picnicking and camping. Closely spaced campsites, landscaped with nonnative pines, offer minimal privacy but serve users well for overnight stays or as base sites for Columbia Gorge outings. A network of interlocking trails and a scenic drive on the Oregon flank unveil the dramatic setting of the Columbia Gorge National Scenic Area.

COLUMBIA GORGE TRAIL TO ONEONTA GORGE

2.1 miles one way
Elevation change: 600 feet
Trail condition: good wide path;
rocky in places
Moderate

Year-round
Access: Beginning at camp, climb
the spur to the Gorge Trail and go
west.

In the state trail plan, the long-distance Columbia Gorge Trail will one day connect Portland to the town of Hood River. This sampling tours a multistoried forest, rounds towering cliffs, passes behind Ponytail Falls, and overlooks the narrow Oneonta Gorge. This breathtakingly dramatic chasm, with moss- and fern-draped vertical walls, is a designated botanical area and a delight for photographers. Upstream lie white, churning water and chutes and a scenic bridge crossing.

A side trip to Triple Falls, off trail 424, adds another mile but is worth it. The trail tours a forested canyon along a crystalline creek draped with maple and accented with moss-capped boulders and treefalls. A rock outcrop provides a direct view of these three side-by-side 100- to 135-foot, white-streaming waterfalls cutting deep into a broad, dark cliff.

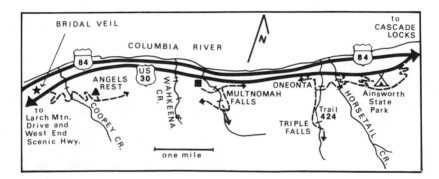

Multnomah Falls

ANGELS REST TRAIL

4.4 miles round trip
Elevation change: 1,500 feet
Trail condition: steady, sometimes
steep, climbing
Moderate to difficult
Year-round
Access: From camp, go 6.5 miles

west on the Columbia Gorge
Scenic Highway. Find the
unmarked trailhead on the road's
south side, just east of the Bridal
Veil Junction. The intersection
creates a triangular space ideal for
trail parking.

This trail streaks up the slope in a no-nonsense style. Touring a temperate Douglas fir rain forest, it follows the ridge above Coopey Creek, bypassing Coopey Falls at 0.3 mile. Coopey Falls is a beautiful, stepped cascade, with a tower of spray-fanned red roots along one side. The broad, windswept summit offers exciting views of the Columbia Gorge to the west. Runty, wind-shaped trees cling to the crest.

SCENIC HIGHWAY DRIVE

22.0 miles one way
Road quality: paved; winding, with
many turnouts

Estimated speed: 25 to 35 mph
Access: From the campground, go
west on the old highway.

Moss-etched Italian stonework graces this vista-packed road. Towering basalt cliffs, temperate rain forest, record-sized waterfalls, and eye-catching canyons flavor the journey. The mouth of Oneonta Gorge is a popular pullout spot and a magnet for photographers. During times of low water, a stone-hopping journey up the creek leads to Oneonta Falls, a 50- to 75-foot drop.

At Bridal Veil Falls State Park, the 0.5-mile, all-ability Overlook Loop Trail tours the bluff meadow, which features the largest camas lily field on the southwestern plateau of the gorge and provides views of Vista House, Rooster Rock, and the cliffs on the Washington side of the gorge.

Farther west, Vista House, a 1918 memorial to the Oregon pioneers, serves as a visitor center. Portland Women's Forum State Park, to its west, affords the classic gorge view of Vista House atop Crown Point.

The 14.0-mile, mostly paved side tour to Larch Mountain begins with a southeast turn onto East Larch Mountain Road, 0.7 mile west of Vista House. This summit destination (elevation 4,056 feet) holds a picnic area and an outstanding vista: a long-distance Cascade view, with volcanic peaks capping the horizon and the Columbia Gorge slicing through the forested expanse.

MULTNOMAH FALLS

Vista and photo point; trails and
trailheads, service center
For information: Columbia Gorge
Ranger District

Access: From camp, go 3.5 miles
west on the Columbia Gorge
Scenic Highway.

Multnomah is the fourth-tallest falls in the nation, at 620 feet. From the stair-tiered viewing deck (with an all-ability access ramp), a paved 0.3-mile path winds through a maple and fern forest along the west flank of the falls. The trail climbs 200 feet to a stone bridge, directly in front of the upper falls and above the lower falls.

From the bridge, the trail climbs another 0.8 mile to a platform vista above the upper falls. Trails branching west from this segment visit beautiful Wahkeena Falls and mystifying Wahkeena Springs, which immediately gives birth to a full-coursing creek. The activity hub for the falls viewpoint is rustic Multnomah Lodge, with its gift shop, restaurant, food concession, and nature exhibits.

29 EAGLE CREEK CAMPGROUND

19 tent/trailer units
Standard service fee campground
Flush toilets
Water
Open seasonally: Memorial Day
weekend through November

For information: Columbia Gorge
Ranger District
Map: Mount Hood National Forest
Access: Take I-84 east to exit 41,
east of Bonneville Dam (eastbound
access only).

These inviting forested sites above Eagle Creek offer access to some of the finest hiking trails in the Columbia Gorge National Scenic Area, a forested mountain region with cliffs, creeks, vistas, and falls. Nearby, Cascade Salmon Fish Hatchery and Bonneville Dam offer viewing of fish-rearing pens. In the fall, red-sided chinook and silver salmon struggle against the current and up a cascade to spawn in the gravels of Eagle Creek. The steeply climbing Buck Point Trail (1.0 mile, 800-foot elevation gain), which overlooks the gorge, and a segment of the extensive Gorge Trail leave directly from camp.

EAGLE CREEK RECREATION TRAIL

7.0 miles round trip (to High
Bridge)
Elevation change: 400 feet
Trail condition: good; narrow
along cliff stretches

Moderate
Year-round
Access: Find the trailhead at the
south end of the day-use area.

The wealth of scenery tied together by this trail, built in the early 1900s, has made it one of the most popular trails in the gorge. Prior to entering the Columbia Wilderness Area, the trail and its side trails offer vistas of such waterfalls as Wauna, the 100- to 150-foot Metlako (named for the Indian goddess of salmon), the highly photographed Punchbowl (a detour onto the Lower Punchbowl Trail enters the falls canyon for an exceptional vista), and Loowit.

The trail quickly climbs above scenic Eagle Creek as it penetrates the rich, green canyon. Wildflowers accent the moisture-dripping vertical rock walls that frame the footpath. High Bridge, where Eagle Creek tumbles through a rock fissure, marks a scenic turnaround point. From here, the recreation trail draws deeper into the wilderness.

WAUNA VIEWPOINT TRAIL

4.0 miles round trip
Elevation change: 1,000 feet
Trail condition: well maintained;
steady-climbing (in 1990, erosion
had stolen the upper part of the
trail, but flags marked the rerouting
higher along the slope)

Moderate
Year-round
Access: Find the trailhead on the
west side of the Eagle Creek
bridge.

The trail climbs through a beautiful, multistoried, old-growth forest bursting with texture and shades of green. Freeway noises can be heard, but the diverse forest setting is worth the intrusion. Pikas whistle from a scree slope near the 1.0-mile trail junction, where the Wauna Viewpoint Trail turns left. The outpost panorama of the gorge includes Bonneville Dam, the Washington shore, and the Bridge of the Gods. A utility corridor contributes to the openness of the view, but detracts from the naturalness of the setting. The 0.25-mile Shady Glen Interpretive Trail, at the beginning of the hike, provides a study of area vegetation and habitat.

WAHCLELLA FALLS TRAIL (FORMERLY TANNER FALLS)

2.0 miles round trip
Elevation change: 200 feet
Trail condition: old road or good
trail
Easy
Year-round

Access: From the campground, go
east on I-84, and take exit 44 for
westbound I-84 travel. From I-84
west, take Bonneville Dam exit 40,
and turn south for the marked
trailhead and parking.

This hike begins on a gated road and follows the silver ribbon of Tanner Creek. At 0.3 mile, the road ends near a concrete impound. Soon after, the trail passes a small waterfall (or water slide depending on the season) on the left and climbs away from the creek. Basalt cliffs rise above both sides.

Bearing right at the 0.6-mile junction, the trail descends for a couple of

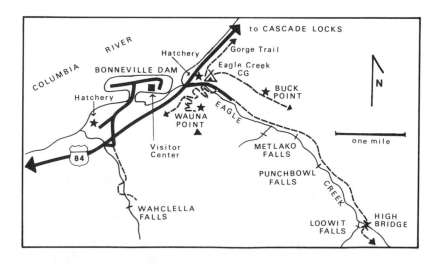

Footbridge over Eagle Creek

creek crossings before reaching one of the most elegant falls in the gorge, with a vertical basalt bowl and a deep pool of waterfall-launched whitecaps swirling around huge boulders. Secondary falls streak the cliff above Wahclella Falls.

BONNEVILLE DAM VISITOR CENTER AND FISH HATCHERY

Free, open to the public; displays, viewing areas
For information: Bonneville Dam

Access: From camp, go east on I-84, and take exit 44 for westbound I-84 travel. From I-84 west, take Bonneville Dam exit 40.

Tours and displays introduce the dam facility and its area offerings. The fish ladder and fish-viewing windows at the center are popular attractions. The hatchery has fifty-eight rearing ponds and five adult holding pens for sturgeon and trout; it produces fifteen million salmon annually. This hatchery is designed to receive visitors and children particularly enjoy feeding the fish.

30 OXBOW COUNTY PARK

45 tent/trailer units
Standard service fee campground;
day-use fee
Nonflush toilets
Water
Open year-round

For information: Oxbow Park
Maps: Mount Hood National
Forest; county park brochure
Access: From Gresham, travel east
via Division Street and Oxbow
Parkway for 8.0 miles.

Wooded campsites provide a base for exploring this 1,000-acre park on the west bank of the Sandy River, with its gorgeous tree-lined canyon, gravel bars, and smooth waters. The second- and old-growth forests house songbirds, pileated woodpecker, common merganser, and nesting osprey. Spawning native chinook salmon are an attraction at the park in the fall.

Straddling a segment of the Sandy Wild and Scenic River, the park offers canoeing, rafting, and swimming. The popular 10.0-mile raft trip from Oxbow Park to Lewis and Clark State Park is mesmerizingly calm. Alphabetically ordered junction posts guide hikers along the park's weblike westside trail system. Exploring the east bank requires a drive, as no nearby bridge links the park's halves. Naturalist-guided walks are offered year-round. No pets are allowed in the park.

DOWNSTREAM LOOP TRAIL

3.5-mile loop
Elevation change: 100 feet
Trail condition: forest and riparian
trail
Moderate

Year-round
Access: From the loop at the end
of the park road, begin at the
trailhead for group camp 2. Carry
a park brochure.

The trail travels through a forest of "teen-age" Douglas fir, Oregon grape, salal, and sword fern before turning right on the equestrian and foot trail

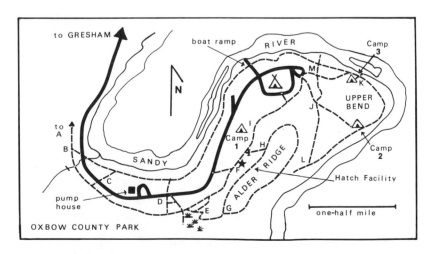

to tour an old-growth stand along the flood plain below Alder Ridge. Spurs from campsites 16-A and 5-B enter at 0.2 mile.

The trail continues along the foot of the slope above the park road and picnic areas to a post marked "B." The overhead canopy alternates between evergreen and alder; stumps and old skid roads hint of former logging days. Along the way, the trail passes a salmonoid hatch facility of tubing, pipes, and barrels (in operation from December to May); old-growth splendor; a wetland overlook; and a small, 30- to 40-foot waterfall. Several spurs lead to the park road and the riverside trail, providing ample opportunities for shorter loops.

From post B, the loop tour trail crosses the road for a return via the river bench. The route is mostly forested, offering branch-framed river views and a few open vistas. Well-tracked side paths lead to the shore. At marker M, a right on the rocky path followed by another right leads to a quick, steep climb to the loop at the end of the road for the end of the hike. Convenient water spigots and pit toilets dot the route.

ALDER RIDGE LOOP TRAIL

2.25 miles round trip
Elevation change: 300 feet
Trail condition: forest path
Moderate
Year-round

Access: From camp, go southwest on the park road to the trailhead parking area near marker D. Find the turnout on the south side of the road west of group picnic area A.

The trail travels east along the foot of Alder Ridge to marker F and an old-growth habitat. After taking a right followed by another quick right, the trail begins a 0.25-mile moderate ascent to the ridge. The trail turns left at marker G to begin a clockwise tour along the perimeter of the ridge. To one side, the forested slope drops away to the Sandy River valley. The other side holds an alder woodland flat, with bigleaf maple, second-growth cedar, sword fern, salmonberry, and massive stumps. At marker H, the trail continues straight to eventually close the loop and retrace the downhill trek. Elk tracks riddle the trail.

UPPER BEND LOOP TRAIL

2.0-mile loop (with detours)
Elevation change: 100 feet
Trail condition: forested and stony
riparian path
Easy

Year-round
Access: From the loop at the end of the park road, begin at the trailhead for group camp 3. Carry a park brochure.

A steep downhill path leads to a four-way junction at 0.1 mile. Here, a right turn begins the loop, which travels inland through a mixed forest of cottonwood, alder, and evergreens, following a low drainage with a rocky bottom. At the junction in 0.3 mile, a right turn leads to the top of a rise and marker J, where the route then turns left. The stone path now tours the multitextured old-growth forest at the base of Alder Ridge. At marker L, a detour to the right leads to a wooden bench and limited river views. The loop continues to the left, staying along the river bank and following the oxbow of the Sandy River downstream to marker M. Side paths break away to gravel and sand bars along the river bend. The main trail offers frequent river views. At post M, a left followed by a right closes the loop at the trailhead.

31 LOST LAKE CAMPGROUND

80 tent/trailer units
Standard service fee campground
Nonflush toilets (some with
handicap access)
Water
Open seasonally: Memorial Day
weekend through September
For information: Hood River
Ranger District

Map: Mount Hood National Forest
Access: The campground is located
about 35.0 miles southwest of
Hood River and 22.0 miles west
of Dee. From Dee follow the well-
marked route along Lost Lake
Road and FR 13.

Wooded and semi-open sites occupy the bench above and along the east shore of this 240-acre lake on the northwest side of Mount Hood. The lake is a favorite location from which to photograph the prized volcanic peak in Oregon's Cascade line-up. The blue waters toss back an unrivaled reflection of the rugged north face. At Lost Lake Resort, visitors can rent rowboats, paddle boats, and canoes; no motors are allowed. A small grocery store and showers are other facilities available at the rustic resort. A separate day-use area hugs the lake's north shore.

LAKE SHORE TRAIL

3.4-mile loop
Elevation change: minimal
Trail condition: good forest path
Easy

Late spring through fall
Access: Begin at the Panorama
Point parking area, on the north
shore of Lost Lake.

Going counterclockwise, the first mile of the lake shore tour is a nature trail (brochures may be purchased at the general store). The trail travels through an ancient forest of large-diameter Douglas and Pacific silver fir,

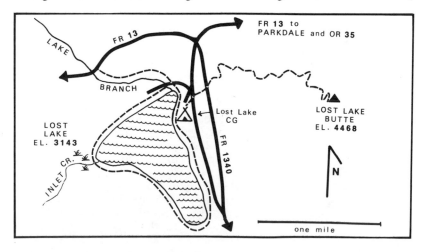

Mount Hood and Lost Lake

western hemlock, and western red cedar. Views of Mount Hood can be captured through the tree cover. In summer, bunchberry, vanilla leaf, queen's cup, and parrots beak sprinkle the forest floor. Leaving the forest, the trail briefly tours the marshy area of Inlet Creek. The rare cutleaf bugbane grows here and nowhere else. The circuit then offers views of Lost Lake Butte, tours stands of cedar, and travels to the more developed east shore to draw to a close.

LOST LAKE BUTTE TRAIL

4.5 miles round trip	Moderate
Elevation change: 1,300 feet	Late spring until first snows
Trail condition: good, steady-climbing	Access: Begin near the campground entrance.

This rock-studded forest trail assumes a comfortable grade throughout its climb to the butte's summit (elevation 4,468 feet). The trail tours a mid-elevation forest, where tree trunks are hairy with lichen. Huckleberry, rhododendron, and beargrass make up the understory. Views of Mount Hood, Mount Adams, Mount Jefferson, the community of Dee, the West Fork of the Hood River, and Hickman Butte Lookout contribute to the panorama. In the basin below, Lost Lake shimmers. Atop the butte rest the remains of a former lookout.

LAKE BRANCH TRAIL

0.8 mile round trip	Late spring through fall
Elevation change: 100 feet	Access: Begin at the north end of
Trail condition: good forest path	Lost Lake, along the Lake Branch
Easy	drainage.

This trail travels along a remnant of the Old Skyline Trail, following Lake Branch. It offers solitude in a beautiful old-growth forest and a bountiful berry harvest in late summer. Huckleberry bushes overwhelm the gentle slope rising above and descending below the trail. A bucket or a plastic bag earns its transport during the harvest season (late August to early September).

*Footbridge over the
East Fork Hood River*

32 ROBINHOOD CAMPGROUND

24 tent/trailer units
Standard service fee campground
Nonflush toilets
Water
Open seasonally: Memorial Day
weekend through October 15

For information: Hood River
Ranger District
Map: Mount Hood National Forest
Access: Find the campground off
OR 35 10.0 miles north of the US
26–OR 35 junction.

Along the East Fork of the Hood River, these campsites, in a mature
Douglas fir forest with cedar and hemlock, provide access to hiking, fishing,
and area sightseeing. Sherwood Campground (22 units), to the north along
the river, offers similar features and access but rests closer to OR 35.

TAMANAWAS FALLS TRAIL

4.0 miles round trip
Elevation change: 500 feet
Trail condition: good forest path,
with steady climbing
Moderate
Late spring through fall

Access: From the campground, go
4.0 miles north on OR 35 to find
the trailhead on the west side of
the highway, just beyond the
Sherwood Campground.

Crossing over the East Fork of the Hood River on a narrow footbridge,
this hike follows the East Fork Trail north, climbing the open-forested slope
of the river's west bank. Where the route turns west to travel upstream along
Cold Spring Creek, the hike setting is at its finest: picturesque pools, swirling
water, and a richly vegetated canyon of trillium, columbine, twisted stalk, lily,
currant, and gooseberry. Douglas fir, Pacific silver fir, and hemlock shade the
path; cliffs frame the canyon.
The trail ends at a broad 100- to 150-foot falls bearing the Chinook Indian name for "Guardian Spirit." Lacy whitewater streamers spill over the
basalt cliff, pounding the jet-black boulders at its base. Behind the curtain of
the falls is a dark cliff hollow. Tree roots and boulders form nearby gallery
seating, while two stout conifers offer shade.

EAST FORK TRAIL

4.1 miles one way
Elevation change: 500 feet
Trail condition: modestly rolling
forest path
Moderate

Late spring through fall
Access: Find trailheads near the entrance to Robinhood Campground
and 0.25 mile north of Sherwood
Campground.

Robinhood Campground is the best place from which to sample a portion
of this river trail, as it is the farthest removed from the traffic of OR 35. From
here, the trail circles behind the campground, passing through a marshy area
with skunk cabbages and waterleaf to follow the west bank of the East Fork
Hood River downstream. Winding along the forested bank, the trail provides
frequent views of the cloudy, rushing water. The area sports a truly mixed
forest, with pine, fir, cedar, spruce, and hemlock. The patchy groundcover
includes prince's pine, twin flower, bunchberry, and vanilla leaf. The trail hugs
the river course much of the way; the tension-erasing river rush is the trekker's
companion.

CLOUD CAP–TILLY JANE HISTORICAL DISTRICT AUTO TOUR

8.6 miles one way
Road quality: good, two-lane,
improved-surface, winding
mountain road
Estimated speed: 25 mph
Access: From Robinhood
Campground, go 5.9 miles north
on OR 35, and turn west onto

Cooper Spur Road. In 2.3 miles,
turn left onto FR 3512 for the
Tilly Jane Recreation Area. Stay
on FR 3512 for the auto tour.
(Brochures are usually available
at the turnout on FR 3512, where
the gravel surface begins.)

En route to Cloud Cap Inn, the road travels just below Ghost Ridge,
winds through the forest of the historic Tilly Jane mining district, and
crisscrosses the routes of the 1884 and 1889 wagon roads. It stitches together
impressive volcano views of Mount Hood and the distant Mounts Adams, St.
Helens, and Rainier. Cloud Cap Inn, the oldest building on Mount Hood
(built in 1889 and being restored), holds the finest close-up view of Mount
Hood to be obtained by motorists. This bold view features the rugged, snowy
mountain, Eliot Glacier, and Barrett and Cooper spurs. Mount Hood is best
seen and photographed in the morning light.

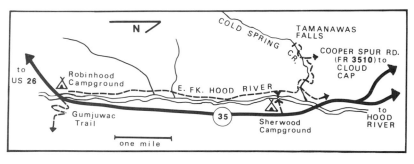

33 GREEN CANYONS CAMPGROUND

15 tent/trailer units
Standard service fee campground
Nonflush toilets
Water
Open seasonally: Memorial Day
weekend through September

For information: Zigzag Ranger
District
Map: Mount Hood National Forest
Access: From US 26 at Zigzag,
turn south on Salmon River Road
(FR 2618).

This scenic campground, set amid an ancient forest along the Salmon River, offers an ideal base for exploration or for just lounging around. East of Rhododendron on US 26 are two alternate campgrounds: Tollgate (15 sites) and Camp Creek (24 sites). Both are forested campgrounds with area access but more road noise.

OLD SALMON RIVER TRAIL

2.3 miles one way (downstream)
Elevation change: 200 feet
Trail condition: reworked path,
with some rock-hopping crossings

Easy
Spring through fall
Access: Begin at camp, along the
riverside.

This section of trail follows the Salmon River downstream, tracing the ancient forest corridor between Salmon River Road and the river's east bank. Brief sections of alder–salmonberry woodland interrupt the forest. Groundcover spills down to the trail. In places, the pinched corridor pushes the trail out onto the road for short distances. The nearly continuous river views and the beauty of the large-diameter trees outweigh any audio-visual disturbance from the road. The Salmon River is a scenic host, with its exceptionally clear water (alternately smooth and churning), gravel bars, moss-decked shore, and side creeks cascading over its banks.

SALMON RIVER TRAIL

6.6 miles round trip
Elevation change: 800 feet
Trail condition: mostly forested;
rocky in places
Moderate

Late spring through fall
Access: From camp, hike the river
trail upstream 0.3 mile, and cross
Salmon River Road to the trailhead,
near the bridge.

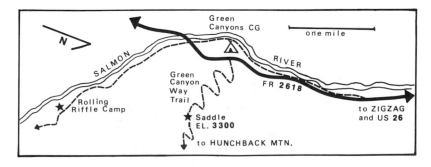

This trail offers a glimpse of the 45,000-acre Salmon–Huckleberry Wilderness and views of the Salmon Wild and Scenic River. The trail follows the river upstream through an old-growth Douglas fir–western hemlock habitat. A plant-draped rock wall frames one side.

At 2.1 miles, the trail enters the wilderness and, at 2.3 miles, bypasses Rolling Riffle Camp, a flat area on the river bench. Ultimately, the trail reaches a number of waterfalls and plentiful huckleberry fields, although this trek concludes at 3.3 miles. Here, as the main trail turns inland, a spur leads out onto an open ridge, offering a panoramic overview of the Salmon River Canyon. Penstemon, larkspur, Indian paintbrush, fritillary, and other wildflowers dot this rocky slope above the river, which hosts wild salmon and steelhead runs.

GREEN CANYON WAY TRAIL

4.0 miles round trip (to the saddle)
Elevation change: 1,700 feet
Trail condition: strenuous, climbing, good forest path

Difficult
Summer through fall
Access: Begin across from the campground entrance on FR 2618.

This leg- and lung-taxing trail tours the ancient forest of the Salmon–Huckleberry Wilderness to reach Hunchback Mountain and its trail, where wilderness loops for long-distance travel are possible. Day hikers find a wilderness sampler. From the semi-open white oak patches, which interrupt the rich western hemlock–Douglas fir slope, hikers can snare infrequent, limited views of Salmon Mountain. The trail advances, contouring and following switchbacks up the slope. Lush oxalis, pathfinder, Oregon grape, and sword, bracken, lady, and deer fern blanket the forest floor. The thorny devils club is also among the mix, with rhododendron present at the higher reaches.

At 1.7 miles, the trail tops a small ridge and then rounds its side to reach an open, up-canyon vista looking deep into the wilderness. Salmon River Canyon, Hunchback Mountain, and Devils Peak are prominent. Just beyond the vista point lies the small saddle marking the end of this hike.

34 McNEIL CAMPGROUND

34 tent/trailer units
Standard service fee campground
Nonflush toilets
Water
Open seasonally: May through September
For information: Zigzag Ranger District

Map: Mount Hood National Forest
Access: From US 26 at Zigzag, go north 4.1 miles on FR 18 (Lolo Pass Road). Then head east 0.8 mile on FR 1825 for the campground.

This campground occupies a semi-open, lodgepole pine–forested area of Old Maid Flat, a lahar (volcanic mud and ash flow) cut by the Sandy River. It offers easy access to Mount Hood Wilderness Area trails and to nearby river

Ramona Falls

fishing. At its entrance is a Mount Hood vista, with a plaque honoring Fred H. McNeil, a prominent newspaperman who promoted the mountain. To the east on FR 1825.382 lies Riley Horse Camp (14 sites).

RAMONA FALLS LOOP TRAIL

4.3-mile loop (6.9 miles round trip via the lower trailhead)
Elevation change: 700 feet (1,000 feet via the lower trailhead)
Trail condition: comfortable grade, ashy, some rocks
Moderate
Spring through fall

Access: From camp, go east 1.5 miles on FR 1825 to FR 1825.100. Continue 0.3 mile to find the trailhead junction. The road to the lower trailhead is paved. The one to the upper trailhead is a little-maintained, rough, rock-studded road suitable only for four-wheel-drive, high-clearance vehicles.

A 1.3-mile, mostly shaded trail links the lower and upper trailheads, passing through a narrow forest corridor between the Sandy River and FR 1825.100. This popular family hike follows Old Maid Flat, a lahar formed during a Mount Hood eruption some 200 to 250 years ago. At the Sandy River footbridge (the shared loop access for both trailheads), an eye-catching view of Mount Hood slows the stride.

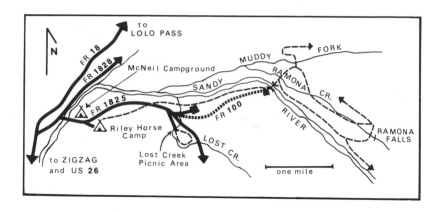

A clockwise tour of the loop begins to the left, through a forest of small hemlock, lodgepole pine, and fir. The trail parallels Ramona Creek to the falls, offering views of stark, pinkish-gray cliffs, clear spilling waters, and a mottled, moss-lichen forest carpet. The falls is a beauty—broad and spreading, with irregular short drops splashing over moss-capped basalt. Leaving the falls, the loop travels mainly through lodgepole pine forest—a forest-type uncharacteristic of the western slopes of the Cascades. Where the trail traces the edge of the Sandy River Canyon, a richer, mixed forest shades it.

LOST CREEK NATURE TRAIL

0.5-mile loop
Elevation change: none
Trail condition: paved; all-ability
Easy
Spring through fall

Access: From camp, go east 1.6 miles on FR 1825 to Lost Creek Picnic Area (with handicapped-accessible sites and toilets).

This loop tours a forest of fir, cedar, and hemlock, with alders crowding Lost Creek. It offers plant study, views of a remnant buried forest, a beaver pond visit, and Lost Creek vistas. From a bench at the edge of the beaver pond, a view of Mount Hood invites a stop. Picnic sites dot the loop.

MOUNT HOOD LOOP DRIVE

70.0-mile loop
Road quality: paved, with short
gravel stretch on north side
Estimated speed: varying from
25 to 45 mph

Access: From camp, return to FR 18 (Lolo Pass Road), and go north for a clockwise loop around the mountain.

This seasonal tour (dictated by the snow on Lolo Pass) skirts the Mount Hood Wilderness, which encompasses 47,000 acres of the mountain and its surrounding forest. An optional side trip takes the 7.0-mile spur to Lost Lake (see trip 31), a scenic mountain lake which mirrors Mount Hood's north face. The loop proceeds toward Dee, crossing the Middle Fork Hood River and turning south toward Parkdale; from Parkdale, the route goes east to OR 35 and travels south on OR 35 and west on US 26. Another side trip off US 26 goes up Timberline Road to the base of Mount Hood and historic Timberline Lodge (see trip 35). The main tour continues west to Zigzag and FR 18, bringing the loop to a close. Along the way, the tour offers exciting views of Mount Hood (elevation 11,235 feet), with USFS camps, picnic areas, and trailheads inviting a closer look. (Brochures are usually available at the Mount Hood Visitor Center at Mount Hood RV Village in Zigzag.)

35 ALPINE CAMPGROUND

16 tent/small-RV units
Standard service fee campground
Nonflush toilets
Water
Open seasonally: July through
September

For information: Zigzag Ranger
District
Map: Mount Hood National Forest
Access: From US 26 east of
Government Camp, take Timber-
line Road north 4.2 miles to the
campground.

The campground rests in an alpine forest–meadow setting, below Timberline's year-round ski area. It's a popular summer base for the younger, snowboarding set. Quieter campgrounds with trailer sites are located at the base of the mountain, east on US 26; Still Creek has 27 sites, and Trillium Lake has 39.

Mount Hood is one of the most climbed glaciated peaks in the world and the most climbed peak in the United States. The first full ascent occurred in 1845. Hikers find easy access to Mount Hood's rugged majesty at alpine and timberline levels. This area is featured along the 70.0-mile Mount Hood Loop Drive (see trip 34). To reach the loop, take US 26 west to Zigzag, and turn north on FR 18 (Lolo Pass Road) to begin a clockwise tour.

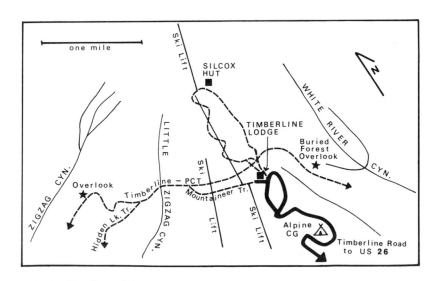

SILCOX HUT TRAIL

2.0-mile loop
Elevation change: 1,000 feet
Trail condition: dusty service roads
Moderate to difficult
Summer through fall
Access: From the east side of
Timberline Lodge (1.0 mile north

of camp), follow the service road
uphill, and go east (right) via the
rock-bordered path crossing a
drainage to the Pacific Crest Trail
(PCT) junction. Look for a sign
marking the mountaineer trail to
the hut.

The hike begins in a patch of alpine trees and silver snags and then pulls out onto an open, wildflower-dotted, rock and sand slope. Views to the south include Timberline Lodge, Trillium Lake, Mount Jefferson, and the forested ridges between Mounts Hood and Jefferson.

Silcox Hut, a stone shelter on the high moraine below Palmer Icefield, (elevation 7,000 feet), was the terminus of the original Magic Mile Chairlift—the second ever built in the United States. The hut is listed on the National Register of Historic Places. Renovation plans include overnight sleeping quarters and food service.

The loop returns to the lodge via the service road on the opposite side of the ski run, for a sidewinding downhill trip beneath the present Magic Mile Ski Lift.

BURIED FOREST TRAIL

1.2 miles round trip
Elevation change: 500 feet
Trail condition: dusty; well-marked; some loose sand
Moderate

Summer through fall
Access: Follow the above directions
to the Pacific Crest Trail junction,
and take the south (right) branch
of the PCT.

Traveling east along the PCT, this hike passes through patchy, snag-pierced alpine forest and open, wildflower-dotted slopes and crosses the headwater drainages of the Salmon River to arrive at an overlook of White River Canyon. This desolate volcanic canyon spilling from the base of Mount Hood houses ridges of rock and sand that buried trees in the last eruptions (200 to 250 years ago). Wind and rain have revealed a few tree tops and limbs. Mount Hood dominates the view to the north, Mount Jefferson the view to the south. Continue another 0.5 mile to a lower canyon vista by descending the PCT along the dividing ridge between the White River and Salmon River canyons. At the broad plateau where the PCT drops steeply away, hikers can peer into the headwater bowl of the White River Canyon.

TIMBERLINE TRAIL TO ZIGZAG CANYON OVERLOOK

5.0 miles round trip
Elevation change: 500 feet
Trail condition: easy-to-follow,
sandy path
Moderate

Summer through fall
Access: Behind Timberline Lodge,
take the paved uphill path to the
Timberline Trail (which is part of
the PCT), and head west.

Following the contour of the slope beneath the ski lifts, this trail crosses alpine forest, meadow, and spare, open slope. Views to the south feature Mount Jefferson and Trillium Lake, with Mount Hood reigning supreme in the north.

Lupine, aster, phlox, paintbrush, and dwarf star tulip add color to the gray slope, where snow patches linger into August.

The trail crosses the shallow headwater drainages of Sand Canyon, dips into Little Zigzag Canyon (for a rock-hopping stream crossing), enters the Mount Hood Wilderness, and begins its descent, passing the junction with Hidden Lake Trail. Leaving a shady forest, the trail rounds the meadow slopes of another drainage to arrive at the open east ridge overlooking Zigzag Canyon. Mount Hood heads the canyon—another deep, rugged volcanic cut with steep eroding slopes, more vegetated than White River Canyon. The trail continues into the canyon as it rounds Mount Hood.

TIMBERLINE LODGE

Open to the public; USFS-guided tours
For information: see page 98

Access: Go 1.0 mile north of the campground on Timberline Road.

In 1937, President Franklin D. Roosevelt dedicated this large lodge, located at timberline (elevation 6,000 feet). Now on the Register of National Historic Places, it is still in operation. Built by master-taught craftsmen, the lodge features many carvings and inlays of native wildlife and serves as a living, functional museum.

36   RAINBOW CAMPGROUND

17 tent/trailer units
Standard service fee campground
Nonflush toilets
Water
Open seasonally: mid-April through October

For information: Clackamas Ranger District
Map: Mount Hood National Forest
Access: Find the campground off FR 46 near its junction with OR 224, just east of Ripplebrook.

These riverside sites in a natural forest setting provide access to two wild and scenic rivers (the Clackamas and the Roaring), reservoirs, a national recreation trail, and remnants of old-growth splendor. Off OR 224 and FR 46 are more than 100 Forest Service campsites. The upper Clackamas River is a popular rafting and kayaking waterway.

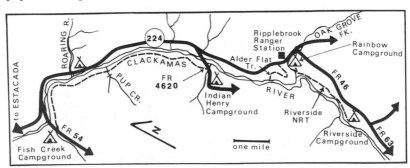

Kayaker, Clackamas River

RIVERSIDE NATIONAL RECREATION TRAIL

4.6 miles one way
Elevation change: 200 feet
Trail condition: good forest path
Moderate
Year-round (except during low-
elevation snows)

Access: Find trailheads at Rainbow
and Riverside campgrounds
(Riverside Campground lies south
off FR 46).

The best sampling of this trail begins at Rainbow Campground. From here, the trail travels along Oak Grove Fork to follow the east bank of the Clackamas River upstream. Old-growth splendor frames the path, which generally travels inland and above the river. Duckboards aid the crossing of marshy areas, and side trails lead to river views. Nearing Riverside Campground, the canyon opens up, with an alder-shaded gravel bar framing the river. The trail alternates between old-growth forest and dry meadow slope. Road noise intrudes along the final leg of the trail.

CLACKAMAS RIVER TRAIL

7.8 miles one way
Elevation change: 400 feet
Trail condition: good, with some
protruding and loose rock
Moderate
Year-round (except during low-
elevation snows)

Access: From the campground, go
northwest on OR 224. Find
trailheads on FR 4620 opposite
Indian Henry Campground and
on FR 54 near Fish Creek
Campground.

This trail follows the southwest bank of the Clackamas River, touring a low-elevation forest of ancient fir, cedar, and hemlock, with brief sections of second-growth forest and utility-corridor meadow. The roller coaster trail travels between the slope and the river bench, offering river overlooks and approaches. Scattered camps along the river offer day-hike destinations. A scenic, moss-softened cliff along the trail's southeast end reveals waterfalls and a "weeping wall" in winter and spring. For the most part, the trail escapes the intrusions of OR 224.

For round-trip day hikes, Pup Creek marks the midway point. From the trailside rock cairn above Pup Creek's west bank, a cut across the forested bench leads to an informal path climbing the slope. This path heads upstream to a vista point that features the spectacular, though unannounced, Pup Creek Falls (0.2 mile). The trail is well tracked, but it does require stepping over, under, and around some obstacles; but the 200-foot, showery falls amply rewards the effort.

The Little North Fork Santiam River

ALDER FLAT TRAIL

2.0-miles round trip
Elevation change: 200 feet
Trail condition: good forest path,
with comfortable grade

Easy
Year-round
Access: Find the trailhead 0.7 mile
northwest of camp, on OR 224.

This trail wanders through a wonderful old-growth Douglas fir forest with some mature cedars and smaller western hemlock. It bypasses a beaver pond and a smaller frog pond to arrive at six forested riverside picnic or camping sites. Alders line the gravel bar of the river. The nearby cliffs show landslide scars. A loop trail around the beaver pond extends the hike and offers a look at impressive beaver dams along the outlet and a water-locked lodge of mounting sticks and limbs.

37 ELKHORN VALLEY RECREATION SITE

16 tent/trailer units
Standard service fee campground
Nonflush toilets
Water
Open seasonally: mid-May through
October

For information: BLM, Salem
District
Map: Willamette National Forest
Access: From OR 22 at Mehama,
turn northeast on FR 2209 for
Little North Fork Recreation Area.
Reach the campground in 8.4 miles.

These campsites occupy a remnant old-growth stand along the scenic, clear-flowing Little North Fork of the Santiam River. Hiking, fishing, swimming, and relaxing beside the river engage campers. Numerous day-use areas along FR 2209 provide access to additional swimming holes and shady picnic sites.

HENLINE MOUNTAIN TRAIL

5.4 miles round trip
Elevation change: 2,700 feet
Trail condition: steady-climbing,
rocky in places
Difficult
Late spring through fall

Access: Find the marked trailhead
at the base of a road cut 9.0 miles
northeast of the campground
on FR 2209 (bear left at the Y
junction). Park along the side of
the road.

Mounting the steep flank of a spur ridge to Henline Mountain, the trail tours an old-growth Douglas fir forest culled by fire early this century (hinted at by the evenly sized, 1.0- to 1.5-foot-diameter trees). Sun-catching vine maples form the midstory, while Oregon grape, fern, huckleberry, and salal dominate the floor. A few showings of poison oak dot the sunnier reaches.

Detours to trailside rock outcrops at 0.7 and 0.9 mile offer grand overlooks of the Little North Santiam, the Elkhorn Valley, and the neighboring ridges. Beargrass and manzanita color the higher forest.

As the trail rounds the ridge to the north, it travels through a richer forest before making a rocky switchback assault on the former lookout site. The 360-

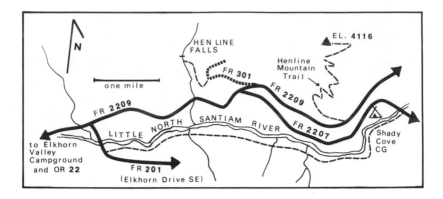

degree panorama features Henline Mountain, the headwaters of the Little North Santiam River, the Elkhorn Valley, rugged slopes, deep canyons, outcrops, and cliffs.

HENLINE FALLS TRAIL

0.6 mile round trip
Elevation change: minimal
Trail condition: forest path; rocky nearing the falls
Easy
Spring through fall

Access: From the campground, go northeast (to the left) 8.4 miles on FR 2209. Soon after bearing left at the Y junction, turn left onto FR 310 (dirt). Reach the unmarked trailhead in 0.5 mile, at a wide turnout on a curve.

An alder gateway frames this needle-softened road-trail as it enters a hemlock–fir forest with huckleberry, vine maple, salal, fern, moss, and wood violets. Some big fir intersperse this forest, which was washed by fire early this century. Mid- to late April finds Oregon grape and lilies in bloom.

The trail ends with an exciting, close-up side vista of the 60-foot waterfall cradled in a corner among dark cliffs. The tunnel of the old Silver King Mine penetrates one wall. The intrepid, armed with flashlights, may venture inside, where crickets mass in the ceiling niches. Scattered concrete and iron remnants recall the mining days.

LITTLE NORTH SANTIAM RIVER TRAIL

4.5 miles one way
Elevation change: 400 feet
Trail condition: good, mostly rolling, with rock-hopping crossings
Moderate
Spring through late fall
Access: To find the downstream trailhead from the campground, go northeast (turn left) for 6.1 miles

on FR 2209. Turn right onto FR 201 (Elkhorn Drive SE) to reach the trailhead in 0.5 mile. Find the upstream trailhead, at Shady Cove Bridge on FR 2207, by going northeast from the campground via FR 2209 and taking FR 2207 at the Y junction.

An upstream hike briefly skirts a replanted harvest site before descending into a classic ancient fir and hemlock forest. The rolling tour stays mainly above the Little North Santiam River but offers frequent views of the clear, rushing, green water with its beckoning pools. Gravel bars, boulders, and bedrock shelves define the river, while rock outcrops dot the forest slope.

At 1.2 miles, sounds of Henline Creek Falls call hikers from the trail for a glimpse through the tree cover. The trail then begins its one major ascent. Vista spurs atop the rock outcrops overlook the Little North Santiam canyon, now flanked by steep rock walls.

At 2.5 miles, the roller coaster trek resumes along the forested flat just above the river (the steep bank discourages detours). Spur trails at 3.2 miles lead to river overlooks of deep, bowl-carved pools, with linking cascades and a free-standing rock pillar. The tree-shaded river tour concludes at Shady Cove Bridge.

38 BREITENBUSH CAMPGROUND

30 tent/trailer units
Standard service fee campground
Nonflush toilets
Water
Open seasonally: end of May through early September

For information: Detroit Ranger District
Map: Willamette National Forest
Access: Find the campground along FR 46 about 10.0 miles northeast of Detroit and just south of Breitenbush Hot Springs.

These forest campsites of hemlock, cedar, and vine maple above the scenic Breitenbush River provide a comfortable base from which to enjoy the area hiking and fishing. Spring Creek threads through the campground. Nearby riverside campgrounds, southwest on FR 46, offer similar services and access.

SOUTH BREITENBUSH GORGE NATIONAL RECREATION TRAIL

2.5 miles one way
Elevation change: 400 feet
Trail condition: good forest path
Easy to moderate
Year-round (except during low-elevation snows)

Access: From camp, go northeast on FR 46, bypassing the junctions to Breitenbush Hot Springs, and turn southeast (right) onto gravel FR 4685. Find marked trailheads at 0.25, 2.0, and 2.5 miles.

A richly textured forest of old-growth Douglas fir, cedar, and western hemlock houses this trail. Rhododendron, Pacific yew, and vine maple dominate the midstory, with scattered dogwood. Twin flower, vanilla leaf, duckfoot, bunchberry, and red huckleberry add to the understory abundance. Nurse trees lace the forest floor. Along the way, mosses and ground vegetation have begun to reclaim snapped limbs and tumbled trees from the January 1990 windstorm.

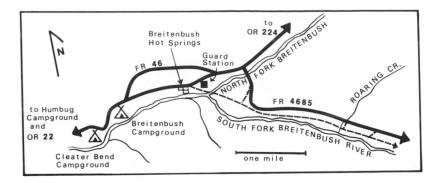

The trail travels well above the South Fork of the Breitenbush River, which rushes in the backdrop.

For a 1.5-mile hike from the northwesternmost trailhead, go left at the early junction to find the parallel-log walkway leading to an overlook of South Breitenbush Gorge—a narrow chasm where deep, clear waters reflect the dark cloak of the gorge. Moss, fern, and water-loving plants ornament the 30- to 40-foot walls. Upstream is a small sparkling falls.

Return to the main trail to find Roaring Creek at 2.0 miles, where moss-covered rocks and clear, cascading waters meet with great flare. A footbridge crossing and creekside stair steps provide good views. The trail continues beyond the southeast trailhead at 2.5 miles, but it loses some of its mystery with the proximity of the road and the admission of light, brought about by some nearby logging activity. The drainages along this stretch tend to be marshy.

For Breitenbush Hot Springs guests, an alternate access to the South Fork Trail begins on FR 4600.050, below the guard station. It adds another mile of distance and another 250 feet in elevation change as it travels an alder–maple riparian environment to the gravel-braided river bottom. Footbridges enable a crossing of the North Fork of the Breitenbush River, just above its confluence with the South Fork. From there, the trail climbs through a corridor of chinquapin, salal, rhododendron, and vine maple to the old-growth splendor.

HUMBUG FLAT TRAIL

2.0 miles round trip
Elevation change: minimal
Trail condition: good forest path
Easy

Year-round
Access: From camp, go southwest on FR 46 to Humbug Campground. Find the trailhead near site 9.

The trail heads through an open forest richly laden with rhododendron and salal to travel an old-growth-forested bench above the Breitenbush River. Paralleling the river downstream, the trail offers glimpses of clear-coursing beauty. Precarious side trails invite anglers to descend the bank. Monarch stout cedars, nurse trees, snags, oxalis, twisted stalk, false Solomon's seal, and a thick moss carpet add their signatures to this multidimensional forest.

Midway, the trail passes down the back of a fallen tree to make a brief river visit. It then climbs steeply away to travel a second-growth forest of young fir and hemlock with some scenic alder stands. The hike ends at the FR 46 trailhead, near the bridge.

39 OLALLIE LAKES SCENIC AREA

96 tent/trailer units
Standard service mostly fee campgrounds
Nonflush toilets
Water (except at Olallie Meadow and Lower Lake)
Open seasonally: June through September
For information: Clackamas Ranger District

Map: Mount Hood National Forest
Access: From FR 46 (which connects Detroit, on OR 22, and Ripplebrook, on OR 224), turn east onto FR 4690 and follow signs to the lakes area (about 8.0 miles off FR 46). The route starts on paved surface and becomes a bumpy, gravel road.

Situated beside lakes and meadows, these open, forested sites offer access to a fine trail system with multiple lake destinations, prime huckleberry fields for autumn harvest, and Mount Jefferson and Cascade Mountain vistas. Still-water rafting, fishing, and photography are other favorite area pursuits.

RUSS LAKE TRAIL

2.0 or 2.8 miles round trip
Elevation change: 100 feet
Trail condition: good forest path
Easy

Late spring through fall
Access: Find the trailhead at the end of Olallie Meadow Campground.

This trail travels a lodgepole pine–hemlock forest with an understory of lupine, dwarf and true huckleberry, and beargrass. In 0.1 mile, a right followed by another right leads to Triangle Lake via the Lodgepole Trail (a 0.4-mile

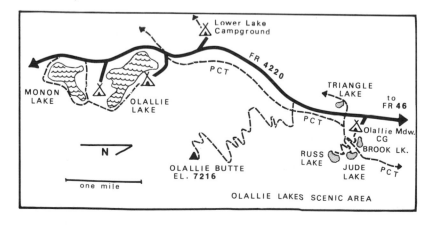

Olallie Lake and Mount Jefferson

detour). Triangle Lake's open meadow shoreline, shallow waters, and Olallie Butte vista create a tranquil retreat.

A left at the 0.1-mile junction leads to a series of scenic lakes: the lodgepole pine–ringed, nearly circular pond of Brooks Lake; the irregular shoreline and scenic outlets of Jude Lake; and finally Russ Lake, the largest one, with its Olallie Butte vista. The trail crosses the Pacific Crest Trail near Jude Lake. Crayfish and newts scurry for shelter in the shallow waters next to the shores.

OLALLIE BUTTE TRAIL

6.0 miles round trip
Elevation change: 2,600 feet
Trail condition: sometimes rocky, steady-climbing grade
Difficult

Late spring through fall
Access: Find the trailhead between Olallie Meadow and Lower Lake campgrounds, where utility lines cross FR 4220.

Crossing the Pacific Crest Trail at 0.1 mile, this trail climbs through a forest complex of mountain hemlock, lodgepole pine, manzanita, and spruce. Midway, it tours an old-growth grove of short, stout spruce and hemlock interspersed by rock-studded patches of high meadow, where the red-orange plumes of Indian paintbrush parade.

Winding toward the summit, the trail unveils grand views of Mount Hood, with Mounts Rainier, Adams, and St. Helens forming its backdrop, followed by tree-filtered views of Mount Jefferson, the lakes basin, and the southern Cascades. Atop the butte, 360-degree viewing pulls together all these attractions, with Mount Jefferson imposing in its snowy finery. The rocky, cindery summit houses the remnant rock walls of a one-time lookout, wind-stunted trees, ground-hugging plants, and lichen-etched rocks. The east face sports rugged cliffs and spires accented by purple penstemon. The upper trail reaches are hot and open, so carry plenty of water.

MONON LAKE TRAIL

2.7 miles one way	Late spring through fall
Elevation change: 100 feet	Access: Find trailheads at the north
Trail condition: good forest path	and south ends of the lake, on FR
Easy	4220.

Rounding three-quarters of the Monon Lake shore, this trail travels through a mixed conifer forest and patchy meadowland threaded by wild huckleberry and blueberry bushes. It offers views of Olallie Butte, Mount Jefferson, and smaller neighboring peaks. Still morning waters reflect the tall, straight trunks of the forest rim. Along the way, the trail affords ample opportunity to pause by the calming blue waters.

Monon Lake Trail connects to the Olallie Lake Trail, which tours the larger, more developed lake. Olallie Lake holds a Mount Jefferson reflection when the wind is still and the day is clear.

40 MARION FORKS CAMPGROUND

15 tent/trailer units	For information: Detroit Ranger
Standard service fee campground	District
Nonflush toilets	Map: Willamette National Forest
Water	Access: Turn north off OR 22 at
Open seasonally: end of May	the community of Marion Forks.
through September	Watch for the sign for the hatchery
	and forest camp.

Located behind Marion Forks Fish Hatchery, these comfortable, forested sites along Marion Creek escape the noise and congestion of OR 22. Nearby trails visit mountain lakes and streams, waterfalls, rock outcrops, and old-growth abundance. Marion Creek invites the cooling of ankles or the casting of a line. Riverside Campground, north on OR 22, holds another 37 sites.

INDEPENDENCE ROCK TRAIL

2.4 miles round trip	Spring through fall
Elevation change: 300 feet	Access: From camp, go 0.1 mile
Trail condition: good forest path,	north on OR 22, and turn east
with loose rock near the top	onto FR 2255 (Marion Road).
Easy to moderate	Find the trailhead in 0.1 mile.

The trail tours a Douglas fir forest. Vanilla leaf, wild rose, red huckleberry, ferns, bunchberry, Oregon grape, and false Solomon's seal fill the understory with texture. An enormous ant mound rests trailside about 0.25 mile in from the road.

Rounding the base of Independence Rock at 1.0 mile leads to the trail junction with the spur to the summit. Use caution on this steep, loose-rock spur, especially upon descent. The summit holds views of the Marion Creek and North Santiam River drainages, Pine Ridge, and the alternating forests and clearcuts. For the return trek, either continue southeast along the trail for a loop hike, which includes walking along Marion Road, or retrace your steps.

MARION LAKE TRAIL

5.2 miles round trip, permit required
Elevation change: 800 feet
Trail condition: wide, packed-earth trail with some roots and loose rock; continuous comfortable climb
Easy to moderate
Spring through fall

Access: From camp, go 0.1 mile north on OR 22, and turn east onto FR 2255 (Marion Road). Find the trailhead in 4.4 miles at the end of this paved and gravel route. Pit toilets are located at the parking area.

This popular Mount Jefferson Wilderness trail travels through old-growth forest, bypassing the smaller, alder- and brush-rimmed Lake Ann to arrive at Marion Lake, a large lake with a forest rim interrupted by talus slopes. Marion Lake offers vistas of Three Fingered Jack, Mount Jefferson, and Marion Mountain. Along both lakes, respect the areas closed for revegetation and marked "no camping."

At the 1.6-mile trail junction, after Lake Ann, both Outlet and Marion trails lead to Marion Lake, allowing a lake circuit. For lake campers or avid hikers, a series of fine trails radiating out from Marion Lake invite exploration. Marion Mountain, a 2.8-mile hike from the lake, overlooks the basin and wilderness. Midweek and off-season visits promise quieter, more enjoyable lake stays.

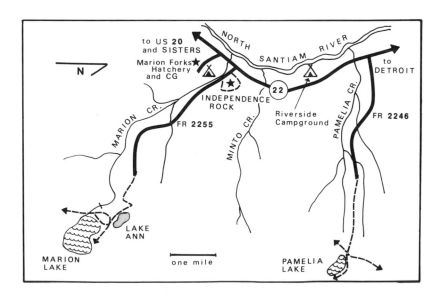

The Marion Lakes Trail

PAMELIA LAKE TRAIL

4.6 miles round trip, permit
required
Elevation change: 700 feet
Trail condition: good forest path,
with well-paced grade
Easy to moderate
Spring through fall

Access: From camp, go north 4.0
miles on OR 22, turning right
onto FR 2246 (Pamelia Road).
Pavement and a good gravel surface lead to the marked trailhead
at road's end.

Paralleling Pamelia Creek upstream to the lake, this trail travels through
an old-growth forest in the Mount Jefferson Wilderness Area. The trail boasts
a cedar–fir–hemlock skyline pierced by scenic snags. False Solomon's seal,
prince's pine, and bunchberry bring spring accents to the trail. The creek fades
upon the approach to Pamelia Lake—a mostly shallow, big mountain lake with
partly submerged logs. Rhododendron thread the forest rim, which is set back
from the open, rocky lake shore; in spring and summer, the bushes put on an
outstanding color show.

Touring the lake shore, hikers find views of Grizzly Peak and Mount
Jefferson. In fall, the racing stripes of red-orange vine maple blaze the drainages
on Mount Jefferson. The Pamelia Lake trail provides access to the Grizzly Peak
and Pacific Crest trails. Pan-sized cutthroat trout attract anglers to the lake.

41 PIONEER FORD CAMPGROUND

20 tent/trailer units
Standard service fee campground
Nonflush toilets
Water
Open seasonally: May through
September
For information: Sisters Ranger
District

Map: Deschutes National Forest
Access: From US 20/OR 126
northeast of Sisters, turn north on
County 14 toward Camp Sherman.
At the junction in 2.5 miles, go
right on FR 14. Find the campground in 9.6 miles.

These sites amid ponderosa pine, fir, and cedar along the Wild and Scenic
Metolius River provide a restful base from which to explore the area trails, enjoy
blue-ribbon fly fishing, tour Wizard Falls Fish Hatchery, and view the surprising origins of this state-treasured waterway. Altogether, some 125 USFS
campsites serve Upper Metolius River visitors.

METOLIUS RIVER TRAIL

5.6-mile loop (via Wizard Falls Fish
Hatchery)
Elevation change: 100 feet
Trail condition: river-bank footpath
(the west-bank path is more
established than the east-bank one)

Moderate
Spring through fall
Access: From camp, head upstream.

In this popular recreation corridor, foot trails travel both banks of the
Metolius River, allowing scenic river touring. From camp, a clockwise loop
travels upstream, crosses the bridge to Wizard Falls Fish Hatchery, loops
downstream to the Lower Bridge crossing, and draws to a close, traveling 0.6

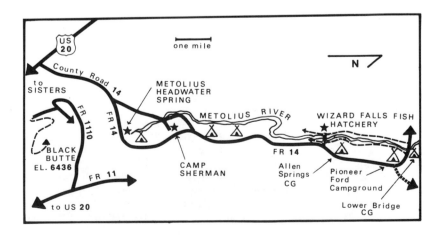

mile upstream via the East Metolius Trail. Ponderosa pine, lodgepole pine, and western larch frame the Metolius. Grass mounds, islands, and silvered logs accent the stream, which reveals various moods as it churns through deep trenches, riffles over stones, and slows to form tranquil pools.

The fish hatchery welcomes visitors to view its displays and holding ponds. The settling pool, detaining the "escapee" fish, is an interesting stop. Large splashes give clues to the size of the fish. Here, eagles, minks, and herons gather to feed.

BLACK BUTTE TRAIL

4.0 miles round trip
Elevation change: 1,500 feet
Trail condition: good, wide,
steady-climbing
Moderate
Late spring through fall
Access: Return to US 20, turn left,
and go southeast for 4.0 miles.

Then turn north onto FR 11, toward Indian Ford Campground. In 3.7 miles, turn left onto improved FR 1110 (Black Butte Trailhead Road). Remain on FR 1110 to arrive at the trailhead and parking lot in 5.0 miles.

The ascent begins by traveling through a mixed-age ponderosa pine forest on the west flank offering tree-filtered views of Mount Washington, Three Fingered Jack, and Hayrick Butte. Ferns, thistle, manzanita, sticky laurel, and chinquapin break the open understory. White-bark pine and grand fir become part of the mix. Midway up, the trail crosses an open shrub slope with manzanita, balsam root, thistle, fireweed, snags, and low pines. The sometimes pungent, sometimes sweet smell of flowering bushes wafts on the breeze or blankets the trail. Open, southerly views of Black Butte Ranch, North Sister and South Sister, Broken Top, Mount Washington, and Belknap, Little Belknap, and Black craters encourage hikers to continue the ascent.

Near the summit, the trail enters a "ghost forest" recovering naturally from a 1981 lightning fire. Here, hikers find views of the high-desert plateau, the Deschutes River plain, and Mounts Jefferson, Hood, and Adams. The summit ridge pulls all the vistas together and adds views of Green Ridge and the Metolius Basin. For safety, the lookout tower has been closed to visitors, so no single site affords 360-degree viewing. The summit's 1924-cupola tower is one of the few of its kind in the Northwest. Ground squirrel marauders abound on top of the butte.

HEAD OF METOLIUS

Public vista; 0.25-mile paved, all-ability trail to the site
For information: see page 112

Access: From the campground, go 8.0 miles south on FR 14 to the marked turn.

At this popular photo point, a mature ponderosa pine forest and lush green pasture cradle the Metolius River headwaters as Mount Jefferson looms in the distance. Here, a full-coursing Metolius River materializes—seemingly without explanation. Springs originating deep beneath Black Butte give rise to the phenomenon.

CAMP SHERMAN FISH-VIEWING PLATFORM

Public vista point
For information: see page 112

Access: Find the platform at Camp
Sherman, below the store near the
bridge.

This viewing deck on the Metolius River holds species-identification plaques, with coin-operated fish-pellet machines nearby. Feeding the fish is popular with all age groups. Large, bully fish stake out the waters just below the platform; under the bridge, smaller fish await the missed morsels.

42 HOUSE ROCK CAMPGROUND

13 tent units; 4 tent/trailer units
Standard service fee campground
Nonflush toilets
Water
Open seasonally: June through
early September
For information: Sweet Home
Ranger District

Map: Willamette National Forest
Access: On US 20, 24.0 miles east
of Sweet Home, turn south onto
Squaw Creek Road (FR 2044).
Find the campground off FR
2044.202 in about 1.0 mile.

The camp and day-use sites occupy a forest of large-diameter fir at the confluence of the South Santiam River and Sheep Creek. Upper-level sites are more spacious, private, and scenic, with some along the banks of the South Santiam. Area trails visit rock outcrops, old-growth habitat, the Old Santiam Wagon Road, and wildflower fields. The Iron Mountain Lookout trail (east of camp on US 20) is the most popular hike in the state for wildflower appreciation.

HOUSE ROCK LOOP TRAIL

1.0 mile round trip (to the falls
vista)
Elevation change: 100 feet
Trail condition: forest path, marshy
and slippery in places

Easy
Spring through fall
Access: Find the trailhead at the
day-use area.

The trail parallels Sheep Creek, steps up between two moss-capped boulders, and crosses a footbridge overlooking the confluence of the South Santiam River and Sheep Creek. The loop tour of an old-growth gallery with rich ground cover begins on the opposite shore. The usually small falls on the river proves incidental to the woodland splendor. Along the loop, a giant boulder creating an overhanging shelter gives the campground its name.

Going to the right (counterclockwise) on the loop finds a snatch of the Old Santiam Wagon Road in 0.1 mile, offering additional exploration. A walkable portion of this state-owned historic route travels the slope above the South Fork of the Santiam River downstream (to the right) for 2.0 miles, ultimately reaching Fernview Campground. As private property and old cabin

Autumn at Lower Soda Falls

sites line the way, keep to the wagon road. The road, reclaimed by moss, ferns, oxalis, and more, tours the Douglas fir–western hemlock forest, alder woodland, and open grassland of the river's south slope. Elk Creek crossing (at 0.6 mile) may turn back springtime venturers.

Midway, the trail offers its first river glimpses. The eroded bank of Stewart Creek at 1.5 miles suggests another turnaround point. Rock-hopping creek fordings and an occasional alder to step over are the lone obstacles.

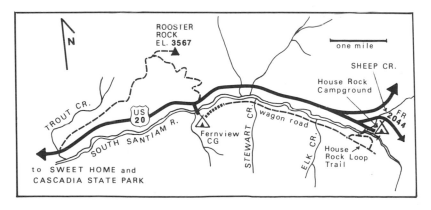

ROOSTER ROCK TRAIL

4.2 miles round trip
Elevation change: 2,100 feet
Trail condition: steady-climbing,
rock-studded in places
Moderate to difficult

Spring through fall
Access: From camp, go west on US
20. Find the trailhead 0.1 mile east
of Fernview Campground (park at
or near Fernview).

The trail snakes skyward through the rich, varied forest of Menagerie Wilderness: ancient Douglas fir, western hemlock, bigleaf maple, vine maple, Pacific yew, madrone, and chinquapin. Dogwood and rhododendron add their floral signatures in spring. From the 1.6-mile junction, the trail grows more steep for its final ascent to the Rooster Rock saddle.

The saddle view reveals the neighboring rock tower with its collapsing viewpoint structure, the South Santiam drainage, the Three Sisters, and the ridges and rock pinnacles dotting the Keith Creek drainage. The area is a popular destination for climbers.

At the 1.6-mile junction, hikers may opt to return to US 20 via the 2.8-mile Trout Creek Trail. The loop hike requires some walking along US 20.

LOWER SODA CREEK FALLS TRAIL

1.5 miles round trip
Elevation change: 500 feet
Trail condition: wide cinder or
earthen path
Easy

Year-round
Access: From camp, go west on US
20 to Cascadia State Park. Find the
trailhead at the lower picnic ground
parking area.

This trail travels the cool, old-growth-forested canyon of Soda Creek to obtain a vista of the 150- to 200-foot ribbon of falls squeezing through a fissure in the moss-decked cliff. Informal side paths at the end of the trail lead to better vantage points.

43 COLD WATER COVE CAMPGROUND

35 tent/trailer units
Standard service fee campground
Nonflush toilets
Water
Open seasonally: end of May
through early September

For information: McKenzie Ranger
District
Map: Willamette National Forest
Access: Find the campground
entrance road on OR 126 south of
its junction with US 20.

These fir-forested sites above cold, blue, crystalline Clear Lake offer access to the area's superior trail system, which visits cold springs, the lake, the Upper McKenzie River and its falls, ancient forest, and lava land. Self-propelled boating, fishing, and sightseeing are other popular pastimes. Ospreys nest above and patrol the lake. Across the lake, a rustic lake-shore resort has a small store and offers boat rentals.

CLEAR LAKE TRAIL

4.6-mile loop	Moderate
Elevation change: 100 feet	Spring through fall
Trail condition: pavement and forest path	Access: Start the hike at the campground boat launch area.

Beginning a counterclockwise lake-shore tour, the trail alternates between a crusted lava flow, accented with vine maple, juniper, and manzanita, and rich stands of old-growth Douglas fir. The trail passes Great Spring, a mesmerizing violet pool, before arriving at the Fish Lake Creek bridge and trail junction (1.8 miles). The loop continues rounding Clear Lake toward the resort, offering limited views of the Three Sisters.

From the resort (3.2 miles), the trail travels the forested slope above the lake, crosses the bridge over the Clear Lake outlet (the McKenzie River headwaters), and tours an older lava flow. The trail then goes left at the McKenzie River National Recreation Trail junction at 4.2 miles to complete the loop and return to camp.

McKENZIE RIVER NATIONAL RECREATION TRAIL (NRT)

3.1 miles round trip (to Carmen Reservoir)	Spring through fall
Elevation change: 400 feet	Access: Start at the campground boat launch area, hiking south (to the left).
Trail condition: forest or lava path Moderate	

This trail travels through forest, crossing OR 126 to reach the McKenzie Wild and Scenic River. With the footbridge crossing to the west bank, the trail leaves the road noise behind and basks in the river glory, passing black pools, blue-ice cascades, and overlooks of tall, broad, rushing Sahalie and Koosah falls (see below) before arriving at Carmen Reservoir.

The trail travels through a cedar–hemlock forest colored by vine maple, rhododendron, and huckleberry. Tree casts dot the lava flows along the trail. Dippers are commonly seen along the river, otters at times in the reservoir. This 27.0-mile national recreation trail offers a variety of shuttle-hike options. For the first miles after the reservoir diversion, the riverbed is usually dry, but downstream springs give it new life.

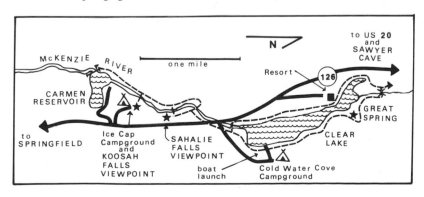

SAWYERS CAVE

Primitive, self-guided tour
100-yard trail to entrance; 200-
foot interior tour
Floor surface: uneven, rocky

Physical requirements: rock
scrambling, some bending
Moderate to difficult
Access: Look for a marked turnout
on the east side of US 20 about 7.0
miles northeast of camp.

From the parking area, small wooden "trail" signs indicate the route to the mouth of the cave, which announces itself with a gust of cold air. Flashlights are needed for all but a mere peek into the cave. The first room narrows, leading to a second room, where jewels of condensation spangle the walls.

SAHALIE AND KOOSAH FALLS VIEWPOINTS

Roadside public sites with short
trails to viewing areas
For information: see page 116

Access: Find the separate parking
lots (both well signed) south of
camp off OR 126, or reach the falls
via the McKenzie River NRT (see
page 117).

Both are beautiful, surging falls along the McKenzie Wild and Scenic River course. Sahalie Falls is a 100-foot plunge; Koosah Falls is a 63-foot split drop in a deep-cut gorge. At both sites, multilevel viewing areas offer different vantages on the falls.

The Three Sisters above Clear Lake

44 LAVA CAMP LAKE CAMPGROUND

12 tent/trailer units
Standard service no fee
campground
Nonflush toilets
No water
Open seasonally: June through
September
For information: Sisters Ranger
District

Map: Deschutes National Forest
Access: From the junction of US 20
and OR 242 in Sisters, go 13.8
miles west on OR 242 (McKenzie
Pass Scenic Route). Turn left on
red-cinder FR 900 to reach the
campground in 0.4 mile.

These established yet informal sites occupy the bench above and the shoreline next to small, green, muddy-bottomed Lava Camp Lake. Mountain hemlock, lodgepole pine, and fir rim the lake and shade the sites. Campers find easy access to trails, volcano vistas, lava lands, and car touring.

MATTHIEU LAKES LOOP TRAIL

5.75-mile loop, permit required
Elevation change: 800 feet
Trail condition: good; brief open
cinder-slope stretches
Moderate

Late spring through fall
Access: Find trailhead parking 0.1
mile below the campground at the
turn marked "Horse Use Area–
Pacific Crest Trail."

This trail heads straight from the trailhead sign to turn south (left) at the 0.25-mile T-junction. From there, it travels a forest of lodgepole pine, mountain hemlock, and fir alongside of a lava flow—a 30-foot high mass of boulders, rocks, and cinders—to enter the Three Sisters Wilderness. Continue straight at the 0.9-mile junction to begin a counterclockwise loop tour.

Leaving a circular pond at 1.5 miles, the trail strikes uphill toward North Matthieu Lake, a mid-sized, murky-bottomed, green-reflecting lake, nearly forest rimmed, with the lava flow on one side. Leaving the lake at 2.4 miles, the trail affords open views of North Sister, Yapoah Crater, The Island, and the lava

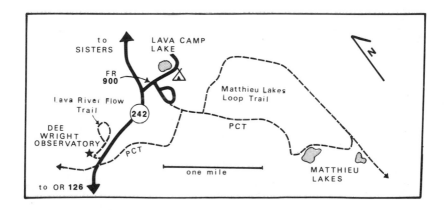

flow, with over-the-shoulder views of Belknap and Little Belknap craters.

From the 2.75-mile junction, South Matthieu Lake rests just below the saddle; the loop trail continues bearing left, contouring the cinder slope. South Matthieu is a small, homely lake, but it holds a grand panorama of North Sister (with Middle Sister just peeking out behind it), Yapoah Crater, and the Chalapaim Cinder Field. Completing the loop and the hike, the trail delivers a 180-degree vista spanning from North Sister to Mount Jefferson before making its slow forest descent and retracing the first 0.9 mile of the hike to return to the trailhead.

PACIFIC CREST TRAIL (PCT)

2.6 miles round trip (to Dee Wright Observatory)
Elevation change: minimal
Trail condition: open, hot, cinder-rock bed (wear boots)

Easy
Late spring through fall
Access: Reach the PCT via the Matthieu Lakes Loop Trail.

Going north (right) from the 0.25-mile T-junction, the PCT travels onto the lava flow, meanders along its edge, and slowly strings together views of Mount Washington, Belknap and Little Belknap craters, Dee Wright Observatory, Black Crater, Black Butte, North Sister, and Middle Sister. The trail offers a close look at the lava flow, providing hints to the nature of lava motion and cooling and revealing the slow process of revegetation. From the point where the trail meets OR 242, a 0.1-mile hike east (to the right) along the highway leads to the observatory.

Dee Wright Observatory

DEE WRIGHT OBSERVATORY

Public roadside vista site, nature trail, interpretive signs; open s easonally
For information: see page 119

Access: Leaving camp, go 0.5 mile west on OR 242, or reach the observatory via the Pacific Crest Trail (see page 120).

Atop its lava-flow rise, this medieval-looking, arch-windowed fortress, constructed of rock from the surrounding flow, holds one of the finest, most accessible volcano-vantage points in all of central Oregon. The windows are arranged to pinpoint Mounts Washington, Jefferson, and Hood, North Sister and Middle Sister, Three Fingered Jack, and a host of nearby craters. The tower roof holds a compass monument identifying the area landmarks and offers a grand overlook of the 65-square-mile flow.

The 0.5-mile Lava River Flow Trail is a paved circuit touring the edge of the flow, revealing the area geology and history and identifying geologic features. It travels beside a portion of the 1866 wagon road that crossed this flow for a torturous overland route.

45 BEDROCK CAMPGROUND

20 tent/trailer units
Standard service fee campground
Nonflush toilets
Water
Open seasonally: May through September
For information: Lowell Ranger District

Map: Willamette National Forest
Access: About 30.0 miles southeast of Springfield, find the campground on FR 18 (Big Fall Creek Road, leaving the northeast arm of Fall Creek Reservoir).

This scenic campground in a Douglas fir forest with a midstory of vine maple, hazel, and cascara and a thickly vegetated floor occupies a bank along Fall Creek. The camp offers access to hiking, fishing, and swimming within this popular recreation corridor, which boasts old-growth groves and creekside abundance.

FALL CREEK NATIONAL RECREATION TRAIL (NRT)

13.7 miles one way
Elevation change: 400 feet
Trail condition: well-defined; marshy after heavy rains
Easy to moderate

Year-round
Access: Find marked trailheads at camp and along and just off FR 18 (a trail brochure is available at the ranger district office).

Broken into segments by FR 18, this national recreation trail provides opportunities for shuttle hiking and short day hikes. Traveling from the campground to the west-end trailhead (4.1 miles west of camp on FR 18), the trail pursues a comfortable, downstream course along Fall Creek through old-growth and mature second-growth forest. The rich texture and diverse vegetation, minimal grade, and uninterrupted creek views recommend this easy, 3.5-mile segment.

The 4.1-mile segment, traveling upstream from the campground to the Alder Creek Trailhead (located on FR 1828, 2.5 miles east of camp via FR 18) holds the greatest challenge of the NRT. It ventures well up the slope, away from the creek, to meet the 5.8-mile Jones Trail. Afterward, it slowly switchbacks down the slope for a creekside tour. Owing to the elevation change, this segment also holds the greatest changes in habitat. Moss-decked cliffs and rocks, old-growth and mature second-growth forest, and mixed deciduous tangles, in turn, frame the trail.

A 1.0-mile hike west from the east-end trailhead (located on FR 1833, 5.9 miles east of camp via FR 18) leads to a 51-acre old-growth grove on the west bank of Marine Creek, where the trees average 40 inches in diameter and are some 300 to 500 years old. Beginning at 0.25 mile, old-growth towers and snags line the trail, hinting of the upcoming glory of the forest.

CLARK CREEK NATURE TRAIL–CLARK BUTTE TRAIL

1.0-mile nature loop, with a 1.5-mile spur to the butte
Elevation change: 100 feet; 1,400 feet (to the butte)
Trail condition: well-defined; marshy after heavy rains

Easy; difficult to the butte
Year-round
Access: Go 1.8 miles west of camp on FR 18.

Taking the nature trail in either direction leads to the butte trail. A clockwise tour travels through a hemlock–fir forest dotted with a few ancient (500- to 600-year-old) Douglas fir. The trail bypasses a rock shelter used by the Calapooya Indians and passes through diverse forest vegetation before arriving at the Clark Butte trail junction. Beyond the junction, other forest species and a marshy flat mark the loop.

Clark Butte Trail climbs steadily and steeply, touring the edge of an ancient forest influenced by the light admitted by a neighboring reforestation site. It crosses forest roads and a narrow, forested drainage to take switchbacks up the ridge to the butte—site of a former lookout, though few clues remain. The butte's full forest rim now blocks all vistas.

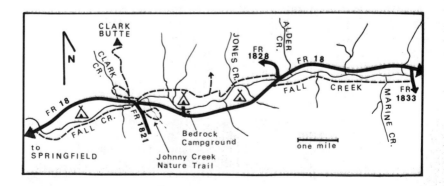

JOHNNY CREEK NATURE TRAIL

0.5-mile all-ability loop
Elevation change: none
Trail condition: wide, paved;
interpretive signs for the visually
impaired
Easy
Year-round

Access: Go 1.3 miles west of camp
via FR 18, and turn south onto FR
1821 for the trailhead. You can
also hike 1.7 miles west on Fall
Creek Trail to the junction of FR
18 and FR 1821.

The circuit tours an old-growth stand along Johnny Creek. Douglas fir, bigleaf and vine maple, cascara, hemlock, and western red cedar generate a thick canopy above oxalis, bleeding heart, bride's bonnet, twisted stalk, false Solomon's seal, and more. April and May find the understory and the dogwood in bloom. Interpretive signs point out subjects to see, touch, or smell, including a tumbled 500-year-old Douglas fir.

46 FRENCH PETE CAMPGROUND

17 tent/trailer units
Standard service fee campground
Nonflush toilets
Water
Open seasonally: end of May
through early September

For information: Blue River
Ranger District
Map: Willamette National Forest
Access: From OR 126 5.5 miles
east of Blue River, go 10.6 miles
south on FR 19.

Situated along the South Fork of the McKenzie River upstream from Cougar Reservoir, this scenic campground, nestled amid an old-growth grove, provides access to premier forest trails; creek, river, and reservoir fishing and recreation; and hot-springs bathing.

FRENCH PETE TRAIL

6.0 miles round trip (to the second
bridge site over the creek), permit
required
Elevation change: 500 feet

Trail condition: good path; rock
hops over side creeks
Moderate
Spring through fall
Access: Find the trailhead opposite
the campground, off FR 19.

Touring the Three Sisters Wilderness, this popular hike pairs old-growth splendor with the pulsing, clear waters of alder-lined French Pete Creek, from which the trail seldom strays. This wonderful ancient-forest "jungle" showcases tall, stout Douglas fir, cedar, and hemlock; showers of hazel, vine maple, dogwood, and rhododendron; and a rich understory tangle of fern, thimbleberry, columbine, pathfinder, and more. Despite heavy use, the trail remains neatly narrow. Only the popular day-use areas and campsites along the creek suffer trampling. Side paths lead to French Pete overlooks and accesses. The creek forever invites viewing and wading with its deep pools and rushing water.

YANKEE MOUNTAIN TRAIL

4.0 miles round trip (to the Yankee Mountain vista site), permit required
Elevation change: 2,000 feet
Trail condition: deliberately unmaintained for wild trekking

Difficult
Spring through fall
Access: Find the trailhead opposite the first parking space in the French Pete trailhead parking area.

This trail provides a wild experience, bridging the gap between a groomed trail and a cross-country outing. It has a well-defined bed, log crossings for marshy spots, and even a log-cut step-over. But it also has encroaching salal and Oregon grape; head-brushing branches of hemlock, hazel, and vine maple; and limbs and downfalls to negotiate. Because of the trail's slapping foliage, it is best to hike in dry weather or to wear rain chaps.

Overall, it is a fun, comfortable, uphill trek for the first mile. After that, added steepness increases the workload. Bald spots on the slope, just off the trail at 1.0 mile and beside it at 1.6 miles, offer vistas looking across the South Fork of the McKenzie River at Hardy Ridge and Lowell Mountain and the forest–clearcut patchwork. At the 2.0-mile turnaround site, the trail travels alongside a larger, grassy bald spot, sprinkled with yellow, pink, and blue wildflowers in early to mid-June. The site offers views of Yankee Mountain and the south wall of French Pete Canyon.

REBEL CREEK TRAIL

5.0 miles one way, permit required
Elevation change: 1,800 feet
Trail condition: good forest path, with some steep sections
Moderate to difficult

Spring through fall
Access: Find the trailhead east off FR 19 about 3.0 miles south of the campground.

This trail tours a mixed forest, dotted with Pacific yew, rhododendron, and vine maple. The lush, diverse forest floor holds many spring wildflowers. At the 0.1-mile junction, a left begins a south-slope tour above Rebel Creek.

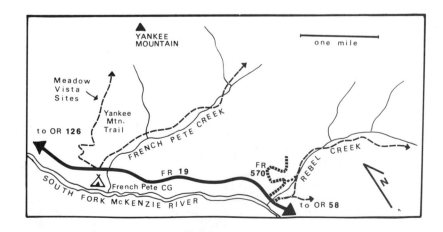

Dense small trees blanket the canyon next to the water. A few large Douglas fir straddle the trail, with old-growth glory claiming the upper slope.

Except for crossings at 0.5 mile and 1.0 mile, the trail remains above the creek, offering only overlooks through the tree cover. After the first bridge, a classic ancient forest houses the trail. Entering the Three Sisters Wilderness, the trail shows a more serious climbing intent. With no specific landmarks within the first 3.0 miles other than the early bridges, day hikers should personalize the hike length according to their interest and physical comfort.

French Pete Creek

TERWILLIGER HOT SPRINGS

Open to the public; donations
accepted for maintenance;
clothing optional but generally
absent; open sunrise to sunset
For information: see page 123

Access: Go 3.3 miles north of camp
on FR 19 to Cougar Reservoir.
Find parking on the east side of the
road; the trailhead is at the north
end of the bay on the road's west
side.

Reached via a 0.25-mile trail, this old-growth-area hot springs, with its open-air series of pools stair-stepping down the creek, is a popular destination. Midweek and off-season visits prove less crowded and more enjoyable than peak-time visits. At 0.1 mile, a trail spur to the left leads to a waterfall vista.

47 FRISSELL CROSSING CAMPGROUND

12 tent/trailer units
Standard service fee campground
Nonflush toilets
Water
Open seasonally: June through
October

For information: Blue River
Ranger District
Map: Willamette National Forest
Access: From the junction of OR
126 and FR 19, about 5.5 miles
east of Blue River, go 21.0 miles
south on FR 19.

Situated in an old-growth stand along the South Fork of the McKenzie River, this campground lies along the Aufderheide Forest Drive, a scenic route with auto-tour tapes available for loan at the Blue River and Oakridge ranger stations. Campers find convenient access to hiking and fishing, both along the river corridor and within the Three Sisters Wilderness. A 0.5-mile upstream trail connects the camp with the Olallie–South Fork McKenzie trailhead.

ERMA BELL LAKES LOOP HIKE

6.6-mile loop, permit required
Elevation change: 400 feet
Trail condition: good, well-used,
comfortable grade
Moderate
Spring through fall

Access: From camp, go 4.2 miles
south on FR 19 to FR 1957. Then
go southeast 3.5 miles on FR 1957
to Skookum Creek Campground
and the trailhead.

A counterclockwise circuit tours the Three Sisters Wilderness, stringing together the three Erma Bell lakes and Mud, Williams, and Otter lakes. At the junction in 0.5 mile, go straight to begin the tour. Douglas and grand fir, spruce, lodgepole pine, chinquapin, and rhododendron frame the path.

At 1.2 miles, the trail reaches Lower Erma Bell Lake, a large circular lake with a rocky shore and a forest rim. As the trail climbs the lake's west ridge, a 30-foot side path leads to an overlook of the waterfall on the inlet creek feeding Lower Erma Bell Lake from Middle Erma Bell Lake. A forest window framed by evergreen boughs offers a view of this white-icing falls spilling over a black

Middle Erma Bell Lake

tiered cliff. Middle Erma Bell Lake lies just ahead. At 2.1 miles, a faint trail leads to the shore of Upper Erma Bell Lake. The rim of trees partly secludes this lake from the main trail.

After taking switchbacks away from the upper lake, the loop continues straight at the 2.6-mile junction, soon rounding the slope above large, shallow Mud Lake. The trail again climbs. At 3.2 miles, take a left on the Williams Lake Trail to continue the loop. The now narrower trail passes Williams Lake, descends through forest, briefly climbs, and skirts meadows to descend to the Irish Mountain trail junction (at 5.4 miles). A left leads to Otter Lake. Elk frequent the area, and pileated woodpeckers sometimes slice through the forest. A right turn at the Erma Bell trail junction brings the hike to an end.

OLALLIE TRAIL

4.0 miles round trip (to Bull Creek crossing), permit required
Elevation change: 700 feet
Trail condition: rock-hopping crossings, comfortable grade
Moderate

Spring through fall
Access: Reach the trail via a 0.5-mile spur from camp, or go 0.1 mile north on FR 19 and turn east onto FR 441 to reach the trailhead in 0.8 mile.

The campground spur enters from the right as the trail leaves the parking area. The main trail soon crosses a small creek via side-by-side logs to tour the Three Sisters Wilderness. At the 0.3-mile junction, the Olallie Trail branches left. Young to middle-aged Douglas firs frame the path, with larger fir, hemlock, madrone, chinquapin, and maple later entering the mix. The first 0.5 mile shows a gradual, steady climb; thereafter, the pace picks up with switchbacks.

A clearing at 1.1 miles offers a broken downstream view of the South Fork of the McKenzie drainage, with its forested ridges and clearcut patches. Grouse are often flushed from cover by approaching boots. Twisted stalk, vanilla leaf, and other forest annuals bring spring color. At 1.4 miles, the trail tours a rich old-growth-forested creek canyon, where stout fir wear the dark badges of fire from long ago. Bull Creek crossing marks the turnaround site.

SOUTH FORK TRAIL

3.2 miles round trip (to the river-fording site), permit required
Elevation change: 100 feet
Trail condition: good; marshy areas; rock-hopping and fording crossings (beware of slippery wet rocks)

Easy to moderate
Spring through fall
Access: See Olallie Trail, page 127

This hike follows the Olallie Trail for the first 0.3 mile, at which point it branches right to journey toward the Elk Creek Trail. It tours the Three Sisters Wilderness, passing through a young to middle-aged Douglas fir forest with Oregon grape, sword and bracken fern, and spring annuals. When newly unfurled or autumn-tinted, the vine maple leaves add visual excitement. Several drainages segment the trail, some cutting deep channels.

Leaving the wilderness, the trail arrives at the South Fork of the McKenzie River. Here, a river fording or a log crossing is required to continue the hike to the Elk Creek trailhead, another 0.25 mile. Day hikers will likely want to end the trek here. The opposite shore holds a few stout cedar, fir, and hemlock amid an old select cut. Rhododendron bushes abound, and the forest floor shows diversity.

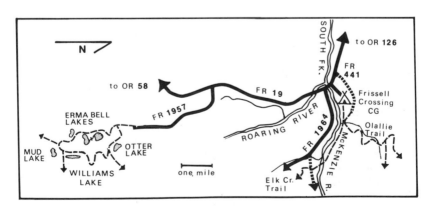

Canoeing, Hosmer Lake

48 HOSMER LAKE CAMPGROUNDS

38 tent/trailer units
Standard service no fee
campgrounds
Nonflush toilets
No water
Open seasonally: June through
September

For information: Bend Ranger
District
Map: Deschutes National Forest
Access: From Bend, go 33.0 miles
southwest on Cascade Lakes High-
way/FR 46, and turn east onto FR
4625 to reach the campgrounds in
1.2 miles.

South and Mallard Marsh campgrounds occupy the lodgepole pine– and fir-forested shore of scenic Hosmer Lake, where open waters reflect Mount Bachelor and Red Crater. Mallard Marsh, with its 15 pull-through sites, is most popular with trailer campers. Premier canoeing, birdwatching, fishing, and nature study draw campers to the lake. Wilderness hikes and swimming invite off-site exploration. Regulations call for fly fishing only (with barbless hooks) and for the unharmed release of Atlantic salmon. Only self-propelled or electric-motor boats are allowed on the lake.

SENOJ TRAIL

2.5 miles round trip (to Lucky
Lake), permit required
Elevation change: 400 feet
Trail condition: good, slow
climbing; may be dusty
Easy
Spring through fall

Access: From camp, return to FR
46, and go south 3.1 miles to the
trailhead parking lots. The hiker
trailhead is in the lower lot, and
the horse trailhead is in the upper
lot.

Crossing the footbridge over a seasonal drainage, the hiker path briefly
ascends a diverse forest corridor above a small meadow. It merges with the
horse path to enter a homogeneous lodgepole pine forest, with a few small
mountain hemlock claiming the lower story through forest succession. Lupine,
currant, and kinnikinick add patchy accents to the pole-tangled floor.

As the trail enters the Three Sisters Wilderness, approaching the lake, the
forest again becomes mixed, with larger fir and mountain hemlock sharing the
skyline with lodgepole pine. Lucky Lake is a large mountain beauty rimmed by
forest, with silver logs collecting against its shore.

SIX LAKES TRAIL

5.4 miles round trip (to Doris
Lake), permit required
Elevation change: 500 feet
Trail condition: good, slow
climbing

Easy
Spring through fall
Access: From camp, return to FR
46, and go north 0.5 mile to the
trailhead.

Entering the Three Sisters Wilderness, this split-character trail introduces
two more Cascade lakes. A semi-open, lodgepole pine–forested route with
partial shade begins the hike, traveling to Blow Lake. A mostly shaded trail
segment then continues the hike, touring a fuller, mixed forest to Doris Lake.

Blow Lake is another quiet beauty in the Cascade lakes system. A square
slide outcrop interrupts its forest rim. Doris Lake is a large, rounded, mountain
lake with a forested peninsula and a low, forested peak with a rock outcrop
overlooking the lake. Silver logs lie on the shore and in the water; small
boulders dot the water's edge.

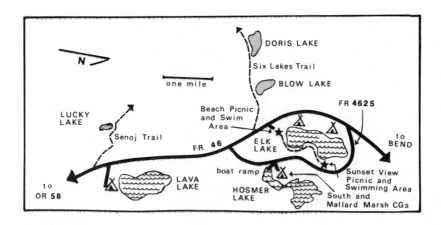

HOSMER LAKE CANOEING

Public access, ramp and side-water anchoring site
For information: see page 129

Access: Find the boat ramp 0.1 mile east of the campground area.

At this wetland lake, two open-water bodies, connected by a marshy neck of cattails, reeds, grasses, and lily pads, invite canoeists in tranquil pursuit of nature. Cameras can capture the still reflection of Mount Bachelor or the back lighting of a cattail. Herons, swallows, ospreys, ducks, geese, cormorants, kingfishers, and gulls send hands groping for binoculars. A muskrat spreading the waters is a common sighting.

The upper lake body, three to four times the size of the open-water area near the boat ramp, offers views of Mount Bachelor and Broken Top. Nearby Lava and Little Lava lakes hold further wetland-lake exploration, with views of South Sister, Broken Top, and Bachelor.

SUNSET VIEW PICNIC AND SWIMMING AREA

Public beach, picnic area, changing rooms, nonflush toilets
For information: see page 129

Access: From camp, continue north 1.1 miles on FR 4625 along the east shore of Elk Lake to the marked site.

This site looks west, catching sunset colors on Elk Lake. Lodgepole pine–shaded picnic tables rest above the long gravel beach, which has an attractive swimming area. Beginners launch their sailboards here. A 2.5-mile east-shore trail links the Sunset View and Beach day-use areas. The Beach Picnic and Swim Area, on Elk Lake's south shore, offers a grand view of South Sister, with Broken Top and Devils Hill, but it lies closer to the main road and has a less attractive beach and lake access.

49 CULTUS LAKE CAMPGROUND

54 tent/trailer units
Standard service fee campground
Nonflush toilets
Water
Open seasonally: June through September

For information: Bend Ranger District
Map: Deschutes National Forest
Access: From Bend, go southwest 43.0 miles on the Cascade Lakes Highway (FR 46). Turn northwest (right) onto FR 4635 for the campground.

These forested sites occupy the shore of Cultus Lake, which offers swimming, boating, waterskiing, and wind-sailing opportunities. The campground holds a boat launch, a gravel beach, and a trailhead for Winopee Trail, which visits a series of wilderness lakes for quieter relaxation. Cultus Butte overlooks the lake.

WINOPEE TRAIL

6.0 miles round trip (to Teddy Lakes), permit required	Easy
Elevation change: 300 feet	Late spring through fall
Trail condition: good, sometimes dusty forest path	Access: Find the trailhead near campsite 35.

The trail travels the pine- and grand fir–forested rim of Cultus Lake, offering tree-filtered lake views. Twin flower, false Solomon's seal, lupine, and kinnikinick dot the forest floor. At 0.6 mile and 1.4 miles, side trails lead to sandy beaches with nearby primitive forest campsites, approachable by foot or boat. The trail continues straight, past the Corral Lakes Trail junction, and turns right at 2.1 miles for Teddy Lakes. An alternative, equidistant hike travels straight ahead from the 2.1-mile junction, continuing the lake-rim tour to West Cultus Lake Campground—a large, developed, boat campground and beach.

En route to Teddy Lakes, the Winopee Trail makes a gradual climb through an open lodgepole pine forest. As it enters the Three Sisters Wilderness, the trail flattens. A right turn at the 2.6-mile junction quickly leads to the first lake, a good-sized mountain lake with a scenic grass-and-rush shoreline and a thick forest rim. Rounding the forested slope above it leads to the second lake (at 3.0 miles). It is a much larger mountain lake than the area maps suggest. Shading its shoreline is a rich forest rim of white pine, spruce, and fir.

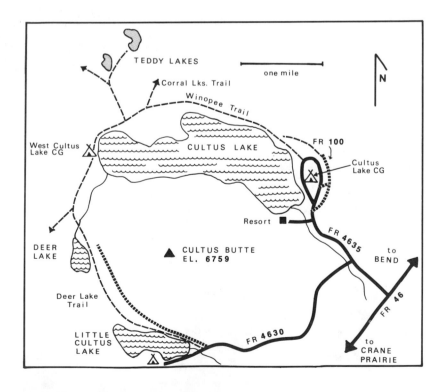

Snags, Crane Prairie Lake

DEER LAKE TRAIL

3.2 miles round trip
Elevation change: minimal
Trail condition: good earthen path,
with brief dirt-road segments
Easy
Late spring through fall

Access: Find the trailhead at Little
Cultus Lake Campground about
4.0 miles south of Cultus Lake.
From FR 4635, turn southwest
onto FR 4630, a gravel, washboard
road.

From the isolated campsite where FR 4630 first arrives at Little Cultus
Lake, the smaller dirt road closest to the lake soon becomes a rolling trail,
touring the mixed-forest base of Cultus Butte just above the lake. Farther along
the trail, the parallel Deer Lake Road is sometimes visible through the tree
border. At 0.7 mile, the trail draws away from the lake shore for a restful,
multitiered forest tour. With a gentle rise, the trail arrives at circular Deer Lake,
the end of this hike. The trail continues to West Cultus Lake Campground for
a longer hike.

CRANE PRAIRIE OSPREY OBSERVATION POINT

Public-access birdwatching site on a
reservoir; trails open May through
October
For information: see page 131

Access: From the junction of FR 46
and FR 4635, go 2.1 miles south
on FR 46 to reach the turnoff.

More than half of Oregon's osprey population nests along Crane Prairie
Reservoir. Arriving in April, the ospreys nest in the snag tops and lay three eggs,
which hatch in 4 to 5 weeks, with the young remaining in the nest 8 to 10
weeks. Winter migration occurs in September and October.

The 0.3-mile Osprey Point Trail travels a thinned lodgepole pine forest
to the interpretive site at the edge of a broad meadow shore. In early August,
tiny newly hatched toads hop along the trail. Paths web the meadow shore;
some prove marshy. Nesting platforms dot the flat. Vistas include Bachelor and
Cultus buttes, and South Sister. Herons, cormorants, ducks, geese, and bald
eagles are often sighted.

The 0.1-mile Billy Quinn Nature Trail visits the grave of a pioneer
shepherd, the tree-carved notations of an early-day forest worker, and Quinn
Springs, which give rise to a short river feeding Crane Prairie Reservoir.

50 NORTH WALDO CAMPGROUND

58 tent/trailer units
Standard service fee campground
Flush and nonflush toilets
Water
Open seasonally: July through
mid-October
For information: Oakridge Ranger
District

Map: Willamette National Forest
Access: From OR 58 about 23.0
miles southeast of Oakridge, turn
north onto FR 5897. Find the
campground in 12.7 miles, off FR
5898.

These fully shaded, spacious sites rest in a mature mountain hemlock–fir
forest above Waldo Lake. A small amphitheater and benches overlook the lake.
A boat dock, swim area, and trailheads are within easy access. Waldo Lake is one
of the purest lakes in the world. With rocky spits, islands, and bays, it is a scenic
lake to tour by canoe. The 22.0-mile Waldo Lake Trail rings this 10-square-
mile lake, usually touring the forest just in from the shore.

SHORELINE TRAIL

3.2 miles one way
Elevation change: none
Trail condition: rolling forest path,
with some rocks

Easy
Summer through fall
Access: Find trailheads at North
Waldo and Islet campgrounds.

From the North Waldo day-use area, a 1.0-mile segment heads north to
tour the small, island-protected northeast bay of the lake. Mountain hemlock
and white and lodgepole pine rim the lake, with dwarf huckleberry, kinnikinick,

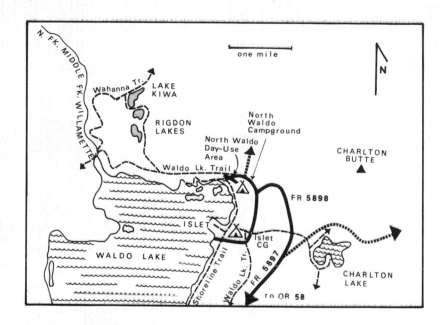

and beargrass laced among the rocks and logs on the forest floor. Lake views include the uneven forest rim and near and far peaks: The Twins, Mounts Ray and Fuji, and Diamond Peak. The hike dead-ends at a quiet, modestly sized bay and beach—a popular canoeist retreat as well.

From North Waldo Campground, a 2.2-mile stretch follows the forested shore south, bypassing North Waldo and Islet campgrounds. Benches dot the route for leisurely viewing of the lake. At 1.0 mile, Islet Point, a narrow peninsula, beckons for a 0.1-mile detour.

On the south side of Islet boat launch is a newer trail segment, which will one day extend to Shadow Bay Campground. Presently, it tours the forested shoreline, passing patches of forest blown down in winter 1990 and visiting isolated small, sandy beaches and rocky points and coves. The trail concludes at a long, crescent-shaped, sandy beach with a few drift logs, shore-lapping waters, and a view of Waldo Mountain and Mount Fuji.

WALDO LAKE TRAIL TO RIGDON LAKES TRAIL

6.8 miles round trip (to Lake Kiwa)
Elevation change: 200 feet
Trail condition: good, wide forest path
Easy to moderate

Summer through fall
Access: Find the trailhead at the upper parking lot for the North Waldo day-use area.

Rounding the lake in a counterclockwise direction, this inland trail travels through a true fir–mountain hemlock–white pine forest, bypassing a series of small ponds, with lily pads and open, shallow water. By 1.2 miles, the trail leaves the pond area and begins a modest ascent and descent, tracing the rolling terrain of the lake basin, to arrive at the 1.6-mile trail junction.

The Rigdon lakes trail turns right, entering the Waldo Lake Wilderness.

The southern lake, at 2.3 miles, is a deep, steep-banked, elongate body of water below Rigdon Butte. Just over the rise lies the northern lake, a rounded mid-sized mountain lake, mirroring another face of the butte. After following the lake shore, the trail crosses over the next rise to Lake Kiwa, a large lake with inviting small points, bays, and beaches—a good destination. With the ease of the trail and the proximity of the lakes to one another, some hikers portage one-person inflatable rafts to the area.

Alternatively, continuing straight from the 1.6-mile junction finds the North Fork of the Middle Willamette in 1.4 miles, for a 6.0-mile round-trip hike. Continuing to follow the mildly rolling terrain, which now boasts more huckleberry bushes, this hike option passes the foot of a large pond at 2.1 miles. A Waldo Lake detour lies just beyond. Ospreys and gulls soar over the indigo waters of the lake. After a slow ascent, the trail bypasses a rhododendron-rimmed pond with a small creek spilling over a flat rock outcrop to arrive at the Wild and Scenic North Fork of the Middle Willamette River. Upstream, at the river's lake headwaters, are a gauging station, a levee, a beach, and a primitive boat camp.

CHARLTON LAKE TRAIL

5.0 miles round trip	Easy to moderate
Elevation change: 300 feet	Summer through fall
Trail condition: good, steady grade, fragmented by forest roads	Access: Find the trailhead near sites 22 and 23 at Islet Campground.

This hike follows the Waldo Lake Trail east for 0.2 mile. Look for the small marker on a trailside tree showing the Charlton Lake Trail bearing left. A slow climb through a mountain hemlock–dominant forest and across forest roads leads to Charlton Lake (1.5 miles). (This large mountain lake is also a drive-to destination.) The Twins peek over its low forested rim, and conical Gerdine Butte presides.

Rounding the lake trail to the southwest provides a view of Charlton Butte across the lake. The trail crosses a grassy meadow shore with a few false hellebore and bypasses some wooded campsites, arriving at a trail junction at 2.25 miles. A trail uphill to the right leads to Round and Long meadows. The shoreline trail continues another 0.25 mile before becoming too faint to follow.

51 CEDAR CREEK CAMPGROUND

8 tent/trailer units	For information: Cottage Grove
Standard service no fee campground	Ranger District
	Map: Umpqua National Forest
Nonflush toilets	Access: Go 23.0 miles east of Cot-
No water	tage Grove via Row River and Brice
Open year-round	Creek roads.

Situated on a bench above scenic, broad, clear-flowing Brice Creek, at the foot of the Calapooya Mountains, this campground offers access to creekside and rugged climbing trails, fishing holes, mountain-biking routes, and a tour

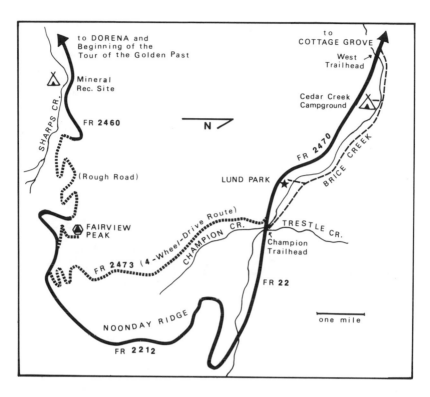

of the historical Bohemia Mining District. Large cedar, fir, and hemlock populate the shady grove of the campground, while understory plants flourish between the sites.

BRICE CREEK TRAIL

5.5 miles one way
Elevation change: 400 feet
Trail condition: good, rolling, loose rock in places; small drainages to rock-step over
Easy to moderate
Year-round (except during low-elevation snows)

Access: Find trailheads at the campground entrance, at Brice Creek bridge (1.3 miles west of camp), and at Lund Park and Champion trailheads (2.2 miles and 3.5 miles east of camp, respectively).

While the trail is good for shuttle hiking, it readily lends itself to two round-trip hikes right from camp. Heading downstream, a 3.0-mile round-trip hike branches left soon after the campground footbridge and begins contouring a rocky, old-growth-forested canyon slope above and away from Brice Creek. At 0.25 mile, the trail rounds an outcrop overlooking the creek but then draws away. A rich, multistory forest separates the creek from the trail. By 0.7 mile, the trail is again above the creek, with a steep, forested slope offering only filtered views. After rounding a forested flat, the trail briefly tours an open slope to the West Trailhead.

Heading upstream, a 5.0-mile round-trip hike to Lund Park offers a split-character tour, featuring first scenic Brice Creek and then the rich forest canyon. Turning right past the footbridge, the trail hugs the creek course, revealing a pair of 5- to 6-foot falls (at 0.25 mile), deep pools, riffles, shallow stretches, chutes, and channels. Gravel-bar beaches and bedrock shores invite sunbathers, swimmers, and anglers to the water's edge. Only the campground and periodic views of Brice Creek Road, on the opposite shore, mar the wild setting.

For the second leg of the journey, the rich, mixed forest of fir, cedar, hemlock, hazel, dogwood, and rhododendron commands attention. The trail

A historic mine building

occasionally pulls out of the forest, rounding the rocky slopes well above the creek. At 2.5 miles, a trail spur leads to a footbridge and Lund Park, once a mining-freight warehouse site and now a shady picnic ground. The main trail continues upstream another 1.5 miles to Champion trailhead.

TOUR OF THE GOLDEN PAST DRIVE

37.5-mile loop (four-wheel-drive tour)
Road quality: narrow, winding, climbing; much of it rock-studded; some carved drainage channels
Estimated speed: 10 to 20 mph

Access: Go 7.8 miles west of camp to the junction of Row River and Sharps Creek roads. A brochure available from the USFS describes a counterclockwise tour of the route.

A tour of interest primarily to historians and modern-day prospectors takes visitors past sites that were significant in the early days of this mining district but leave little to see today. Visitors can, however, appreciate the rugged setting, the difficulty of freighting equipment and supplies, and the isolated existence of the miners. The brochure proves an interesting read even if you don't take the tour, describing boom sites, colorful characters, early-day tales, and hardships.

Some of the tour is accessible to conventional vehicles, but by far the most interesting stops lie along the less-accessible roads. Watch mileages in the booklet and look for the "old gold panner" markers that identify many of the sites (some are private). From Bohemia Saddle, a side trip to Fairview Lookout is worthwhile. The road is good, and the tower is open to visitors. Clear-day vistas extend from the Coast Range to the volcano chain of the Cascades.

Respect private property along the entire loop, and stay away from adits (mine entrances), as timbers decay, tunnels crumble, and gases may escape.

52 TIMPANOGAS LAKE CAMPGROUND

10 tent/trailer units
Standard service fee campground
Nonflush toilets
Water
Open seasonally: June through September
For information: Rigdon Ranger District

Map: Willamette National Forest
Access: Find the campground about 42.0 miles southeast of Oakridge on a paved and gravel route. From OR 58, follow FR 21 and FR 2154 southeast.

Here, spacious, forested, lakeside sites rest above an incredibly blue mile-high lake bordered by meadow, forest, and rugged slope. A smaller lake nudges one end of the campground. The setting is a camper's dream—except for voracious mosquitoes during the early part of the camping season. The pristine setting usually outweighs the aggravation of spray and netting. Hiking, photography, still-water rafting, berry picking, and fishing fill campers' days.

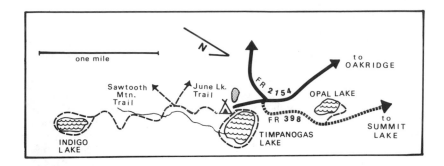

INDIGO LAKE TRAIL

3.75 miles round trip
Elevation change: 700 feet
Trail condition: well-marked
forest path, with steady grade

Moderate
Late spring through fall
Access: Find the trailhead at camp,
above the smaller lake.

The trail travels through a forest of Pacific silver fir and Engelmann spruce above a floor of huckleberry and heather, arriving at the trail junction in 0.5 mile. Go straight to continue the Indigo Lake trek. (The center right fork leads to Sawtooth Mountain in 3.5 miles, and the far right fork arrives at June Lake in 2.1 miles.)

Leaving the junction, the trail follows a nearby creek for the next leg. The trail then laces through forest, stringing together small meadows and views of Sawtooth Mountain, before arriving at Indigo Lake. Rugged Sawtooth Mountain (elevation 7,302 feet), with its scree slopes and vertical broken cliffs, looms above the lake setting. A 0.75-mile trail rings the blue brilliance, touring a mixed conifer forest and crossing a scree slope. The whistles of pikas chastise hikers who invade the rocky complex. The water is its deepest near the scree slope, offering a hole for swimming or fishing. A five-site backpacker camp occupies the lakeshore.

TIMPANOGAS LAKE TRAIL

1.0-mile loop
Elevation change: none
Trail condition: mostly good path,
marshy in places

Easy
Late spring through fall
Access: Begin the hike at the camp-
ground lake shore.

The trail travels just in from the lake shore, offering views of Sawtooth Mountain and the forested ridges above Timpanogas Lake. Dwarf and true huckleberry, vanilla leaf, bunchberry, and prince's pine mat the floor beneath the forest of Pacific silver fir, pine, and spruce. Rocky areas sport penstemon, while marshy areas sport false hellebore and shooting stars. Unfortunately, the peak wildflower season coincides with the peak mosquito season. On the east and southeast shores, hikers encounter inlets and marshy reaches, but usually adequate numbers of fallen logs and patches of high ground help keep your boots dry.

OPAL LAKE TRAIL

0.5 mile round trip
Elevation change: 100 feet
Trail condition: good earthen path
Easy
Late spring through fall

Access: From the campground, go
north (right) about 1.0 mile on FR
2154.398 to the marked roadside
parking area.

The trail descends from the road through a forest of Pacific silver fir and mixed conifer to the shore of Opal Lake. A couple of walk-in campsites are located in an opening along its bank. Opal Lake is a small, rounded mountain lake, offering a quiet retreat. Its thickly vegetated rim defies easy lake-shore passage beyond the campsites.

53 SUSAN CREEK CAMPGROUND

33 tent/trailer units
Standard service fee campground
Flush toilets
Water
Open seasonally: end of May
through September

For information: BLM, Roseburg
District
Map: Umpqua National Forest
Access: Turn off OR 138 about
28.0 miles east of Roseburg.

High-rise firs, bigleaf maple, and alder shade spacious river-bank sites above the hypnotic, blue-green North Umpqua River. Fly-cast fishing and exploration of the area's healthy trail system, which visits old-growth forest, falls, and an ancient Indian spiritual grounds, keep visitors entertained during a stay. A web of short trails covers the camp area, including a 0.5-mile spur to the day-use area and a 0.5-mile barrier-free trail overlooking the river. To the east, Bogus Creek Campground offers additional sites with access to the same offerings.

SUSAN CREEK FALLS–INDIAN MOUNDS TRAIL

2.0 miles round trip
Elevation change: 500 feet
Trail condition: rocky in places;
steep grade to the mounds

Easy
Year-round
Access: Find the trailhead across
OR 138 from the day-use area.

The trail travels through a mixed evergreen forest of small-diameter trees with a lush understory of salal, black huckleberry, fern, and moss to Susan Creek Falls, which drops 60 to 70 feet down a narrow cliff to a pool squeezed by large boulders. Spring finds a rushing white veil, while summer finds silvery threads spilling over uneven black rock. Beware of poison oak near the falls.

Continue across the footbridge and up the hill for 0.3 mile at trail's end to find the Indian mounds. The trail travels along a rocky, open utility corridor and then switches back through a conifer–madrone forest to arrive at the ceremonial rock piles laid by Indian boys seeking the supernatural on a spiritual

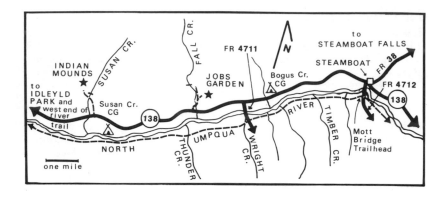

journey into manhood. A fence protects the historical mounds. Mounds made by contemporary hands and what appear to be authentic, moss-bound ones lie outside the enclosure.

FALL CREEK FALLS NATIONAL RECREATION TRAIL

1.5 miles round trip	Easy
Elevation change: 300 feet	Year-round
Trail condition: good, steady-climbing earthen path	Access: Take OR 138 about 3.4 miles east of the campground.

A scenic footbridge ties together the columnar basalt blocks of the creekbed and launches the trail. The path then snakes through a natural rock fissure to travel along Fall Creek in a richly forested canyon of remnant old-growth splendor. Views of cascades and pools accent the trek. A side spur at 0.25 mile leads to Jobs Garden, a lichen- and moss-etched cliff with a bountiful fern gallery. On the main trail, lower and upper vista points present the two-part, angled falls.

NORTH UMPQUA TRAIL

77.5 miles one way (multiple short-hike options)	Spring through fall (year-round at lower elevations)
Elevation change: depends on trail segment	Access: Find any of twelve trailheads along OR 138 and its side roads. The westernmost is at Swiftwater County Park, the east-ernmost at Kelsay Valley Trailhead. (A brochure is available at the Roseburg BLM office.)
Trail condition: rolling, marshy in places	
Easy, moderate, and difficult tours possible	

This long-distance trail travels a roller-coaster route, touring above and alongside the North Umpqua River, journeying deep into its side canyons, visiting ancient and second-growth forest, and passing scenic cliffs and water-falls.

The 1.5-mile Swiftwater to Fern Falls tour starts at the county park 6.8 miles west of the campground. Traveling through old- and second-growth forest of Douglas fir, sugar pine, cedar, and maple, the trail offers tree-filtered upstream views of the North Umpqua. The hike ends at a footbridge over another Fall Creek, providing a view of Fern Falls, a 10-foot split drop launching a series of cascades at the mouth of a fern-lined canyon.

The 2.3-mile Wright Creek–Thunder Creek tour takes a downstream, high-slope route through a mid-sized forest to arrive at a side canyon housing the spectacular, quick-dropping Thunder Creek—a series of slides, waterfalls, and cascades tumbling between moss-decorated banks to the river far below. To reach this segment, go 4.8 miles east of camp, and turn south off OR 138, crossing the bridge to the trailhead.

Heading upstream from the same trailhead, the 5.5-mile Wright Creek– Mott Bridge National Recreation Trail is ideal for a shuttle or an all-day hike. It takes a low-level upstream route along the river bank, with nearly continuous views of the still waters, rapids, and river bends. The trail passes moss-etched cliffs, scenic side creeks, and the site of Zane Grey's fishing camp and travels through an old-growth-forested flat. The noise from OR 138, which travels the opposite shore, is only a minor annoyance when compared with the natural bounty of the North Umpqua Trail.

STEAMBOAT FALLS

Public USFS campground and vista site
For information: North Umpqua Ranger District

Access: From the campground, go 9.6 miles east on OR 138, and turn north onto Steamboat Creek Road (FR 38). Go 5.5 miles, and turn right onto FR 3810 for the campground and vista in 1.0 mile.

This spectacular series of multiangle, multitiered falls stretching across the 70- to 100-foot breadth of scenic Steamboat Creek thrills viewers and inspires photographers. In September and October, visitors have the added excitement of watching the spawning chinook salmon jump the falls. Steamboat Creek is closed to fishing.

54 BOULDER FLAT CAMPGROUND

10 tent/trailer units
Standard service no fee campground
Nonflush toilets
No water
Open year-round

For information: North Umpqua Ranger District
Map: Umpqua National Forest
Access: Turn north off OR 138 about 16.0 miles southeast of Steamboat.

A second-growth mixed conifer forest threaded by maple and alder houses this North Umpqua River campground with spacious sites. Fern, salal, and Oregon grape spill between the sites. The campground holds rafting and fishing access; nearby trails draw visitors away from camp. The river drowns much of the road noise from OR 138.

BOULDER CREEK TRAIL

4.4 miles round trip (to the Boulder Creek fording site)
Elevation change: 700 feet
Trail condition: old road and good earthen path, with some sharply climbing stretches
Moderate
Spring through fall

Access: From the campground, go east for 2.7 miles on OR 138, and turn north onto Soda Springs Reservoir Road (FR 4775). Take an immediate left onto FR 4775.010. Find the trailhead in 2.5 miles at the end of this narrow, dirt-track road, passable for conventional vehicles (no RVs).

The trail climbs steeply from a gated road, rising above the North Umpqua River and overlooking Boulder Flat. At a fork in 0.2 mile, the Boulder Creek trail branches to the right, while the Illahee Flat trail heads downhill to the left. Fir, pine, and chinquapin frame the now narrow, needle-littered road path. Around the upcoming bend is a vista of three rock spires on Rattlesnake Ridge, including Old Man Rock; utility lines mar the view.

A foot trail replaces the former road as the hike approaches the Boulder Creek Wilderness. Douglas fir, sugar pine, oak, madrone, and manzanita offer shade and block views as the trail climbs. At 1.0 mile is Pine Bench, the most popular site in the wilderness. This large flat sports a magnificent old-growth ponderosa pine stand with a bracken fern floor.

At the Bradley Trail junction, continue straight for the Boulder Creek trail. At the north end of Pine Bench, the fork straight ahead leads to a small spring and a lower ledge overlooking the steep, forested ravine of Boulder Creek. The main trail journeys right, on a rolling trek through a mixed forest with Oregon grape, salal, and mosses. Continuing straight ahead from the Perry Butte Trail junction, the trail descends quickly into Boulder Canyon. Boulder Creek invites a stay before the return trek or a continuation of the hike on the opposite shore. Upstream from the fording site are inviting, ankle-cooling pools fed by a 2-foot cascade.

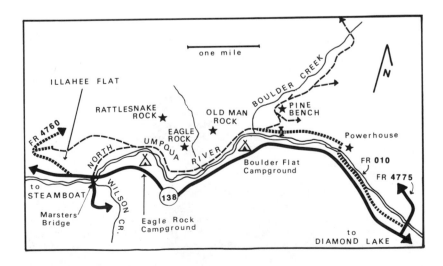

ILLAHEE FLAT TRAIL

2.75 miles one way
Elevation change: 800 feet
Trail condition: good earthen path,
rolling grade, with some steep
climbs
Moderate
Spring through fall

Access: Use the same trailhead as
Boulder Creek Trail, or, from the
campground, go west on OR 138
and turn north onto FR 4760, west
of Eagle Rock Campground. Go
uphill for 1.5 miles, and turn right
onto FR 4760.040 for the
trailhead in 0.25 mile.

Leaving from the Boulder Creek trailhead, this trail forks downhill to the
left to cross the Boulder Creek bridge. Angling left across a forest road, the trail
enters a classic low-elevation Douglas fir–western hemlock forest to follow the

Boulder Creek

North Umpqua River downstream. Cedars and maple accent the forest, and signs of beaver activity mark the shore. Despite the proximity of OR 138, the trail holds exciting river views, some featuring scenic boulder islands.

At 0.6 mile, near a gauge station with an old river-pulley system, is the rock-hopping crossing of Eagle Creek. At 1.2 miles, the trail runs opposite Eagle Creek Campground. Soon after, it takes switchbacks uphill, offering teasing glimpses of Rattlesnake Rock through the tree cover (best viewed in fall and winter, when the deciduous trees lose their leaves). The trail then levels out, contouring a steep, forested slope, with the utility corridor above some-times intruding on the setting.

At the junction in 1.6 miles, a 0.6-mile segment of the extensive North Umpqua Trail branches left, ending at OR 138 near Marsters Bridge. The Illahee Flat trail continues climbing to the right, skirting an oak woodland and offering over-the-shoulder looks at Rattlesnake Rock and Eagle Rock, to conclude at an old-time select-cut flat, the site of an early homestead.

55 LAKE IN THE WOODS CAMPGROUND

9 tent/trailer units
Standard service fee campground
Flush toilets
Water
Open seasonally: mid-May through September

For information: North Umpqua Ranger District
Map: Umpqua National Forest
Access: Drive 45.0 miles east of Roseburg via OR 138, County 17 (Little River Road), and FR 27 (mostly paved).

An old-growth forest shades the campsites ringing this small, shallow lake rimmed by cattails and topped by lily pads. The lake is a former swampy meadow drained for horse pasture and later flooded. Frogs abound in the lake, and a restored log cabin rests beside it. In spring and early summer, flowering rhododendron bushes accent the forest. Visitors pass their time hiking, fishing, and lounging at camp.

YAKSO FALLS TRAIL

1.5 miles round trip
Elevation change: minimal
Trail condition: wide earthen path
Easy

Spring through fall
Access: Find the trailhead across the road from the camp entrance.

This trail tours an old-growth forest of Douglas fir, cedar, and hemlock. A neighboring clearcut admits light along the first stretch, altering the understory vegetation mix. Bigleaf maple and vine maple, rhododendron, Oregon grape, and prince's pine color the mid- and understory. Sounds of the Little River and Yakso Falls add to the enjoyment and cause anticipation. The trail halts at the pool fed by this 70-foot conical drop, for a first-rate view. Moss-decked canyon walls form a partial bowl housing the falls. Some beautiful cedar and fir accent the setting. The force of the falls fans the nearby patches of maidenhair and sword ferns.

Yakso Falls

HEMLOCK FALLS TRAIL

1.0 mile round trip	Easy
Elevation change: 100 feet	Spring through fall
Trail condition: wide, switchbacked forest trail	Access: Find the trailhead near campsite 1.

The trail quickly descends through an old-growth-forest habitat. Rhododendron, twin flower, oxalis, and Oregon grape contribute to the floral abundance. The first sounds of rushing water signal a falls on a side creek, visible through the tree cover. Hemlock Falls is an 80-foot, narrow drop splashing over a boulder base. Downstream, the creek races through the scenic, steep-sided canyon. Mimicking the falls is a streamer of maidenhair ferns adorning the cliff face. Logs crisscross the base of the falls and crowd its pool.

WOLF CREEK FALLS TRAIL

2.0 miles round trip	Access: Find the trailhead 15.5
Elevation change: 400 feet	miles west of camp on County 17.
Trail condition: wide, forest path	Across the road from it is a small
Easy	picnic area.
Year-round	

A photographic, moon-shaped footbridge over the Little River launches this trail. Where it branches, the upstream path follows the Little River for 0.2 mile to a playing field across from the Wolf Creek Civilian Conservation Center. The main falls trail turns away from the river, crossing Wolf Creek. Bigleaf maples overhang the water, while vine maples crowd the shore. Branches of hemlock and Douglas fir create a light-blocking canopy.

At 0.3 mile, the trail travels across a bedrock floor, skirting a rock outcrop embroidered with moss and fern. Occasional dogwood and lichen-dressed yew punctuate this classic low-elevation Cascade forest. The trail concludes along the slope opposite the upper falls—a 60- to 80-foot vertical slide streaking the

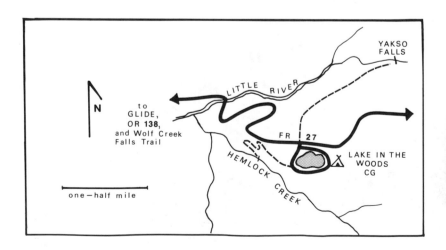

smooth face of the cliff. Moss, maidenhair and sword ferns, a few cedar, and bigleaf maple add to the setting. The lower falls consists of short, thin, rapid chutes spilling over a rocky confine. Shiny logs, wet from spray, litter its pool.

56 DIAMOND LAKE RECREATION AREA

494 tent/trailer units
Standard service fee campgrounds
Flush and nonflush toilets
Water
Open seasonally: mid-May through
October

For information: Diamond Lake
Ranger Station
Map: Umpqua National Forest
Access: Turn off OR 138 about
7.0 miles north of Crater Lake
National Park.

An extensive community of forested campsites rings this large, nearly mile-high lake—a winter–summer sport complex. Campers find easy access to water sport, fishing, and a prized network of hiking, cycling, and equestrian trails. Cinnamon Butte Lookout, north off OR 138 via gravel FR 2711, offers a sweeping southern-Cascade vista. Weather and sunset watchers find an ideal vigil post atop the cinder cone (elevation 6,417 feet). Do not disturb the electronic site at its summit.

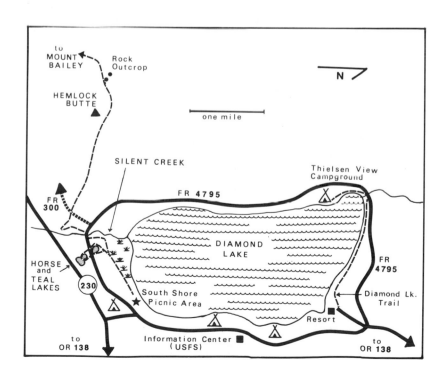

DIAMOND LAKE TRAIL

1.75 miles one way (to Mount
Thielsen View Campground)
Elevation change: minimal
Trail condition: wide, paved lane
Easy
Spring through fall

Access: Find the trailhead off the
access road to the cabins, about
200 feet uphill from the Diamond
Lake Resort lodge and store
parking area.

The trail rounds the north end of the lake via a forest bench about 10 feet above it, with occasional dips to the shore. Ponderosa pine and grand and Douglas firs climb the slope. At 0.2 mile, the trail affords an open lake vista that includes Mount Bailey.

At 1.0 mile, the trail briefly exits onto FR 4795 before returning to the lake shore, where open views of Mount Thielsen (paired with a lake reflection on windless mornings) greet hikers. Lodgepole and sugar pines, grand fir, and mountain hemlock now form the forest complex. Marsh occupies the lake fringe as the trail draws closer to the road. The hike ends at the campground, with additional views of Mount Thielsen. Cyclists may continue on a lake loop via the road and bicycle-path segments.

HORSE AND TEAL LAKES TRAIL TO SILENT CREEK TRAIL

5.7 miles round trip
Elevation change: minimal
Trail condition: wide, paved lane or
earthen footpath
Easy to moderate

Spring through fall
Access: Find the trailhead near the
fish-cleaning station at the South
Shore Picnic Area.

The trail tours the lodgepole pine–mountain hemlock fringe of an extensive meadow with cow-lily ponds. Diamond Lake occupies the far edge, while Mount Bailey reigns over the setting. Geese, barely visible, wade amid the grasses.

At 0.75 mile, the paved lane draws away from the meadow, arriving opposite Teal Lake at 0.9 mile. Go left on the earthen path for a figure-8 loop encircling Teal and Horse lakes. (The paved path ahead is Silent Creek Trail.) The loop trail finds low forest rims encircling the shallow lakes, which support a few lily pads, flooded grasses, and silver logs. At Horse Lake, the trail passes between two shallow ponds; in spring, a watery arm links the ponds, severing the trail.

The paved Silent Creek Trail travels through planted and multistory lodgepole pine forests to tag the east bank of Silent Creek. The enchantingly broad, smooth-faced stream shimmers yellow, green, and black as the water passes over a floor of yellow rock, moss, and sand. Logs lace the creek, forming pools. The opposite shore holds forest–meadow habitat.

In 0.5 mile, the trail arrives at FR 4795, where it crosses a bridge to travel the west bank upstream on an earthen bed. Boardwalks across the moist meadow stretches bow to a dry-forest path paralleling the creek. Bypassing the headwater springs, the route veers away from the creek canyon, following a blazed course through the open lodgepole pine forest to FR 4795.300.

Mount Theilsen above Diamond Lake

MOUNT BAILEY NATIONAL RECREATION TRAIL

4.0 miles round trip (to the trail-
head on FR 380)
Elevation change: 800 feet
Trail condition: good forest path,
with steady climbing
Moderate

Late spring through fall
Access: From FR 4795 at the
southwest end of the lake, turn
south onto dirt FR 4795.300 (Bailey Road). Find the trailhead opposite Silent Creek Trail in 0.4 mile.

The trail crosses a small drainage—at times active with frogs—to ascend
through an open lodgepole pine forest. At 0.75 mile, a break in the tree cover
allows a brief view to the south. The forest mix now includes fir, mountain
hemlock, Shasta red fir, and white-bark, white, and lodgepole pines, with
patchy chinquapin, prince's pine, huckleberry, and kinnikinick.

At 1.5 miles, as the trail rounds a bend approaching a forest flat, a detour
north (to the right) off the trail to nearby rock outcrops provides a Diamond
Lake vista with Mount Thielsen, Sawtooth Ridge, and Tipsoo Peak. Mount
Scott can be seen peeking over the saddle to the south. A tour of the forest flat
leads to the conclusion of this hike at FR 380. (Mount Bailey's summit is
another 2.5 miles of intense climb from there.)

57 CRATER LAKE NATIONAL PARK

198 tent/trailer units (Mazama Campground)
Standard service fee campground
Flush toilets; showers
Water
Open seasonally: June through October 20
For information: Crater Lake Lodge Company

Map: park map-and-guide brochure
Access: The park, located about 54.0 miles northwest of Klamath Falls, has entrances on OR 62 and OR 138. The entrance fee allows seven-day access to the park.

Pine-forested sites on a rim above deep-cut Annie Creek gorge serve as a convenient base for park exploration. Trails, scenic drives, and lake tours display the park's beauty and tell the tale of its geologic origins. Lost Creek Campground offers twelve additional campsites within the park's boundaries.

ANNIE CREEK CANYON TRAIL

1.7 miles round trip
Elevation change: 200 feet
Trail condition: dusty pumice path with footbridges
Easy

Summer through early fall
Access: Find trailheads at Mazama Campground loops C, D, and G. (Interpretive brochures are available at the trailheads.)

From the rim, the trail quickly descends to the bottom of Annie Creek Canyon. Open mountain hemlock–fir forest, steep, unstable pumice slopes, and wildflower grasslands characterize this deep canyon. The trail crisscrosses Annie Creek, a 3- to 4-foot-wide, clear, bubbling stream with meadow banks and a gravel bottom. Larkspur, monkey flowers, scarlet skyrockets, and more comprise the wildflower showcase.

Following a 0.5-mile creek tour, the trail climbs to close the loop via a canyon-rim tour. From the south end of the tour, cross-canyon views include the fumarole spires of a pyroclastic (heat-melded volcanic ash) cliff. Benches on switchbacks invite hikers to pause.

GARFIELD PEAK TRAIL

3.4 miles round trip
Elevation change: 1,000 feet
Trail condition: wide, good, steady-climbing

Moderate
Summer through early fall
Access: Find the trailhead behind the historic lodge at Rim Village.

The trail rises in switchbacks up the flank of this crater-rim peak, traveling through forest of mountain hemlock and Shasta red fir, dry meadow-wildflower grassland, open rocky terrain, and alpine forest–meadow habitat. The trail begins with overlooks of the historic lodge and Crater Lake and continuously broadens its view to include the entire caldera, with Garfield Peak's own steep-dropping cliff wall to Crater Lake, Wizard Island and the Phantom Ship, Mount Thielsen, the Klamath Basin, Union Peak, Mount McLoughlin, and even California's Mount Shasta on clear days.

Deer, pikas, marmots, and Clark's nutcrackers are commonly spied along the trail. The tufted heads of western anemone adorn the upper rocky reaches, along with Indian paintbrush, phlox, and some small, yellow composite flowers.

RIM DRIVE

33.0-mile loop
Road quality: two-way, paved
(open July to mid-October)

Estimated speed: posted speeds
(averaging 35 mph)
Access: Begin the drive northeast of
the campground.

This tour with multiple turnouts examines the caldera from all perspectives, its lichen-etched, plunging walls and deep, blue-reflecting waters, the forested cinder cone of Wizard Island, and the descriptively named rock Phantom Ship. The tour also offers looks at Mount Scott, Mount Thielsen, Mount McLoughlin, Red Cone, and the Pumice Desert.

North of Discovery Point, the Watchman Tower trail climbs 1.0 mile and 400 feet to the lookout (elevation 8,025 feet) for a lofty vista of Crater Lake, its rim, and Wizard Island. The 0.5 mile Castle Crest Wildflower Trail, near the park headquarters, tours the wildflower bounty of Munson Creek, cradled by Castle Crest. Lewis monkey flowers bloom in July and August, along with monkshood, groundsel, larkspur, and lupine.

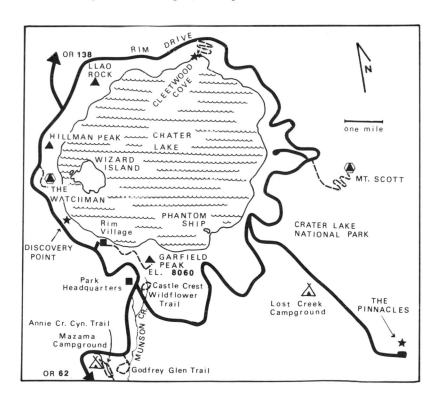

Crater Lake

THE PINNACLES

Geologic-interest area, canyon overlook, photo point
For information: Crater Lake National Park

Access: From the Rim Drive 3.8 miles south of the Mount Scott trailhead, go southeast past Lost Creek Campground to The Pinnacles viewpoint (5.7 miles).

A "five-star stop" well worth the Rim Drive detour, this Bryce Canyon-like landscape along Wheeler Creek sports a rich collection of gray spires and towers mirroring the shape of the evergreens threading between them. Time and stream action have unveiled these mineral-welded fumaroles formed during the Mount Mazama eruption 6,800 years ago. Mount Scott overlooks the dramatic landscape.

LAUNCH TRIP

Two-hour narrated tour; fee; July through early September, hourly boat departures from 10:00 A.M. to 4:00 P.M.
For information: Crater Lake Lodge Company

Access: From Cleetwood Cove on Rim Drive, take the 1.1-mile trail descending 700 feet to the dock—a hot, dry, steep trek. Wear sensible shoes and carry water. Benches dot the route.

This 25.0-mile shoreline tour with a Wizard Island stop treats visitors to an inside look at the caldera and a close view of the cobalt-blue depths. The narration reveals facts, history, and geology that increase appreciation of the spectacle. While there's no beach—only a rocky shore—many visitors yield to the lake's call, taking a cooling plunge before the dusty hike back up to the rim.

58 UNION CREEK CAMPGROUND

72 tent/trailer units
Standard service fee campground
Nonflush toilets
Water
Open seasonally: late May through
October

For information: Prospect Ranger
District
Map: Rogue River National Forest
Access: Turn west off OR 62 1.3
miles south of its junction with OR
230.

Spacious forested sites along the Rogue River frame both sides of Union Creek and provide access to the Upper Rogue–Crater Lake–Diamond Lake recreation complex, featuring premier hiking trails and fishing waters, old-growth galleries, and geologic oddities. Farewell Bend Campground, 1.0 mile north, provides similar access, with flush-toilet facilities; Natural Bridge Campground, 1.0 mile south, offers similar access, with no water and no fee.

The 48.0-mile Upper Rogue National Recreation Trail travels the shore opposite Union Creek Campground. Natural Bridge Campground offers access to this trail via its upper-footbridge and viewpoint-parking trailheads.

UNION CREEK RECREATION TRAIL
4.5 miles one way
Elevation change: 500 feet
Trail condition: good, well-marked, few "toe catchers"
Easy to moderate

Spring through fall (in winter it's a Nordic ski trail)
Access: Find the trailhead opposite the campground, on the east side of OR 62 near the Union Creek Resort.

Hugging the shoreline of Union Creek, the trail tours the wonderful old-growth corridor of this broad creek valley. Tall, stout Douglas fir, grand fir, and western white pine tower above a rich mid- and understory of dogwood, Pacific yew, alder, chinquapin, prince's pine, twin flower, starflower, bunchberry, and more. The creek reveals a variety of moods as it spills through snug, moss-decked gorges, tumbles over rocks, and forms still, deep pools near washed-down logs. With continuous creek access, the trail offers ample opportunity to linger on the bank. A car shuttle is possible, with another trailhead upstream, just 1.0 mile off OR 62 via FR 6200.600 and a short distance on 6200.610 (turns are marked).

ROGUE GORGE TRAIL
3.5 miles one way
Elevation change: 300 feet
Trail condition: good earthen path
Easy

Spring through fall
Access: Find the trailhead at the campground, near the Union Creek–Rogue River confluence.

Union Creek to Natural Bridge, a 2.5-mile hike, follows the east bank of the Rogue River downstream. Skirting the campground and bypassing cabins, the trail makes a relaxing tour along a broad, quiet river stretch marked by a few riffles. Fir, pine, maple, dogwood, chinquapin, and hazel border the path. Approaching the upper footbridge near Natural Bridge Campground, a narrow basalt gorge squeezes the water into a white, rushing channel, hinting of features to come.

A hike downstream along the Rogue Gorge Trail, across the lower footbridge, and briefly upstream via the Upper Rogue Trail leads to vista points overlooking the geologic oddity of Natural Bridge. Here, a lava tube swallows the river whole, only to release it 200 feet downstream. Blow holes, potholes, and river caves add to the unusual view.

Union Creek to Rogue Gorge Viewpoint, a 1.0-mile hike, travels upstream, skirting the campground and bypassing cabins for an equally relaxing riverside tour leading to another geologic eye teaser. At 0.9 mile, the trail offers a view of the mouth of the gorge, with its forested cliffs, white, rushing water, and scattered boulders. Just ahead lies the mesh-fence-enclosed, paved vista trail, which provides multiple gorge overlooks of the powerful match-up of steep, rugged basalt and churning water. Caves, bowls, hollows, and rings

The Upper Rogue River

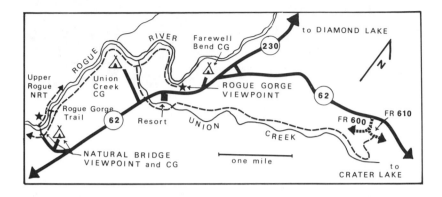

riddle the basalt walls, while the mist-fed moss provides contrast to their blackness.

Both vista sites have roadside access off OR 62.

MAMMOTH PINES NATURE TRAIL

0.4-mile interpretive loop (contact the ranger district for a brochure)
Elevation change: none
Trail condition: wide, with finely ground cinder bed

Easy
Spring through fall
Access: From the campground, go 5.0 miles south on OR 62, and turn west on FR 6200.060.

Some twenty stations along this loop identify area vegetation and explain life processes within the forest habitat. The tour travels through mixed forest—primarily fir, with some outstanding, giant ponderosa pine and a few large sugar pine. Mid- and understory plants include Pacific yew, hazel, dogwood, bracken fern, vanilla leaf, twin flower, iris, and prince's pine. Walking alongside a tumbled colossus brings a new appreciation of its size.

59 JOSEPH P. STEWART STATE PARK

201 tent/trailer units
Full service fee campground
Flush toilets; showers
Water
Open seasonally: mid-April to late October

For information: State Parks, Bend Regional Office
Map: Rogue River National Forest
Access: Go 35.0 miles northeast of Medford on OR 62.

Sites amid lawns, young pines, and deciduous trees occupy a mostly open flat above dammed Lost Creek Lake, in Rogue River country. Hiking, bicycling, swimming, boating, river floating, lake and river fishing, and fish-hatchery touring keep campers busy. Osprey nests top river and lakeshore snags. Generally, high lake levels are maintained behind the dam during visitor season.

A Rogue River fisherman

VIEWPOINT MIKE TRAIL

5.0 miles round trip
Elevation change: 1,000 feet
Trail condition: comfortable grade, with fine gravel bed
Moderate
Year-round (except during low-elevation snows)

Access: From camp, go 4.8 miles west on OR 62, and turn south onto Crowfoot Road. Find the trailhead on the left in 0.2 mile, opposite a day-use parking area.

The trail begins climbing an oak-grassland slope, with small ponderosa pine, madrone, manzanita, and California lilac. Lupine, clover, blue-dicks, wild geranium, balsam root, and other wildflowers decorate the slope in late May and early June. Poison oak, too, is well represented. The trail suffers from some road noise as it draws above OR 62, but it's mostly a pleasant tour, passing through oak woodland, buckbrush-dotted grassland, and fir–pine forest.

En route to the vista, the trail offers fleeting views of the Rogue River, the fish hatchery, Lost Creek Lake, and neighboring forested hills. The rock-wall-rimmed vista site occupies a rocky point on the foothill crest overlooking multi-armed Lost Creek Lake. Twisted manzanitas accent the vista seating area.

ROGUE RIVER TRAIL

4.5 miles round trip (to the Grotto)
Elevation change: 100 feet
Trail condition: sometimes rolling, with fine gravel bed
Easy to moderate
Year-round

Access: From camp, go east on OR 62, crossing Peyton Bridge for a left turn onto Lewis Road. Go west for 1.0 mile to find the day-use area with the trailhead.

This lake portion of the Rogue River Trail tours the wilder, less developed north shore, offering nearly continuous views of Lost Creek Lake and early views of Catfish Cove and distant Needle Rock. Meandering along the ragged, multiarmed lake shore, the trail travels through a mixed forest of small fir, pine, white and black oak, maple, manzanita, madrone, and poison oak. Patches of Indian paintbrush, iris, dwarf star tulip, and blue-dicks accent the trek, as does the blue-flowering California lilac.

At 0.6 mile, the trail passes through a semi-open shrubland recovering from the fire of 1979, and at 1.0 mile, it passes the walk-in campsites of Fire Glen. At the marked Grotto junction (at 2.1 miles), a right leads uphill to a light-colored, steep-walled box canyon. A small waterfall spills into the canyon during the rainy season; at other times, the water-stained rock hints of its presence.

The paved, more developed south shore segment of the Rogue River Trail ties together the campground, the marina, and the day-use area. Leaving from camp to tour the forest–shrub bench, the trail offers limited lake views before reaching the marina at about 2.5 miles. Beyond the marina and the day-use area, the trail holds more open lake views and access points. A richly textured shelter of fir, pine, madrone, oak, maple, hazel, rhododendron, and lilac houses the trail. An earthen footpath continues the westward trek after 3.0 miles. In all, the south shore holds 5.25 miles of trail between camp and the dam. Side roads to the lake offer shuttle-hike options.

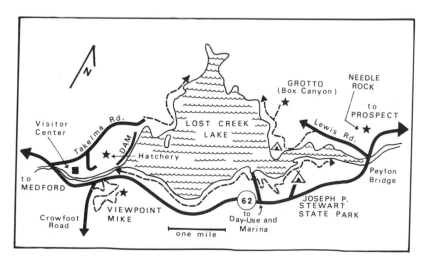

COLE M. RIVERS FISH HATCHERY

Open to the public; self-guided
facility tour (a brochure is available
at the lake's McGregor Park Visitor
Center)
For information: Oregon Department of Fish and Wildlife

Access: From camp, go 5.0 miles
west on OR 62, and turn north on
Takelma Road, following signs to
the hatchery.

Along the Rogue River stem of Lost Creek Lake rests the largest fish-hatchery operation in Oregon. The complex holds a fish ladder, an extensive setup of holding and rearing ponds, a hatching room, and a public lobby. Storyboards and brochures describe the operation.

60 SOUTH FORK CAMPGROUND

6 tent/trailer units
Standard service no fee
campground
Nonflush toilets
No water
Open year-round
For information: Butte Falls
Ranger District

Map: Rogue River National Forest
Access: Going 1.0 mile east of
Butte Falls (located northeast of
Medford, off OR 62), turn north
onto Butte Falls–Prospect Road. In
8.5 miles, turn right onto Lodgepole Road/FR 34 to reach the
campground in another 7.3 miles.

The campground sits on a bench above FR 34, within easy walking distance of the South Fork of the Rogue River. Tall trees amid the select-cut grove of Douglas fir and ponderosa pine shade the well-spaced sites with grasses and wildflowers spreading between them. This lightly used campground offers access to hiking and fishing along the South Fork as well as to the foot and horse trails of the neighboring Sky Lakes Wilderness. Big Ben Campground, off FR 37 to the southeast, offers two tent sites.

SOUTH FORK ROGUE RIVER TRAIL

4.8 miles one way
Elevation change: 400 feet
Trail condition: rolling earthen
trail, a few protuding roots
Moderate
Spring through fall

Access: Find trailheads 0.5 mile
east of camp off FR 34 and 5.2
miles south of the first trailhead
(take a right onto FR 37 from the
junction of FR 34 and FR 37).

An upstream hike from the trailhead nearest camp crosses a forested flat above the South Fork of the Rogue River to reach the canyon slope in 0.3 mile. From there, it begins a rolling tour above the river that continues for 4.5 miles. The trail meets the river along a gentle, boulder-riddled bend with deep pools and brief riffles. The bridge on FR 34 is visible downstream. A rich forest corridor of Douglas and grand fir, spruce, white and ponderosa pine, chinquapin, and some large Pacific yew houses the trail. Some big trees and some eye-disturbing and -delighting snags appear in the mix.

The South Fork Rogue River

As the trail continues upstream, side creeks become smaller and more scenic, slipping through tighter canyons. The river undergoes a character change, becoming more creeklike by the end of the hike. Both side creeks and the river invite detours for water fun or angling. Although the trail seldom strays far from the river, some areas provide easier access than others, being less vegetated or less steep. At 4.0 miles, the trail passes above a large riverside flat (also reached off FR 3700.800). It offers picnicking and dispersed primitive camping, with a pit toilet being the only service.

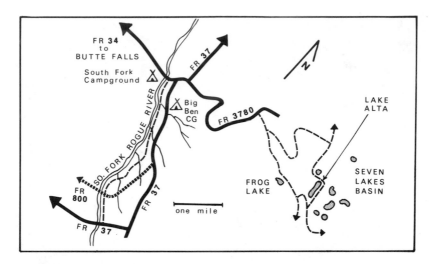

SEVEN LAKES–LAKE ALTA LOOP

9.0-mile loop
Elevation change: 1,800 feet
Trail condition: dusty or rocky,
with some steep ups and downs
Difficult
Late spring through fall

Access: At the junction of FR 34
and FR 37, 0.5 mile east of camp,
go straight on FR 37 and gravel FR
3780 to find the trailhead and
roadside parking in 4.5 miles.

Entering Sky Lakes Wilderness, a steady climb finds forest changes, with big-diameter trees bowing to smaller, more open forest. Douglas, grand, and Shasta red fir, mountain hemlock, and a few spruce and white pine, together with woodpecker-drilled snags, comprise the forest mix. The open floor sports patchy prince's pine, Oregon grape, huckleberry, and kinnikinick.

At the 0.6-mile junction, the Seven Lakes Trail begins a counterclockwise loop that strings together the Seven Lakes, Lake Alta, and King Spruce trails (all junctions are well marked). The trail reaches the shallow waters of Frog Lake at 1.8 miles and climbs again, capturing a semiblocked view of the South and Middle forks of the Rogue River drainages before topping a ridge at 3.0 miles.

A descent and a left turn leads to Lake Alta, a long, serene mountain lake reflecting a low, steep, open forest rim. The deep north end is best for water play and angling. Jupiter–Lucifer Ridge accents the lake view to the south.

From the lake's north end, the trail ventures left, bypassing Boulder Pond. Stretches of flat, dry lupine meadow with bare spots interrupt rocky forest descents. With a left on King Spruce Trail, more rocky descents follow. Dipping into a canyon, the trail makes a rolling, downhill tour of grassland, forest, and spring-fed meadow habitats before bottoming out in a vast huckleberry patch. It then angles up a slope for the close of the loop and a 0.6-mile downhill trek to the trailhead.

KLAMATH BASIN

With Upper Klamath and Agency lakes and extensive scattered bulrush marshes dominating much of the region's landscape, it's not surprising that this area is best noted for its place along the Pacific Flyway. The basin hosts a great number and variety of wintering waterfowl and the state's largest eagle population—some 500 bald eagles winter here. Driving the back roads, one may be surprised at seeing as many as four bald eagles roosting in the same tree.

The wintering waterfowl add to an already varied bird population: sandhill cranes, terns, grebes, avocets, red-winged and yellow-headed blackbirds, white pelicans, white-headed and pileated woodpeckers, ospreys, and more. Flocks of snow geese peel off the waters in white clouds of beating wings. That single-minded lumberjack, the beaver, also draws its share of attention. Lodges, dams, pencil-point stumps, and scent mounds dot area waterways. A raft or canoe, binoculars, and telephoto lenses enhance a basin stay.

Spring Creek

The region's boast of being the eastern gateway to the southern Cascade wilderness areas and to Crater Lake National Park is its calling card to hikers. Icy, clear, spring-swollen streams entice anglers. The wetlands, however, remain central to recreation and nature appreciation in this region.

Uprises among area Indian populations, most notably the Modocs (whose historic homeland is present-day Lava Beds National Monument in northern California), delayed settlement of this region. In 1863, the establishment of Fort Klamath cleared the way for homesteaders. Western explorer John C. Fremont, too, left his mark on the land, as his party attempted to lay out north–south and basin–Cascade transportation routes.

The Collier State Park Logging Museum preserves the lumbering heritage of the region. Housed on its grounds are the historic tools and machines used to cut, groom, and haul logs. Forests of ponderosa and lodgepole pine, white fir, and Shasta red fir claim the flanks of the mountains framing the historic wetland. Bitter-brush and sage flats spill from the foothills to the valley floor.

The Klamath Basin bottomland holds year-round recreation opportunities, with summer and fall recreation in the overlooking mountains. Winter days may be wet or snowy; summer days are often capped with afternoon thunderstorms. ∎

61 DIGIT POINT CAMPGROUND

64 tent/trailer units
Standard service fee campground
Flush and nonflush toilets
Water
Open seasonally: mid-June through September

For information: Chemult Ranger District
Map: Winema National Forest
Access: From US 97, turn west 1.0 mile north of Chemult onto gravel FR 9772. Find the campground in 12.0 miles.

Lakeside and land-bound sites occupy a broad, forested peninsula on Miller Lake. Boating, swimming, fishing on this large, natural mountain lake (elevation 5,600 feet) and hiking and birdwatching entertain visitors in the immediate vicinity of camp.

MILLER LAKESHORE TRAIL

4.2-mile loop
Elevation change: minimal
Trail condition: sand and pumice path with footbridges

Easy
Summer through fall
Access: Find trailheads at the boat launch and the day-use swim area.

A counterclockwise lake tour from the boat launch begins on the steps heading up the slope just inland from the launch. The circuit travels just above the lake, through a forest of fir, mountain hemlock, spruce, and mixed pine. Dwarf huckleberry spots the forest floor. Beyond Gideon Creek, picnic tables occupy an open bench, where one finds easy lake access to an anchored floating dock.

At 0.9 mile, the trail travels atop the lake shore's 20-foot high sandy cliffs. Trees cling tenuously to the eroding edge. Bald eagles roost in the trees above the lake. The trail then passes through a meadow cut by meandering Miller Creek (the lake outlet). Beaver harvests line the bench above the meadow. Trails branching to the right lead to FR 9772.

By 1.7 miles, the trail begins offering tree-filtered views of Sawtooth Ridge, Red Cone, and Mount Thielsen. Along the north shore, understory vegetation is more varied, with prince's pine, sticky laurel, chinquapin, and fern. A few areas along the shore are adequately open to allow angling, but the lake is better suited for boat fishing. Inlet creeks fragment the next stretch of trail. The Skyline–Maidu Lake trail departs to the northwest, paralleling Evening Creek, at 3.6 miles. Beaver-gnawed trees line the final leg of the circuit. The trail ends at the day-use picnic and swim area below camp.

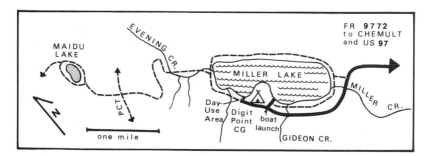

MAIDU LAKE TRAIL

6.5 miles round trip
Elevation change: 700 feet
Trail condition: well-designed
climbing grade with bridges
Easy to moderate

Summer through fall
Access: Reach the trail via the
Lakeshore trailhead at the day-use
swim area.

The Lakeshore trail enters the forest, traveling a slope just above Miller
Lake, crossing inlet creeks, and touring a grassy shoreline flat to arrive at the
trail junction for Maidu Lake at 0.6 mile. Here, the Maidu Lake trail turns left
to follow a wide, pole-lined path away from Miller Lake, beginning a lodgepole
pine–basin tour. Spruce guard the Evening Creek footbridge at the entrance to
the Mount Thielsen Wilderness.

The trail now travels a small rise above and along Evening Creek; its
meadowlike border provides a contrast to the maze of silver logs and absence
of greenery along much of the forest floor. With a second creek crossing, the
trail begins a comfortable diagonal ascent of the slope offering overlooks of
Miller Lake. A few white pine, fir, and mountain hemlock enter the forest mix.
Prince's pine, kinnikinick, and manzanita provide patchy ground cover. The
trail then crosses the Cascade Crest and the Pacific Crest Trail to begin its
descent to Maidu Lake, a mid-sized mountain lake rimmed by low, forested
slopes (at 3.25 miles). Gray jays, Clark's nutcrackers, ducks, herons, kingfishers, and shorebirds entertain hikers along the 0.75-mile Maidu Lake Loop.
Midway along the loop is a junction for Lake Lucile (another 1.25 miles).

---

62 COLLIER STATE PARK

68 tent/trailer units
Full service fee campground
Flush toilets; showers
Water
Open seasonally: mid-April through
October

For information: State Parks, Bend
Regional Office
Map: Oregon State
Access: The campground lies off
US 97 about 30.0 miles north of
Klamath Falls.

Set back from the highway, these tree-shaded, closely spaced sites rest on
an elevated bank above the Williamson River–Spring Creek confluence,
opposite the park's open-air logging museum. Some 1.5 miles of trail intercon-

nect the park's day-use, campground, and museum segments via a US 97 underpass. The campground serves as a convenient base for explorations of Upper Klamath Lake country. Area enjoyment calls for a full gas tank, binoculars, a raft or canoe, hiking boots, and a sturdy rod.

UPPER KLAMATH CANOE TRAIL

3.5- and 6.0-mile loops
Moderate
Spring through fall, during
daylight hours

Access: Find access at or near
Rocky Point Resort on Upper
Klamath Lake, 28.0 miles north-
west of Klamath Falls or 20.0 miles
southwest of Fort Klamath, off
Westside Road.

This marked route through the marsh of Upper Klamath Lake explores a narrow strip of the Upper Klamath Wildlife Refuge. Paddlers tour reeds, rushes, lily pads, and the low-water islands of Recreation and Crystal creeks and Pelican Bay. Eagles, blackbirds, geese, cormorants, marsh hawks, coots, and more keep binoculars moving. Beaver lodges and scent mounds dot the route. Mount McLoughlin and Pelican Butte preside over the setting. Sunglasses, sunscreen, insect repellent, and foul-weather gear should be carried along with boating-safety items. Canoe rentals and brochures are available at the resort.

KLAMATH LOOP TOUR DRIVE

100.0-mile loop
Road quality: paved main road
Estimated speed: 45 to 55 mph

Access: From the campground, go
south on US 97 to take OR 62
northwest.

As the tour heads northwest on OR 62 for a counterclockwise loop, Fort Klamath Military Outpost is an early attraction. The site features the rebuilt 1863 frontier post of Oregon's volunteer cavalry, a museum, and a cemetery for the executed Modoc leaders who, with a ragtag band of fifty-two Indians, led a cavalry standoff in 1872, in what is today California's Lava Beds National Monument.

Continue to Fort Klamath (the town) and head south. The tour route then journeys west on Sevenmile Road, which becomes Westside Road as it turns south. Mares Egg Springs Botanical Area, a roadside site 0.6 mile down Westside Road, houses a rare colonizing, egg-shaped, blue-green algae found in only four or five places in the world. Informal footpaths descend from the east side of the road to the spring; a signboard beside the spring marks the site. Do not disturb these unusual plant forms.

Continuing south, the route bypasses several USFS primitive day-use areas situated in the fir–pine forest fringe of the marsh. At these areas, visitors can have picnics, scope the Pacific Flyway, pursue nature study and photography, launch a boat, or cast a line. Malone Springs and Odessa Creek have active beaver populations. Eagles, pileated woodpeckers, geese, white pelicans, sandhill cranes, terns, and shovelers number among the winged sightings. These areas hint at the natural riches of the Upper Klamath Wildlife Refuge, which is inaccessible by vehicle.

Rocky Point Resort, about 2.0 miles south of Malone Springs, offers canoe rentals and canoe-trail access (see above). South of Odessa Creek, Denny Creek Historical Monument notes where Indians attacked the John C.

Fremont camp; look for a small roadside marker. The loop tour then enters Klamath Falls via either OR 140 or Lakeshore Drive, which tours the south shore of Upper Klamath Lake, passing Moore Park. From Klamath Falls, swinging the loop north via US 97 provides a fast return to camp. Side trips find recreation sites on Upper Klamath and Agency lakes and the Williamson River. The loop tour's scenery includes Pelican Butte, Mounts McLoughlin and Shasta, forest, marsh, and open water.

OUX KANEE VIEWPOINT–SPRING CREEK HEADWATERS

Public day-use and picnic sites, short trails
For information: Chiloquin Ranger District

Access: From the campground, go 2.6 miles north on US 97, and turn west onto gravel FR 9732 to reach the sites in 1.0 and 4.0 miles.

On a natural rim, Oux Kanee Viewpoint houses a deck and picnic sites overlooking the broad, aquamarine back of Spring Creek, its rural and forested valley, and the distant southern Cascades. Vultures ride the thermals and roost on nearby snags. Eagle sightings are common. A planned interpretive trail along the rim (scheduled for construction in 1991 or 1992) will reveal area history and geography.

At the bottom of the rim, Spring Creek is another spring-launched, full-coursing waterway. Ground water percolates the sands of the creek bottom and gives rise to small pockets of mares egg, a rare algae (see Klamath Loop Tour Drive). From the picnic area, a 1.0-mile path travels the west bank, while a 0.25-mile path beginning at the creek's headwaters travels the east bank. The clear waters invite wading, but their chilly temperatures discourage it.

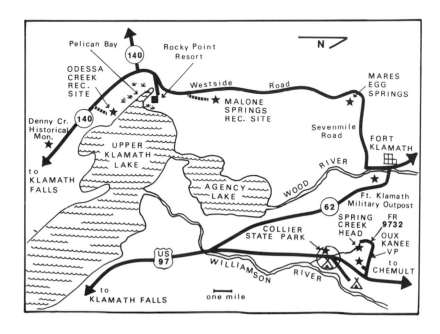

63 SUNSET CAMPGROUND

67 tent/trailer units
Standard service fee campground
Flush toilets
Water
Open seasonally: mid-June through
early September
For information: Klamath Ranger
District

Map: Winema National Forest
Access: Go 34.0 miles northwest of
Klamath Falls or 44.0 miles east of
Medford, and turn south off OR
140 for Lake of the Woods. Follow
FR 3704 and Dead Indian Road
along the east shore to reach the
campground turnoff in 2.2 miles.

Well-spaced sites occupy a fir–pine forest inland from Lake of the Woods,
with some sites located near the shore. The campground holds a boat launch,
a swim area, a Mount McLoughlin vista, and a 1.0-mile lake-shore trail linking
the camp to the Rainbow Bay picnic and swim area. The campground also offers
access to nearby trails, which explore wilderness lands, lakes, vistas, and lava
beds.

BADGER LAKE TRAIL

8.8 or 7.2 miles round trip (to
Long Lake)
Elevation change: 400 feet
Trail condition: good, comfortable
grade
Moderate
Late spring through fall

Access: From the campground, go
about 8.5 miles northwest via Dead
Indian Road, FR 3704, OR 140
west, and gravel FR 3661 to reach
Fourmile Lake Campground and
the trailhead.

From the formal trailhead, the trail rounds the campground, passing
through a lodgepole pine forest, skirting a pond, and crossing a forest road.
However, beginning the hike at the gated campground road near Fourmile
Lake Dam reduces the round-trip distance to 7.2 miles while sacrificing none
of the scenic value. Following the gated road briefly downhill, this shorter hike
meets the main trail near the canal.

From here, the route mounts the forested bench above the canal and

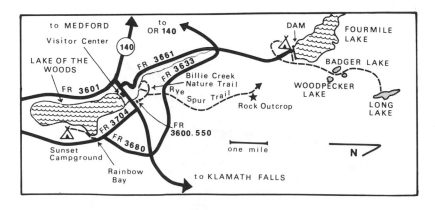

heads north away from the dam (look for the Badger Lake Trail sign posted on a tree atop the bench). Now, a mixed forest frames the footpath, which soon affords views of Fourmile Lake, with its silver drift-log ring, and towering Mount McLoughlin. At 2.2 miles (or 1.4 miles, taking the shorter route) the trail passes mid-sized, shallow Woodpecker Lake, with larger, deeper Badger Lake just beyond. Moist wildflower meadows house the middle portion of the hike, while forest dominates the final leg to the aptly named Long Lake, with its cross-lake view of Lost Peak.

BILLIE CREEK NATURE TRAIL

1.5 miles round trip
Elevation change: 100 feet
Trail condition: good, with foot-bridge crossings
Easy
Spring through fall
Access: Going north from Sunset Campground, find the trailhead on FR 3600.550 on the north side of OR 140, west of the OR 140–FR 3704 junction and east of the visitor center. The trailhead bulletin board is visible from OR 140. As the exit requires a high-clearance vehicle, it's best to park along the road or at the visitor center.

The trail travels along the foot of a slope above OR 140, touring a mature fir forest with ponderosa and white pine. Prince's pine, false Solomon's seal, star- and wind flowers, and needle mat and cones add color and texture to the forest floor.

By the 0.25-mile junction, the broad forest buffer filters out much of the road noise. The Rye Spur trail heads uphill to the right, while the Billie Creek trail continues straight ahead, splitting for a loop in 100 feet. The loop tours an old-growth grove with stout trees and snags and a huckleberry-filled, moist creek bottom. Billie Creek is a rock-bottomed, clear, shallow waterway with greenery spilling over its banks.

RYE SPUR TRAIL

6.0 miles round trip (to the outcrop vista site)
Elevation change: 1,200 feet
Trail condition: good, some rocks, steady climb
Moderate
Late spring through fall
Access: See Billie Creek Nature Trail, above.

From the 0.25-mile junction, the Rye Spur trail climbs uphill to the right through mature mixed forest. After entering a select cut at 1.0 mile, the trail crosses FR 3633, and at 1.7 miles it crosses over a canal. Throughout the day, the forest shades much of the route. Interesting pock-marked snags dot the way.

At 2.5 miles, the trail begins rounding a slope. A brushy opening at 2.8 miles affords the first vista, featuring Klamath Basin, Pelican Butte, Whitefaced Peak, and Mount Harriman. At 3.0 miles, a jutting rock outcrop with a straight-dropping cliff and a talus-bottomed slope expands the north–south views to include Great Meadow and a tree-filtered glint of Lake of the Woods. Penstemon and lichen accent the rocky perch. Traveling beyond the outcrop, the trail descends to the Fourmile Lake basin.

*Fourmile Lake and
Mount McLoughlin*

64 HYATT LAKE CAMPGROUND

28 tent/trailer units (plus a separate
overflow camp area)
Standard service fee campground
Flush toilets; showers
Water
Open seasonally: mid-April
through mid-October

For information: BLM, Medford
District
Map: Oregon State
Access: From Ashland, go 16.3
miles east on OR 66, and turn
north on paved East Hyatt Lake
Access Road. Go 3.0 miles for the
campground and day-use area.

The campground occupies the open fir-forest rim of the southeast shore
of Hyatt Lake. This reservoir is managed for irrigation first and recreation
second; its water level depends on the rainfall of recent years. Boat speed is 10
miles per hour. Osprey nest atop snags along the west shore, and nesting boxes
dot the meadow edges of the lake. The campground provides a convenient base
for exploring the Pacific Crest Trail (PCT). To the north, the larger Howard
Prairie Reservoir offers additional water recreation and hiking opportunities,
including a 14.0-mile lake trail.

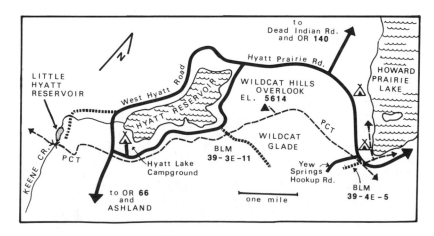

PACIFIC CREST NATIONAL SCENIC TRAIL

9.0 miles one way (Little Hyatt Reservoir to Howard Prairie Lake, with shorter hike options)
Elevation change: 1,000 feet
Trail condition: good, rolling grade, dusty in places
Easy to moderate
Spring through fall
Access: Begin at any of four trailheads: at the junction of East and West Hyatt roads, 0.1 mile south of the campground; at Little Hyatt Reservoir, southwest of the campground off West Hyatt Road (a high-clearance-vehicle access); at Wildcat Glades Road (BLM 39-3E-11), 2.3 miles north of camp off East Hyatt Road; and at the south end of Howard Prairie Lake.

Hyatt Lake to Little Hyatt Reservoir: This 3.0-mile round-trip hike begins near the junction of East and West Hyatt roads (close to camp). It heads west, touring a select-cut forest of large fir, a snag-riddled open forest, a tree plantation, and a prairie grassland threaded by Keene Creek. Old utility and forest roads fragment the trail. At 0.5 mile, the open snag forest affords views of California's Mount Shasta to the south and the ski-run-streaked face of Mount Ashland to the west. Blue-dicks, Oregon iris, lupine, and clover add splashes of spring color to the prairie. Little Hyatt is a scenic, pond-sized reservoir, generally maintained high, with a meadow border and a ponderosa pine and fir rim. Mother ducks weave their broods across the pond in early summer. The PCT continues south via the Keene Creek footbridge.

Hyatt Lake to Wildcat Glade Road: This rolling-grade section of the PCT (3.2 miles one way) heads north from the junction of East and West Hyatt roads. It alternately travels through open meadow, select cut, and mature natural forest after briefly skirting the edge of a harvest site. Yellow, white, and purple wildflowers sprinkle the rock-studded meadows framed by small oak and cedar. Midway, hikers find limited views of Mount Ashland and Hyatt Lake. Occasionally, an eye-catching big trunk leads the look skyward. Deer are often seen along the trail, which exits onto Wildcat Glade Road, 0.1 mile east of its junction with East Hyatt Road.

Wildcat Glade Road to Howard Prairie Lake: This north-bound segment (4.3 miles one way) holds the greatest elevation change of the three identified segments. It tours a green-carpeted, select-cut forest, a moist tall-grass–false hellebore meadow, a cedar–oak–grassland knob, open hillside, harvest zone, and shady forest.

At 1.4 miles, a 400-foot side trail leads to Wildcat Hills Overlook, a rocky summit post with a broken 360-degree view that includes Mount Ashland, Hyatt and Howard Prairie lakes, and Table Mountain Lookout. Raptors soar over the setting.

Continuing northeast from the vista detour, the main trail affords views of Mount Shasta, Wildcat Glade, and Howard Prairie Lake. Along the way, the trail passes some giant sugar pine and fir. At 3.0 miles, the trail offers a view of Howard Prairie Lake, with conical Mount McLoughlin in the distance. The trail descends, crossing over paved Yew Springs Hookup Road to exit onto gravel BLM road 39-4E-5. The route then crosses an open gravel apron and the paved lake road to descend at a marked spur to reach the Howard Prairie Lake shore and its trail.

A nesting box by the Hyatt River Reservoir; Mount McLoughlin in the distance

DESCHUTES–UMATILLA PLATEAU

A marker near Deschutes River State Park

Arid open range, far-spreading wheatland, and sage flats comprise much of the Deschutes–Umatilla Plateau. Large tracts of this region are private or otherwise inaccessible, but a few special public lands provide an introduction to this hard, dramatic landscape of thin-soiled steppes and bluffs, rugged basalt rims, deep-cut canyons, and remnant historic marshes.

The Oregon Trail cuts a scar of human history across this sweeping expanse. Roadside markers and a few BLM sites dot the backroads that parallel the overland route. Using the pioneers' words and observations, interpretive signs unfold the tale of one of the most notable human migrations of all time.

The Columbia River is an ancient Indian fishing and trading ground. Prehistoric Indians wintered in huts along the Deschutes River, one of the state's premier water-recreation lands. The John Day Wild and Scenic River also threads this arid region; with few accesses, this river is best discovered via raft. The Deschutes and John Day rivers are two of the state's most popular rafting waters.

John Day Fossil Beds National Monument preserves three outstanding canyon caches, featuring rainbow-colored rounded hills, terraced palisades, eroding tilted slopes, fluted cliffs, and prehistoric fossil beds.

John Day, a member of the John Jacob Astor Expedition, was reportedly robbed of his clothing and possessions in this area. His name lingers, touching many of the region's features. Ghost towns across the John Day country tell the tale of the 1860s gold rush and the bypassing of towns by contemporary transportation routes.

Despite limited public access, the region boasts a diversity of recreational pursuits: river rafting, prized fishing, wildlife viewing, canoeing among the islands of the Columbia River wildlife areas, boating and windsurfing, the tracking of Oregon history, and hiking.

This sun-baked land is best toured in the off-season: Early spring touches the grassland with a color palette; during fall and winter, mild temperatures prevail.

Visitors should be alert to the presence of ticks in the spring and to snakes and poison oak almost anytime. Boots or sturdy-soled shoes are recommended for all foot touring of this rugged terrain. ■

65 DESCHUTES RIVER STATE RECREATION AREA

34 tent/trailer units
Standard service fee campground
Flush toilets
Water
Open seasonally: mid-April to late October

For information: State Parks, Bend Regional Office
Map: Oregon State
Access: East of The Dalles, take exit 97 off I-84 and go 3.0 miles east on OR 206.

These tree-shaded sites alongside the Deschutes River provide campers access to one of the premier fishing and recreation waterways in the state. This semi-arid river canyon also invites hiking, photography, and stargazing. An overflow camp area accommodates summer numbers. The history of the Columbia River—a traditional Indian fishing and trading ground and the final obstacle along the Oregon Trail—flavors area adventures. The campground houses an Oregon Trail display.

VIC ATIYEH LOOP TRAIL

4.5 miles round trip
Elevation change: 500 feet
Trail condition: good, defined path
Moderate to difficult

Year-round
Access: Find the trailhead at the south end of the overflow camping area.

This trail travels upstream along the Deschutes River shoreline, serving hikers, anglers, and birdwatchers. Hawks, gulls, ducks, and geese keep eyes moving. Duckboards aid crossings of spring-fed areas. Near the start of the hike, abandoned fruit trees, an old homestead, and an alder-entangled, weathered frame with rusting gears rest along the trail. White alder and sumac shade the river's edge, while sage and bunchgrass dominate the canyon expanse.

For 1.5 miles, the trail closely hugs the river line, unfolding prized river views. At 1.5 miles, the loop streaks up the slope to tour the top of the basalt rim (the riverside tour continues but is unmaintained). The loop offers upstream vistas before crossing the former railroad grade to a stair step over a fence, which marks the beginning of the hillside tour. Here, the trail ascends through the grassland and sage of the canyon's east slope.

After crossing Ferry Springs Canyon, the trail offers an overview of the Deschutes River mouth and the Columbia River. A canyon descent follows, and the trail again crosses the former railroad grade (at 3.6 miles). From there, it meanders downstream along the arid river slope, with sagebrush reaching 10 feet high. The loop ends at the old road, near the homestead. Retracing your steps north (downstream) along the riverside path leads back to camp. Beware of ticks in the sage and grass.

WEST BANK TRAIL

3.0 miles round trip
Elevation change: minimal
Trail condition: good, unmaintained; marshy springs
Easy
Year-round

Access: Find the trailhead 0.2 mile south of the Heritage Landing day-use area and boat launch, across the river from camp. Stairs step over the fence, marking the start of the hike.

The trail begins following the grass-overtaken tracks of an old ranch road, bypassing weathered, collapsed stock pens and loading ramps being reclaimed by tall sage. At 0.6 mile, near the river relay station, the old road fades, and former cattle trails—well tracked by anglers—now lead the way. Sagebrush, isolated alder stands, boulder outcrops, river cascades, and stony islands set the stage for the trail.

The entire way holds easy river access. Waving-grass hummocks dot the river course. Ducks, herons, gulls, cormorants, and kingfishers sweep and churn the waters, while kestrels and marsh hawks patrol the sage. Anglers in waist-deep water make their fly lines dance.

Beyond 1.5 miles, the primary path becomes less well defined, but hikers and anglers can still make their way upstream. A natural spring along the way has been tapped for a drinking fountain. Pit toilets serve river users.

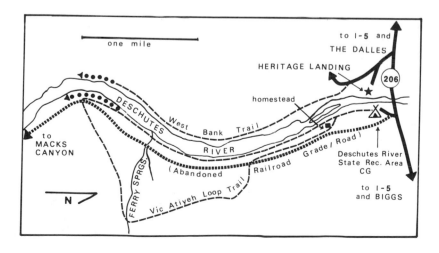

OREGON TRAIL FRAGMENT

Roadside stop; historical interest site
For information: N/A

Access: Find the pullout alongside OR 206 about 2.3 miles east of the campground.

A wooden post quietly marks a tiny fragment of the 1,900-mile overland pioneer route not claimed by I-84. Here, wagon ruts can still be seen. At stops along I-84 and in a walking tour of The Dalles (settled by early immigrants), visitors can learn more about the Oregon Trail.

---

66 BOARDMAN PARK CAMPGROUND

63 tent/trailer units (reservations by mail or phone)
Full service fee campground
Flush toilets; showers
Water

Open year-round
For information: Boardman Parks
Map: Oregon State
Access: Turn north off I-84 at Boardman.

Landscaped sites with lawns and planted deciduous shade trees and shrubs occupy the Lake Umatilla shore on the Columbia River. Wind fences shelter sites (the Columbia River is noted for its winds). Low, flat plateaus rim the river lake. Next door, a marina for water-sport enthusiasts, a roped swimming area, and sports areas entertain campers at the park. Salvaged petroglyphs, displaced by the artificial flooding of the Columbia River, rest at the day-use area. Wildlife lands draw visitors away from camp.

UMATILLA NATIONAL WILDLIFE REFUGE, MCCORMACK UNIT

Public access, boat launch (for small, car-top boats, no motors), visitor information; most areas open year-round, 5:00 A.M. to 10:00 P.M. (from early October to mid-January, it is best to visit on nonhunting days: Monday, Tuesday, Thursday, and Friday)

For information: Refuge headquarters (in Umatilla)
Access: From the campground, go east on I-84, and exit north onto US 730. From US 730, travel north along Paterson Ferry Road to reach the refuge, located about 10.0 miles from camp.

The refuge houses river, slough, wetland, and desert habitats supporting more than 180 bird species. During mid- to late November, waterfowl populations peak with the fall migration, which also brings bald eagles to feed on the sick and injured birds. In fall, winter, and spring, Canada geese congregate on the river islands—vital nesting grounds. Burrowing owls nest in abandoned badger dens. Mule deer may be seen wading the wetland grasses of McCormack Slough or crossing the sage dunes.

Canoeing is the most popular way to enjoy the refuge, although all designated open areas invite hiking. The mowed 1.0-mile Wildlife Foottrail begins along the levee at the end of McCormack Slough. It then drifts away to tour a moist riparian environment and sage-reclaimed dunes. The trail offers

Boardman Lake Campground

only blocked views of the slough through its false indigo–Russian olive frame. Great blue herons, white pelicans, and songbirds claim the attention of birdwatchers. The path exits near parking lot B.

IRRIGON WILDLIFE AREA
Public access, trails, wildlife viewing
For information: Oregon Department of Fish and Wildlife

Access: Find the wildlife area at the north end of Irrigon, next door to Irrigon Park, off US 730 about 12.0 miles northeast of the campground. Access is from the east side of Irrigon Park or via the gravel road one block east of the park entrance road.

Within 0.75-mile, interlocking, well-traveled footpaths visit a half dozen of the forty-four ponds occupying this 8.0-mile-long wildlife corridor on the Columbia River–Lake Umatilla shore. Ponds have varying character: Some are overtaken by cattails, some are marshy, and some sport open water. Signs of beaver abound. Red-winged blackbirds, painted turtles, and waterfowl are among other wildlife in the area. Prickly pear cactus and wildflowers color the sage and grassland dividing the ponds.

The shoreline may hold additional opportunities for exploration, depending on lake levels. Low-hanging willows or pinched beach stretches invite brief detours away from shore. Open clam shells and the tracks of nighttime raiders are commonly seen along the beach. Gulls and terns are passersby. Cottonwood, poplar, olive, and willow trees shade the river, shore, and ponds. Additional accesses are found east along US 730. Look for the triangular wildlife area signs.

MCNARY WILDLIFE AREA

Public access, nature trail, wildlife-viewing area
For information: U.S. Army Corps of Engineers, Walla Walla (Washington) District

Access: The area is located about 22.0 miles northeast of camp via I-84 east and US 730 east. Go 1.5 miles east of Umatilla, turn north, and go 1.0 mile on McNary Dam Road.

A 0.75-mile nature trail tours ponds, creeks, open wetland, and wooded areas. Bridges, boardwalks, viewing platforms, and benches improve access and aid nature study. Frogs, ducks, pheasants, orioles, magpies, and muskrats keep the eyes darting. Birdhouses and platforms encourage nesting. Cattails, rushes, and reeds crowd the ponds; Russian olives offer shade.

A wood-shaving trail connects the area's east and west entrances, traveling across an open sage flat. East of the wildlife area, the McNary Dam visitor facility offers restrooms, picnic grounds, fish-viewing windows, and an information center.

67 MACKS CANYON CAMPGROUND

16 tent/trailer units
Standard service fee campground
Nonflush toilets
Water
Open year-round
For information: BLM, Prineville District

Map: Oregon State
Access: About 8.5 miles east of Tygh Valley, turn north off OR 216 for Deschutes River Recreation Lands. Go 17.0 miles on the (sometimes rough) gravel road to the campground.

These comfortable, mostly open sites with small deciduous shade trees occupy an arid canyon setting along the Deschutes River. The campground offers access to exceptional river sport, fishing, and waterfowl viewing. A former railroad grade provides a trail to downstream discovery, while a 0.25-mile angler path explores upstream.

The region boasts a rich Indian history and houses sites where Oregon-pioneer adventures occurred. The campground itself is a National Historic Site, occupying the river flat used by prehistoric Indian tribes as a wintering

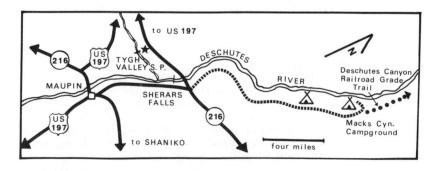

ground some 2,000 years ago. Pit-house shelters once lined these shores. The University of Oregon Museum of Natural History excavated the site in 1967 and 1968.

DESCHUTES CANYON RAILROAD GRADE TRAIL

3.5 miles round trip
Elevation change: 100 feet
Trail condition: rocky, with a cross-country side-canyon crossing (boots recommended). (This newly proposed trail is not yet developed. No improvements will be made until the final River Management Plan is announced, probably in 1992.)

Difficult (in its yet undeveloped state)
Year-round
Access: Find the trailhead at the wide turnout where the road turns to descend into the campground.

As this shadeless hike begins contouring the slope, tall sagebrush crowds the trail but does not prohibit passage. At a former trestle site at 0.25 mile, hikers must descend into Macks Canyon. Once across, they find the railroad grade that travels the east wall of the Deschutes River Canyon to the Deschutes River State Recreation Area (see trip 65). Railroad grades stripe both walls of the canyon, recording the historic race to build the first railroad serving Central Oregon.

This tour offers river overlooks and views of the rugged, semi-arid canyon with its basalt rims, reddish cliffs, and rounded grassland slopes. At 1.4 miles lies Allison Canyon. Here, the path dips around shallow side-canyon depressions. Lupine, balsam root, yarrow, and other wildflowers add color to the river corridor in spring.

At 1.75 miles, beyond a fence line, a short cross-country jaunt through the sage leads to the river. (Earlier, a scree slope prevented easy river access.) The river stop proves a nice ending for the hike. Throughout the hike, beware of rattlesnakes in this rugged, rocky terrain.

TYGH VALLEY STATE PARK TRAIL

1.5 miles round trip
Elevation change: 200 feet
Trail condition: rocky or steep in places (boots or sturdy footwear recommended)

Moderate
Year-round
Access: Find the state park on OR 216 about 22.0 miles southwest of the campground.

A paved path leads to a fenced overlook showcasing a scenic, broad, 100-foot falls on the White River. The cliff creates angles and channels in the surging white flow. A second path downstream, toward the old powerhouse, ties together views of the upper and lower falls and the awaiting deep, circular pool. Along this path, beware of the gulch bridge, which is in disrepair, and the crumbling stair steps approaching the powerhouse. Giant turbines are still housed in the stone structure. Swallows nest in the rafters and in the niches of the cliff.

Bluffs, steppes, and semi-arid terrain create the backdrop to this trail. Yellow, white, and violet wildflowers color the canyon wall, and alder, cottonwood, and an occasional ponderosa pine dot the canyon bottom. An informal path continues downstream via sageland and rocky rim to find additional river accesses and overlooks. Orange-sided lizards slip over the basalt. The hike ends atop a bluff offering a yawning canyon vista. In spring, beware of ticks amid sage and of poison oak along the trail.

Clarno Arch, Clarno Unit, John Day Fossil Beds National Monument

SHERARS BRIDGE AND FALLS

Roadside historic site; Indian
fishing grounds
For information: N/A

Access: From camp, return to OR
216, and go briefly west to where it
crosses the Deschutes River.

Sherars Bridge marks the site where an ancient Indian trail crossed the
Deschutes River. Above the falls, pioneer members of the "Lost Wagon Train
of 1845" floated their wagons to the west bank in a desperate drive toward The
Dalles, having endured the hardships of being misguided through south-
central Oregon by mountainman Stephen H. L. Meek. The first bridge strad-
dled these waters in 1860.

The overhanging basalt bluffs and serial cascades of Sherars Falls are a
historic Indian dip-net fishing ground. During the seasonal fish runs, visitors
discover members of the Confederated Tribes of Warm Springs Reservation
perched on the rock ledges and dipping for their catch, in the tradition of their
ancestors.

68 SHELTON STATE PARK

36 tent/trailer units
Standard service fee campground
Nonflush toilets
Water
Open seasonally: mid April to late
October

For information: State Parks, Bend
Regional Office
Map: Oregon State
Access: Turn off OR 19 about 10.0
miles southeast of Fossil.

Situated in a ponderosa pine–Douglas fir–forested canyon below OR 19,
this campground offers central access to the three units of John Day Fossil Beds
National Monument, which features rainbow-colored hillsides, dramatic cliffs,
and fossils dating back forty million years. A 1.0-mile trail tours the forested
ridge above camp. From mid-May to mid-June, wildflowers—fairy slipper,
lupine, false hellebore, larkspur, sunflowers, and more—sprinkle the forest and
meadow of the trail

CLARNO UNIT, JOHN DAY FOSSIL BEDS

Nature trails, picnic area; open year-
round, dawn to dusk; picnic area
closed in winter
For information: John Day Fossil
Beds Headquarters

Access: From camp, go northwest
on OR 19 to Fossil. From there,
take OR 218 west for 20.0 miles to
the Clarno Unit.

Beautiful gray-orange spires pierce the desert sky above a sage–juniper–
bunchgrass floor in this land that was once a subtropical rain forest. This unit
boasts the oldest fossil-bearing rock in the monument. Three 0.25-mile trails
unravel the tale of the Eocene era while exploring the present-day Palisades (the
name given to the central formation of eroding spires).

The Wayside Nature Trail tours the base of the Palisades, linking the
picnic area to the trailheads. The Trail of Fossils introduces the area geology

and points out the location of fossils amid the rubble of boulders, tumbled from the cliff.

The third trail, the Clarno Arch Trail, climbs 150 feet to view an arch in the mud-flow deposit—a natural skylight above a weather-sculpted grotto. Next door to this feature, fossil trees are locked in the bronze-colored rock of the cliff. Swallows, rock doves, hawks, and ravens put on an aerial show. The lyrical song of the meadowlark mingles with the wail of the coyote for an odd harmony.

Morning lighting proves best for photography, while morning and late-afternoon hours are most comfortable for summer-time outings.

PAINTED HILLS UNIT, JOHN DAY FOSSIL BEDS

Nature trails, overlook, picnic area; open dawn to dusk, year-round
For information: see page 181

Access: From camp, go south via OR 19 and OR 207 to Mitchell. From there, go west 3.0 miles on US 26, and turn north onto the marked county road for the Painted Hills Unit (in 6.0 miles).

Rainbow-striped, rounded hills punctuate the setting of this highly photographed unit of the park. Painted Hills Overlook offers vistas of the colorful landscape from both the parking area and the end of a short trail. (As turnaround space for large RV and trailer units is limited beyond Painted Hills Overlook, park there and continue on foot.)

Nearby, the 0.75-mile Carroll Rim Trail mounts a ridge of welded volcanic ash for still more views of the hills and neighboring Sutton Mountain. Farther along the monument road, the 0.25-mile Painted Cove Trail offers close-up viewing of the clay-cinder formations and the brilliant color bands, which display maximum color following a rain shower. Trail brochures (available at the trailhead) unravel the geologic tale of the cove. Spring is a favorite time to visit this unit, when yellow wildflowers shower the slopes and the desert floor.

SHEEP ROCK UNIT, JOHN DAY FOSSIL BEDS

Monument Visitor Center (hours: 8:30 A.M. to 6:00 P.M. daily, mid-March through October); nature trails, vistas, picnic area (open dawn to dusk, year-round)

For information: see page 181
Access: From camp, go south, staying on OR 19 to Sheep Rock Unit, located 2.0 miles north of US 26.

This unit holds the visitor center; a fossil laboratory, where visitors can view technicians at work; and exhibits of early area ranch life. Its Sheep Rock Overlook offers views of the rock feature that lends the unit its name, the main stem of the John Day River, and the grassy fields and badlands of John Day country.

Blue Basin, located north of the visitor center, has two trails exploring its eroding, weather-chiseled amphitheater of blue-gray cliffs. The 0.6-mile Island in Time Trail is punctuated with replica fossils and offers interior views of the basin. The 3.0-mile Overlook Trail climbs a slope to peer into the bowl of the basin and overlook the valley. This trail is steep in places and slippery when wet. Do not stray from the trails when touring this sensitive landscape.

HIGH LAVA PLAINS

In the rain shadow of the Cascades, the high lava plains sport habitats of high desert sage, grassland, and lodgepole and ponderosa pine forests, intermixed with volcanic features. The landscape parades extensive lava flows, craters, cinder cones, obsidian ridges, and caldera lakes. The scenic, productive waters of the Deschutes River thread south to north through this region.

The plains are home to Oregon's Newberry National Volcanic Monument. Its 56,000 acres protect a sweeping area of volcanic interest. The rugged terrain has defied development, thus preserving its natural value. Newberry Crater, centerpiece of the monument, is the largest volcano (in area) in Oregon. Paulina and East lakes occupy the depression of this once great shield volcano. Their crystalline cobalt waters rival that of Crater Lake in clarity.

Fort Rock

A lodgepole pine branch

Drive-to vista sites at Paulina Peak, Pilot Butte State Park, and Lava Butte reveal the expanse of the Cascade volcanic peaks, cinder cone–riddled lava lands, and the outward-spreading desert.

Tree casts dot the lava flows, evidence of the forests that once stood. Below the ground snake lava tubes, caves that invite the adventurous to enter; across the threshold lies the black unknown. A narrow flashlight beam brushes ribbed floors, archways adorned with mineral leaching, galleries of icicles and frost, and of "lavacicles" and pull-offs—not the color and drama of the limestone caves.

Lava tubes form when the surface of a flow cools rapidly and hardens while the interior flow rushes hot, eventually emptying the outer encasement. Caves in this region are primitive and semiwild; three light sources, boots, gloves, and headgear are required for their exploration.

Such geologic oddities as a mile-wide depression and a natural crescent-shaped rock fortress promise mind-stretching discoveries. Smith Rocks State Park challenges the climber.

This semi-arid country knows weather extremes, with winter snows and hot summer days. Amazing stargazing opportunities exist in remoter reaches. The high lava plains are home to Pine Mountain Observatory, which holds one of the largest telescopes in the Northwest. ∎

69 TUMALO STATE PARK

88 tent/trailer units
Full service fee campground
Flush toilets; showers
Water
Open seasonally: mid-April through October

For information: State Parks, Bend Regional Office
Map: Oregon State
Access: Find the park turnoff on US 20 5.0 miles northwest of Bend.

Semi-open sites, some landscaped, other situated among the native vegetation, occupy a flat along an irrigation-reduced segment of the Deschutes River. The campground provides a good base for exploring the geological highlights of Newberry National Volcanic Monument and for enjoying relaxation and sport on or along the river. The day-use area across the road from camp holds shaded lawns and a small swimming hole, attractive on hot afternoons. The lava country outings on the outskirts of Bend suffer the drawback of city traffic en route.

LAVA RIVER CAVE TOUR

Semi-primitive, self-guided
(brochure available), lantern rental
available in summer
1.2 miles round trip
Floor surface: rippled, crusted lava

Physical requirements: stairs, some
ducking required
Easy
Access: After taking US 20 to Bend,
go south on US 97 for 12.0 miles
to the marked turn for the cave.

The longest lava tube in Oregon, this cave provides a good introduction to lava-tube caving. This lava tube's features include arched ceilings, shadow and light play, echoes, coolness, and modest ornamentation: hardened motion, lavacicles, pull-offs, lichen, and glazing.

CAVES DRIVE (FR 18)

Distance: 15.0 miles one way, plus
mileage on cave spur roads
Road quality: improved-surface
forest road
Estimated speed: 15 to 35 mph

Access: After taking US 20 to
Bend, go south on US 97 for 4.0
miles. Turn east on China Hat
Road (FR 18).

The route strings together a series of primitive lava tubes. Boyd Cave, in 9.0 miles, is 0.25-mile long, with a couple of dead-end galleries at its entrance. It sports a high ceiling, a mostly lava-surface floor interrupted by a few rock jumbles, and such features as lavacicles, pull-offs, benches, and gutters.

Skeleton Cave is longer, with a sandy floor to the junction. There, a rippled lava floor with a few rock jumbles replaces the sandy avenue. The main cavity sports a high ceiling, although there is one short passage where adults will

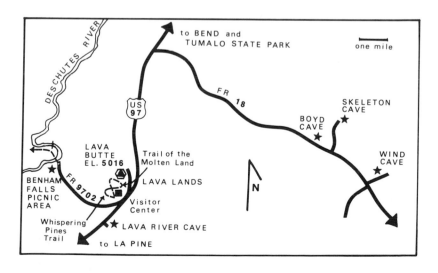

need to duck. The cave boasts atmosphere more than beauty. Passing through it is like being Pinocchio in the whale or a food particle passing down the throat. The cave has defined arches, mottled walls, lavacicles, and mineral leaching.

Wind Cave is more rugged, with rock jumble the entire 3,200-foot length. Boots, hats, and gloves are recommended.

LAVA LANDS VISITOR CENTER

Open 9:00 A.M. to 4:00 P.M. daily during late spring to early fall, with extended summer hours
For information: Fort Rock Ranger District

Access: After taking US 20 to Bend, go south on US 97 for 11.0 miles. Turn west at the marked exit.

At the visitor center, displays and programs introduce the geological significance of Newberry National Volcanic Monument, while the center's immediate area holds nature trails, Benham Falls, and Lava Butte, allowing

Deschutes River, Tumalo State Park

first-hand discovery. The Trail of the Molten Land and the Whispering Pines Trail (both short, all-ability trails beginning at the visitor center) examine lava-flow characteristics and the vegetation of the region, respectively.

A paved winding road leads to the top of Lava Butte (elevation 5,020 feet), with a small parking area, lookout tower, and 0.25-mile rim trail. Summit vistas include forest and flow, Mount Bachelor, the Three Sisters, Mount Jefferson, Mount Washington, and Three Fingered Jack. Hiking the red cinders of the crater requires sturdy-soled shoes.

The road to Benham Falls from the visitor center finds a picnic area amid a remnant old-growth ponderosa pine grove, a 0.25-mile nature trail relating the logging history of the area, and a 0.75-mile trail to Benham Falls, a large river cascade. The falls trail begins downstream, crossing a former railroad logging bridge.

70 LA PINE RECREATION AREA

145 tent/trailer units
Full service fee campground
Flush toilets; showers
Water
Open seasonally: mid-April through October
For information: State Parks, Bend Regional Office

Map: Oregon State
Access: Turn west off US 97 about 22.0 miles south of Bend to reach the recreation area in another 6.0 miles. A park sign marks the exit.

Housing the campground is a generally open forest of lodgepole pine and young ponderosa pine atop a rim overlooking a broad, scenic, slow-winding stretch of the Deschutes River. Sites with sewer hookups are more closely spaced than those without.

The La Pine Recreation Area offers fishing, swimming at its day-use area, sightseeing, and hiking along the former jeep trails that web the park. The park also holds the state's largest (stoutest) ponderosa pine and provides access to Central Oregon's lava country, including Lava River Cave and Lava Lands (part of Newberry National Volcanic Monument), located north on US 97 10.0 and 11.0 miles, respectively, from the La Pine Recreation Area turnoff (see trip 69).

BIG TREE TRAIL
0.4 mile round trip
Elevation change: 100 feet
Trail condition: paved, steady grade
Easy

Year-round
Access: Find the marked turnoff 2.0 miles east of the campground on the park road.

The trail descends through a forest of large ponderosa, living and beetle-killed lodgepole, and new-growth pines. Bitterbrush, wild rose, currant, and bunchgrass are the primary forest-floor species, with yarrow, fireweed, and pine drops adding color accents. A fence provides a wide safety skirt around the record-sized ponderosa pine, which measures 162 feet in height and 8.6 feet in diameter. The thick trunk runs nearly the full height to the tree's broken

Deschutes River, La Pine State Park

forked top. The 500-year-old pine stands watch at the edge of a grassy flat along the Deschutes River—one of the easiest and most attractive river accesses in the park for sightseer or angler.

LAVA CAST FOREST TRAIL

1.0-mile loop
Elevation change: minimal
Trail condition: all-ability trail
Easy
Spring through fall

Access: Returning to US 97, go 7.2 miles north. Turn east onto gravel FR 9720 (opposite the Sun River turnoff), and travel to the road's end.

The trail begins at the picnic area and soon enters a 6,000-year-old flow originating from a side vent in Newberry Crater (visible in the distance). Lodgepole and small ponderosa pine rim the flow, with a few larger ponderosa pine dotting the landscape. Sticky laurel and manzanita occupy the more open areas. Hundreds of tree molds riddle the crusted field. Prince's pine, Indian paintbrush, and purple penstemon lend delicate contrast and color splashes to the lava.

71 NEWBERRY NATIONAL VOLCANIC MONUMENT

300 tent/trailer units
Standard service fee campgrounds
Flush and nonflush toilets
Water
Open seasonally: mid-May through October

For information: Fort Rock Ranger District
Map: Deschutes National Forest
Access: Go 23.0 miles south of Bend on US 97, and turn east onto County 21 for campgrounds in 13.0, 16.0, 17.0, and 18.0 miles.

In the cradle of Newberry Crater, these tightly packaged, pine-forested sites occupy the banks of twin lakes, Paulina and East lakes, that rival Crater Lake in their azure color and clarity. Lake recreation, hiking, sightseeing, nature study, and photography entertain campers.

PAULINA FALLS TRAIL

1.0 mile round trip
Elevation change: 100 feet
Trail condition: good earthen path
Easy
Late spring through fall

Access: Find the trailhead at Paulina Creek Falls Picnic Area, west of the lakeside campgrounds off County 21.

Traveling through the picnic area, a 300-foot trail leads to the upper vista of this 100-foot falls housed in a canyon of reddish-brown volcanic cliffs. The trail continues upstream to arrive at Paulina Lake (0.25 mile).

The lower vista is reached via a 0.5-mile switchback course traveling a pine- and spruce-forested slope with minimal ground cover. The deck offers straight-on viewing of this falls split by a rocky island at the ledge. Downstream waters thread around and over the boulder jumble of this scenic, narrow gorge.

PAULINA LAKE SHORE LOOP TRAIL

6.5-mile loop
Elevation change: 100 feet
Trail condition: forest and cinder
path, lava-studded in places
Moderate

Late spring through fall
Access: Begin at one of the Paulina
Lake campgrounds, the day-use
areas, or the resort.

The trail travels the shoreline of this large, azure lake, which holds reflections of its low, forested crater rim. Jagged lava tongues jut into the lake, creating ideal posts for lake viewing and angling. Craggy Paulina Peak overlooks the setting. Stringing together the campgrounds and the hike-in camps of shore, the trail tours a lodgepole and ponderosa pine forest, the base of an obsidian flow (a ridge of shiny black, glass-sharp rock), and semi-open manzanita and juniper slopes. It visits a grassy, drift-log-littered shore, gravel beaches, and marshy drainages. Where it climbs the red-cinder slope, hikers gain overviews of the lake, Paulina Peak, the lava flow, and Little Crater. Bitterbrush and manzanita cling to the steep cinder slope. Deer, ospreys, eagles, and nutcrackers are common sightings.

OBSIDIAN FLOW TRAIL

1.0 mile round trip
Elevation change: 100 feet
Trail condition: paved trail
Easy

Late spring through fall
Access: Take the marked turn off
County 21 between Paulina and
East lakes.

This trail climbs the flank of a large obsidian flow above Lost Lake. The sharp-edged, glassy black rock catches the eye of the collector, but the area is posted against rock collecting. A link to the long-distance Newberry Crater

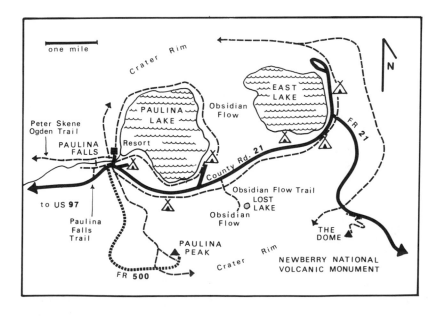

Paulina Peak and Paulina Lake

Rim Trail travels the base of the flow. Following it west, hikers travel between the flow and the lodgepole-pine forest edge, obtaining views of Paulina Peak. At 0.8 mile, the trail leaves the flow, entering the forest.

PAULINA PEAK DRIVE

8.0 miles round trip
Road quality: climbing, winding, improved road; final 1.5 miles to top are bumpy

Estimated speed: 10 to 15 mph
Access: Near the west end of Paulina Lake, turn south off County 21 onto FR 500.

This route features one of the best drive-to vistas in Oregon, atop Paulina Peak (elevation 7,985 feet). Mounts Hood and Jefferson, Broken Top, the Three Sisters, Mount Bachelor, Diamond Peak, Mount Thielsen, the Newberry Crater rim, Paulina and East lakes, Paulina Pinnacles, Fort Rock, and obsidian and lava flows keep the eyes sweeping the 360-degree expanse.

72 CABIN LAKE CAMPGROUND

14 tent/trailer units
Standard service no fee
campground
Nonflush toilets
Water
Open year-round
For information: Fort Rock Ranger
District

Map: Deschutes National Forest
Access: At La Pine, turn east off
US 97 onto Finley Butte Road (FR
22). In 25.5 miles, turn south onto
gravel FR 18 to reach camp in 6.0
miles.

This campground occupies a beautiful semi-open flat of mature ponderosa pine at the door to a pine forest–sage flat transition zone. The name Cabin Lake refers to a small, now dry lake across from the guard station. The campground offers a comfortable, quiet retreat and serves as a base from which to explore this region's interesting geology. Woodpeckers are commonly observed at camp.

SOUTH ICE CAVE TOUR

Primitive, self-guided
2,000 feet round trip (maximum distance)
Floor surface: rough rock, with areas of water and ice
Physical requirements: some step-overs and ducking encountered

Difficult
Access: From camp, go 6.0 miles
north on FR 18, and turn west
onto FR 22 to reach the marked
cave in 1.2 miles. The southeast
opening holds the main passageway.

For the adventurous armed with a pair of sturdy boots and a good flashlight, this natural ice rink in a lava tube offers cool fun. Even the mildly curious will want to scramble over the doorway rocks to view the seasonal ice pond just within the cave. Beyond the pond to the left is a small dead-end passage with an ice plug—a wall of glimmering discovery in the black. To the right, a narrow opening leads to an arch-ceilinged, rock-littered gallery with a perennial ice floor. Frost and icicles adorn the rocks. Late April to early May is the best time to view the ice forms. An open ponderosa pine forest with picnic sites surrounds the cave. Birds nest in the cave-mouth niches.

FORT ROCK STATE PARK

Point of geologic interest, picnic
area, flush toilets
For information: State Parks, Bend
Regional Office

Access: From camp, go 9.0 miles
south on FR 18/County 511 to
the marked turn. Continue 0.7
mile to reach the park.

Featured here is the descriptively named, naturally formed rock fortress. Its walls stand some 325 feet high, and its cavity measures one-third of a mile in diameter. Some 10,000 to 12,000 years ago, a volcanic eruption occurred beneath the shallow lake that stood here, creating a circular fallout that hardened and eventually eroded to the present crescent shape. Camels, mammoths, and mastodons grazed the shore of this one-time lake. Sagebrush

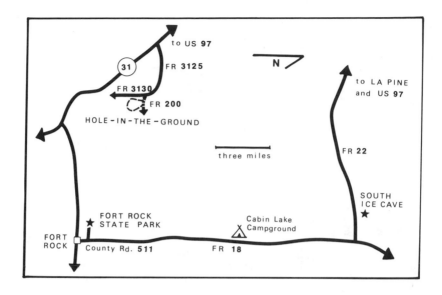

sandals found in a nearby cave date the presence of early humans in this area to some 10,000 years ago.

Exiting a turnstile in the fence, hikers can explore the outer base of Fort Rock via informal footpaths and cow trails. Raptors and ravens soar from the rocks, and swallows nest in the cliffs. Brilliant orange lichens etch the layered, crusted rock. Within the fort cavity, the walls show a more spattered appearance. Their gradual incline allows a rock scramble to the rim, for an overlook of the sweeping semi-arid expanse. Newberry Crater reigns to the north. Jeep trails explore the cavity.

HOLE-IN-THE-GROUND

Point of geologic interest, no facilities, carry water
For information: Fort Rock Ranger District
Access: From camp, turn right and go 11.0 miles south on FR 18/ County 511 to the town of Fort Rock. From there, go west 7.0 miles to OR 31, and turn northwest (right). In another 7.0 miles, turn right onto improved dirt FR 3125. In 3.0 miles, a turn right onto FR 3130 followed by a turn onto FR 3130.200 leads to the viewpoint and the trailhead in about 1.0 mile.

In the forest savannah of the high lava plains, this mile-wide, 300-foot-deep crater represents a violent, short-lived eruption that occurred when groundwater came into contact with molten rock. Near the viewpoint sign, a steep, dusty trail descends to the floor of the crater bowl. Sagebrush, bitterbrush, and mats of small white sand lilies accent the sandy bottom, while a few lodgepole pines offer shade. A jeep trail ascends the opposite wall, allowing a 2.5-mile loop through the crater and along the rim. Fire swept a section of the crater slope, scorching the bases of the larger ponderosa and killing the smaller pines. The dead trees have already attracted woodpeckers.

BASIN AND RANGE

Sunstone

The basin and range region unveils another open expanse of the state, one uniting ancient lakes and playas (dry lakes), fault-block mountains, stone-capped mesas, deserts, sagelands, wetlands, uncommon wildlife lands, hot springs, and even a geyser (just outside Lakeview). Much of the area has no outlet to the sea. The dry harshness explains the isolation of the land to this day. Only in the higher, wetter ranges of the Fremont National Forest do rich evergreen forests grow. A vehicle is mandatory for getting to know this sweeping expanse. Gravel roads provide routes to many of the discoveries.

Faults have shaped this land, creating island mountains with steep, upward-thrusting fronts and gently sloping backs. These mountains feature trout streams, rugged cliffs, high-elevation grasslands, and forests of aspen, mountain mahogany, and juniper.

Malheur National Wildlife Refuge, Warner Basin, Lake Abert, and Goose and Summer lakes provide premier winter stopping areas for waterfowl migration. Warner Wetlands is in the process of adding marked foot and canoe trails to its offering of wonderful waterfowl viewing. Taking flight off Abert Rim, hang gliders soar with the raptors above Lake Abert.

Pronghorn antelope range the sage flats and Hart Mountain. Beavers redesign creeks and preserve ponds throughout the year, protecting fish and other wildlife. Mule deer, coyote, wild horses, bighorn sheep, eagles, hawks, white pelicans, sandhill cranes, and more entertain the naturalist and photographer.

Such wildlife diversity and abundance attracted Indian hunting parties. Arrowheads, hide scrapers, and other tools and shards are sometimes discovered. Admire them, but do not remove them, as all artifacts are protected under the Antiquities Act.

Rockhounding is popular in this region. One area in particular holds special appeal: the Sunstone Collecting Area. At this remote location, the state gemstone sprinkles the desert-sage floor, guaranteeing even the novice a find. Agates, thunder eggs, Hart Mountain nodules, fire opal, obsidian, and petrified wood are among other sought-after rocks.

The higher reaches know winter snows, with the entire basin experiencing chilly winter temperatures and summer extremes. Spring and fall visits promise greater comfort. In spring, check ahead on road conditions, as the freeze-and-thaw cycle renders many roads impassable. ∎

Winter Rim above
Summer Lake Meadows

73   SUMMER LAKE WILDLIFE AREA

4 designated tent/trailer camping
areas
Primitive no fee campgrounds
Nonflush toilets
No water
Open year-round (some closures
between October and January,
depending on waterfowl hunting
season)

For information: Oregon
Department of Fish and Wildlife
Map: Oregon State
Access: At the south end of the
town of Summer Lake, turn east
off OR 31 for the wildlife area
headquarters.

Open campground flats suitable for one to five camp units dot the car-tour circuit through this wildlife area at the north end of extensive Summer Lake. To the west, Winter Ridge (elevation 7,100 feet) rises above the stage, breaking an otherwise open expanse. The area features open water, dense-reed marshland, ponds, alkali-mud flats, and sagelands, preserving the vital wildlife habitats of the high desert country. Spring and fall migrations bring added variety to the bird sightings, which run the gamut from bald eagles, white pelicans, whistling swans, and sandhill cranes to common ducks and shore-birds. Muskrats are often seen plying the waters of channels and ponds. Deer roam the open sagelands.

Amenities are few at these spartan campgrounds, but sightings are numerous. Binoculars, scopes, bird-identification guides, and telephoto lenses bring added enjoyment to a visit. Shade sources bring more comfort. The best time to visit is in late March and early April, when the birds remain numerous, the water high, the grasses low, and the temperatures kind. Insect repellent is a must.

WILDLIFE LOOP DRIVE

8.6-mile loop, plus 1.4 miles of
side-road spurs; maps and brochures
are available at the headquarters
Road quality: dirt dike roads, with
a few narrow places

Estimated speed: 15 mph
Access: From the headquarters,
follow the dirt road heading south.

This little-traveled circuit allows for a relaxing wildlife-area tour, with camp-area stops welcoming a chance for lengthier, more intimate wildlife study. Quail and pheasant dart from the sage. Red-winged blackbirds flash their wing-patch glory while passing amid the reeds. Nesting in open areas, killdeer put on grand wounded displays to divert attention from their eggs. A cacophony of sound rides the breeze.

Some dike roads that are closed to vehicle travel are open to foot travel. These dikes, together with the footbridges crossing the canals, give visitors viewing access to interior ponds and flats and allow for short hiking loops (good leg stretches after a ride).

Crucial nesting times and the like determine visitor freedom. Check at the headquarters about seasonal restrictions. Walks reveal sun-bleached bones in the alkali-mud flats, the salt-resistant vegetation that surrounds the flats, or

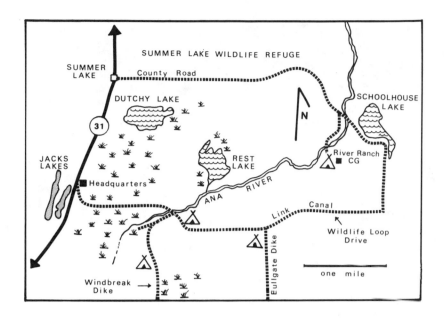

even a mouse scurrying to its protective burrow. Along Link Canal, many night herons are seen. At River Ranch Campground, a swirling parade of swallows exits the barn.

The loop leaves the wildlife area via a county road. Head west to meet OR 31 near the Summer Lake rest stop, 1.3 miles north of the headquarters.

74 CAMPBELL LAKE CAMPGROUND

15 tent/trailer units
Standard service no fee
campground
Nonflush toilets
Water
Open seasonally: mid-June through
October
For information: Paisley Ranger
District

Map: Fremont National Forest
Access: From Paisley on OR 31,
turn west onto Mill Street and
continue west and south via forest
roads 33, 3315, 28, and 2800.033,
following signs to Campbell Lake
and Dead Horse Lake camp-
grounds—in all about 25.0 miles
of gravel-road travel.

At the base of Dead Horse Rim, lodgepole pine–forested, well-spaced campsites ring rounded, scenic Campbell Lake (elevation 7,200 feet). Hiking, fishing, swimming, and boating (either self-propelled or with 5-hp-maximum electric motor) entertain visitors at this remote high-lake retreat. Next door, larger Dead Horse Lake, tied to Campbell Lake via trail and forest road, offers additional camping (21 sites) and similar lake recreation.

Deadhorse Lake

DEAD HORSE RIM TRAIL

3.5 miles one way	Difficult
Elevation change: 800 feet	Summer through fall
Trail condition: steep; faint atop	Access: Find trailheads at both lake
the rim (watch for blazes)	campgrounds.

From the trailhead near sites 13 and 14 at Campbell Lake Campground, the trail immediately enters a climbing mode, bypassing a small pond to arrive at a junction in 0.25 mile. In early summer, a frog serenade may be heard along this stretch. To the right lies the Lower Dead Horse Lake Trail; continue uphill for the rim hike.

The trail climbs through a lodgepole and white-bark pine forest, with spare lupine and kinnikinick floor. Switchbacks advance the climb, while tree blazes mark the trail. Approaching the rim, the trail exits the forest for a brief, steep, dusty, angling ascent along a semi-open rocky slope. The path is narrow and uneven.

Once atop the rim, hikers secure the only true vista of the hike, overlooking the eastern basin and range expanse, including Campbell Lake basin, the dropoff of Winter Ridge, the fault scarp spreading east, and Morgan Butte

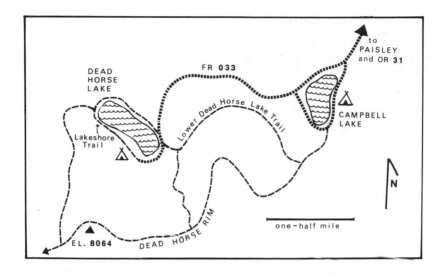

Lookout. With the rim's open floor and undefined path, keep a sharp eye out for markers. Tiny wildflowers sprinkle the rim top.

At the 1.5-mile junction, a shorter hike to Dead Horse Lake heads downhill to the right (it exits at FR 2800.033, near the entrance to Dead Horse Lake Campground). The Rim Trail continues straight to a second junction for the lake, in about another 1.0 mile. Going right at this junction, the downhill trek finds a newly rerouted switchback course through similar forest. It ends at an abandoned road encircling part of Dead Horse Lake (the Lakeshore Trail). Here, a right leads to a gate and Dead Horse Lake Campground in 0.3 mile.

LOWER DEAD HORSE LAKE TRAIL

2.25 miles one way	**Moderate**
Elevation change: 300 feet	**Summer through fall**
Trail condition: steady-climbing, dusty forest trail	**Access: Find trailheads at both lake campgrounds.**

Beginning near sites 13 and 14 at Campbell Lake Campground, this hike shares its first 0.25 mile with the Rim Trail and then turns right at the junction. Touring the lower reaches of Dead Horse Rim, this tree-blazed route journeys through a lodgepole and white-bark pine forest with a patchy kinnikinick floor. By 0.75 mile, true fir have entered the forest mix.

At the 1.5-mile junction, an uphill trek leads to the rim; the Lower Dead Horse Lake Trail continues straight, quickly delivering its only view—an overlook of Dead Horse Lake, a beautiful, forest-rimmed, elongate lake at the base of Dead Horse Rim. Distant landmarks include Black Butte, Green Mountain, and Shake Butte. Mountain mahogany and sagebrush claim the volcanic soils on this east-facing slope. Leaving the vantage point, the trail descends via a gradual switchback course through a pine forest, void of views, to arrive at the trailhead on FR 2800.033, near the entrance to Dead Horse Lake Campground.

Cottonwood Meadow Lake

75 COTTONWOOD MEADOW LAKE AREA

26 tent/trailer units
Standard service no fee campground
Nonflush toilets
Water
Open seasonally: June through mid-October
For information: Lakeview Ranger District
Map: Fremont National Forest

Access: For a paved route, from OR 140 about 26.0 miles northwest of Lakeview and 25.0 miles southeast of Bly, turn east onto FR 3870 (look for a sign for Cottonwood Meadow Lake). Go 5.5 miles on FR 3870, and turn north onto FR 024 to reach the campground in 1.0 mile.

Sites occupy a mixed pine-and-fir-forested bench above narrow, meandering Cougar Creek; others dot the shore of Cottonwood Meadow Lake. Campers enjoy hiking, fishing, swimming, and boating (self-propelled or with 5-hp-maximum electric motor). Day-use areas and boat-launch sites also occupy the shore of Cottonwood Meadow Lake, a small, scenic reservoir rimmed by lush meadows, ponderosa pine stands, and aspen groves. Grizzly and Cougar peaks can be seen while boating. The moist lake meadows produce a spring wildflower bonanza.

COUGAR PEAK TRAIL

5.5 miles round trip (to the summit)
Elevation change: 1,700 feet
Trail condition: closed, abandoned, steady-climbing jeep trail or footpath; rocky upper reaches

Moderate to difficult
Late spring through fall
Access: Find the trailhead at the north end of Cougar Creek Campground, off FR 024.

The hike begins by climbing over a rail fence to follow an abandoned jeep road uphill. Ponderosa pine and white fir frame the unreclaimed avenue but throw little shade over the hiking corridor. Alongside and below the route, 2-

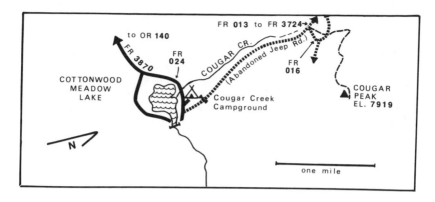

foot-wide Cougar Creek drunkenly slips through meadow and forest. By late autumn, the creek is reduced to a trickle; a few aspen line its course. The lichen-adorned fir trunks reveal distinct winter snow lines.

At 1.3 miles, FR 013 and FR 016 meet at the foot of Cougar Peak. Angle uphill across the meadow to the left or briefly follow FR 016 and bear left below the clearcut to find the marked peak trailhead. The meadow, accented by beautiful large ponderosa pines and adorned by yellow bells and other wildflowers (with peak blooms in May), proves a pleasant alternative ending to the hike (1.5 miles).

Continuing to the summit, the hike follows the jeep trail venturing left, tracing a low contour along the snag-dotted, cut-over slope. The route soon enters a ponderosa pine–fir forest, with large-diameter trees and silver snags. Some lupine, dry grasses, and mats of kinnikinick patch the floor. Lacking a sharp road cut, the jeep trail proves a pleasant, wide path.

From the trail sign at 1.8 miles, the route climbs alongside a fence at the forest edge. A footpath replaces the jeep trail as it approaches a talus slope. Mountain mahogany, low-growing chinquapin, manzanita, and small fir and aspen gain footing in the rocky terrain. At 2.3 miles, hikers obtain the first open views, with Blue Mountain to the west, California's Mount Shasta to the southwest, Bly with the far-distant Cascade volcano peaks to the northwest, and Grizzly Peak to the south.

At 2.4 miles, the trail again meets the jeep road. Here, hikers have the option of following the jeep road to the summit or taking the trail, which continues up the talus slope. The grade and footing are both easier on the jeep road, but the route is longer (3.1 miles vs. 2.75 miles to the summit). At 2.5 miles, the trail briefly merges with the jeep road before continuing up the talus slope at a cairn-marked site. The onetime site of a lookout, the summit unfolds a 360-degree vista. To previous views it adds looks at Lakeview, Cottonwood Reservoir, Abert Rim, Goose Lake, and Drake and Crane peaks.

For the 1.25-mile summit hike alone, campers should return to FR 3870, heading west from camp. In about 1.0 mile, turn north onto gravel FR 3724. On the timber-cut saddle below Cougar Peak, turn east (right) onto FR 013, and park. Skirting the meadow, hike the rock-edged road scrape to the left to find the marked trailhead in 0.1 mile.

76 SUNSTONE AREA

2 to 4 tent/trailer units
Primitive no fee camping area
Nonflush toilets
No water
Open year-round (except during the
muddy freeze-and-thaw period in
spring, when the area is inaccessible)
For information: BLM, Lakeview
District
Map: BLM brochure, available at
the Lakeview District office
Access: From Plush (located 40.0
miles northeast of Lakeview), go
10.0 miles north, and turn right
onto County 3-11, heading toward
Hart Mountain and Frenchglen. In
0.5 mile, turn left onto Road 6155,
at the sign for the Sunstone Area
and Rabbit Hills. In 8.0 miles,
again turn left, to travel Road 6115
(do not take Corn Lake Road). In
1.9 miles, continue straight, and in
another 3.0 miles, turn right to
reach the Sunstone Area in 0.7
mile. It's a paved, gravel, and im-
proved-dirt route, with some heavy
washboard along the final 4.0
miles. While the roads are passable
for trailers and RVs, as a camping
destination, this site is reserved for
the avid rockhound.

This shadeless, windy high-desert sagebrush plain promises seclusion and adventure. The flat near the sign offers open space for primitive camping. Raptors, lizards, jackrabbits, and antelope are the next-door neighbors. Break- ing the open expanse are views of Hart Mountain and Poker Jim Ridge to the east, Rabbit Hills to the south, Juniper Mountain to the northwest, and Abert Rim to the west. The set-aside 4-square-mile special interest area invites cross- country exploration and sunstone sleuthing.

The sunstone is a translucent feldspar, the state gemstone. The area assures even the amateur a find—in fact, a small bag of sunstone finds. Sunstones litter the surface of the dry plain, with higher-quality stones lying beneath the surface. Amateur seekers can simply pluck the stones from the sand. For the avid seeker, a shovel to uncover the matrix rock and a pry bar or screwdriver to liberate the stones are basic tools.

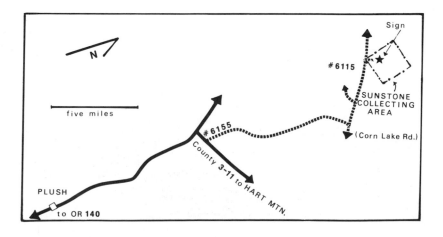

SUNSTONE COLLECTING AREA

Public, self-guided mineral-collecting area

For information: see page 202

Access: The area covers 4 square miles, radiating out from the sunstone sign at camp. Green triangular BLM signs mark the site boundary. Visible from a great distance, the sunstone sign serves as a navigational landmark. BLM lands extend beyond the designated collection area, but they are dotted with private claims. Contact the BLM district office before conducting any off-site excursions.

Scattered atop the dry, cracked sage flats and along the desert washes, these fingernail-sized, yellow-pink translucent crystals catch the sun, drawing collectors to their knees. Look toward the sun to spy the sunstones more easily. Avid collectors use shovels and screens to increase the likelihood of their finding the superior gems—those that are larger and show better fracturing and richer color. Green and red crystals are the most coveted. According to the BLM, the rule of thumb is that for every one hundred colorless stones, a pink-hued stone is found; for every ten pinks, a transparent red stone is found; and for every ten reds, a clear green stone may be found.

Sage at the Sunstone Collection Area

Small excavation holes along the washes reveal where previous seekers tested their luck. The abandoned jeep roads and the washes prove natural avenues of discovery, but they are also the most often walked and searched. A shallow wash bypasses camp, ushering rockhounds deeper into the open expanse.

Periodically venturing away from the washes and jeep roads is likely to improve both the quality and the number of the sunstone finds. Before prowling the open sage expanse, establish your bearings, noting the physical landmarks. Use of a compass is recommended for all but the shortest outings.

---

77 HART MOUNTAIN ANTELOPE REFUGE

12 tent units (approximately)
Primitive no fee camp area
Nonflush toilets
No water
Open seasonally (occasional closures from November to May due to foul-weather road conditions or wet meadow sites)
For information: Hart Mountain National Antelope Refuge
Map: Oregon State
Access: From Plush (located 40.0 miles northeast of Lakeview), go 0.9 mile north of town and turn east (right) for Hart Mountain and Frenchglen. The refuge headquarters is in 23.0 miles; the camp area is in 27.0 miles (go right at the junction beyond the headquarters). This paved and good gravel route is part of the Lakeview to Steens National Back Country Byway. The refuge road to the Hot Springs camp area is not recommended for trailers or RVs.

Informal sites occupy aspen-shaded grassy flats along Bond and Rock creeks, below the juniper- and mountain mahogany–dotted sage slopes. The hot-springs bathhouse is the centerpiece of the camp area. Its 5-foot-deep pool rests in an open-air concrete-block cell. At night, bathers can relax under the stars. The refuge invites car touring, cross-country hiking, photography, and wildlife viewing. A small museum and nature garden are found at the headquarters complex. Mid-May through October is the best time to visit.

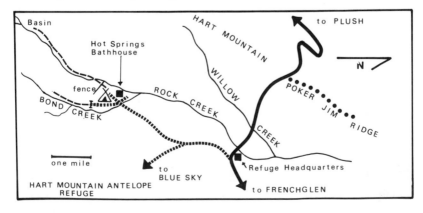

POKER JIM HIKE

4.8 miles round trip (to the canyon overlook)
Elevation change: 200 feet
Trail condition: cross-country, rocky (wear boots)
Difficult

Spring through fall
Access: The hike begins where the refuge road crosses the Poker Jim Ridge–Hart Mountain saddle, 6.3 miles northwest of camp. Parallel roadside parking is limited.

From the refuge road, the trail mounts the sage slope to the north to top Poker Jim Ridge in 0.1 mile. In the loose sand of the slope, obsidian arrowhead shards catch the sun. (Look, but do not disturb; all artifacts are protected under the Antiquities Act.) Paralleling the outer edge of the rim—a natural guide—hikers overlook the corridor of the refuge road, the marbled desert wetland and lakes of Warner Basin, and Juniper Mountain. Lichen etch the volcanic rock of the rim. Coyotes, rabbits, and thermal-riding raptors are among the possible wildlife sightings. Balsam root, desert parsley, Indian paintbrush, phlox, and lupine splash color on the rocky terrain.

By 0.6 mile, the hike destination, a juniper-dotted knob, comes into view. At 2.0 miles is a false top, and at 2.4 miles is the knob summit. The post offers overlooks of the rugged canyon slicing Poker Jim Ridge, as well as looks at the ridge's own imposing front face. On clear days, Steens Mountain adds to the view.

BOND CREEK HIKE

2.0 miles round trip (to a meadow)
Elevation change: 200 feet
Trail condition: abandoned jeep track

Easy
Spring through fall
Access: Begin at the Bond Creek arm of the camp area.

The hike crosses a barbed-wire fence for an upstream tour. The grassy track of the trail journeys alongside the aspen–willow corridor of Bond Creek, cradled in a sage canyon, for two-habitat viewing. Red-winged blackbirds, grackles, raptors, and woodpeckers invite birdwatching. Antelope and mule deer may be seen crossing the slopes.

Go right at the canyon split in 0.5 mile to follow the main canyon fork. A thick grove of mountain mahogany claims the ridge top; some huge aspen line the canyon belly. The hike ends at a beautiful small meadow shaded by a stand of grand old aspen.

ROCK CREEK HIKE

4.0 miles round trip
Elevation change: 400 feet
Trail condition: old cattle trail, with creek fording
Moderate

Spring through fall
Access: An upstream hike begins at the end of the camp road, along the east bank of Rock Creek.

The well-tracked footpath ahead travels the juniper–aspen–willow corridor of Rock Creek. At 0.1 mile is a barbed-wire-fence crossing (an easy step-over with unanchored wire), and at 0.2 mile, the hike requires a creek crossing to the west bank. The fording site lies just below a beaver pond. Several beaver enhancements mark the creek, reserving water well into the summer for fish and wildlife. Hart Mountain rises to the west; the arid dividing ridge between Bond and Rock creeks rises to the east. Follow the cow trails (which prove good footpaths) along the base of the sage slope to avoid the downfalls, branches, and wet meadow stretches right along the creek.

At 1.3 miles, the canyon splits. Continuing along the main stem, the trail enters a pinched canyon with a more rugged western flavor. At 2.0 miles, the canyon opens up to a peaceful mountain basin at the foot of Warner Peak. The crooked ribbon of Rock Creek parts the basin grassland. Deer and flickers are among the common wildlife sightings. Ticks are a springtime problem.

78 PAGE SPRINGS CAMPGROUND

30 tent/trailer units
Standard service fee campground
Nonflush toilets
Water
Open seasonally: mid-April through mid-November

For information: BLM, Burns District
Map: Oregon State
Access: From OR 205 at Frenchglen, go 2.0 miles east on Steens Mountain Loop Road for the campground.

Located where the Donner und Blitzen River leaves its basalt-rimmed canyon to travel the semi-arid land of Malheur National Wildlife Refuge, Page Springs is the ideal base for exploring the wildlife area. It offers open and tree-shaded river-flat sites surrounded by juniper-dotted grassland. The campground lies along the extensive Desert Trail, which at this point follows the river, attracting hikers, anglers, and birders.

DESERT TRAIL

2.0 miles round trip (to the island point below the gauge station)
Elevation change: minimal
Trail condition: good path, with a side-water fording

Easy
Year-round
Access: Find the upstream trailhead at the south end of the campground.

This hike samples a brief, scenic segment of the extensive Desert Trail, proposed for National Scenic Trail distinction. The trail tours the east bank of the wide, fast-flowing Donner und Blitzen River, alternately traveling along the river flat and below the juniper-dotted canyon rim. It bypasses a marshy cattail wetland pond, open grassland, and clear-water springs. Lichen, minerals, and guano streak the dark basalt rim in green, red, and white.

At 0.7 mile, it's best to round the bend just below the rim to avoid the marshy river edge. Swallows nest in the cliff and engage in swirling chaotic flight, snatching at the insect hatches off the river. A side-channel fording ends the hike at a small, grassy island, with an upstream view that includes a gauging station. To hike farther upstream requires frequent wading.

MALHEUR REFUGE CENTER PATROL ROAD TOUR

42.0 miles one way
Road quality: gravel levee roads and OR 205
Estimated speed: 25 mph (refuge road)

Access: From the campground, go 1.4 miles west and turn north to enter the refuge and begin the road tour.

The refuge road tour unveils the various habitats—marsh, grassland, open water, upland sage, river bank, and field—that create this rich wildlife land where native and migratory inhabitants feed, shelter, winter, and breed. Malheur is Oregon's premier waterfowl wintering ground. Basalt rims frame the west edge of the refuge; Steens Mountain looms in the distant southeast. Farther north, rims, tablelands, and buttes break the expanse.

From south to north, interesting stops dot the way. Near the tour start, the Observation Tower hosts forty to fifty roosting vultures at peak periods (during the early morning and evening hours). By midday, most of the vultures have evacuated the tower to ride the thermals in search of food.

The tour later travels along Benson Pond, with its long rush islands and rafts of lily pads. Great horned owls nest in the lake area and are commonly seen amid the cottonwood trees on its north shore. Trumpeter swans also nest near Benson Pond. Beyond the pond is the turn for the 3.5-mile side road leading to Krumbo Reservoir, a small, artificial lake cradled by basalt rims. More interestingly, the side road bypasses a petroglyph rock in 2.2 miles. The rock rests on the south side of the road; there's no sign. Faded painted carvings of lizards and symbols decorate the large basalt boulder.

Returning to the refuge tour, the route follows OR 205 north. The volcanic rim of Buena Vista Overlook, located 0.8 mile from Buena Vista Station, east off OR 205, features a 180-degree overview of the ponds, fields, Donner und Blitzen Canal, and the desert east. Geese, rock doves, and deer, nearly hidden amid the tall grass, are among the sightings.

With a right turn off OR 205 (farther north), the tour then returns to the Center Patrol Road, heading north to the refuge headquarters (the tour's conclusion). For serious birders, the one-room museum houses a code board

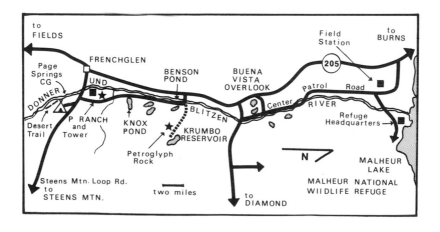

noting when and where to find bird species. The shaded grounds attract songbirds. Headquarters Pond promises sightings of white pelicans, cormorants, and coots. A greater variety and number of birds can be seen on Malheur Lake.

FRENCHGLEN HOTEL

**State wayside, historic site; open
from March 1 to November 15
For information: State Parks,
LaGrande Regional Office**

**Access: Go west from the camp-
ground to Frenchglen.**

A public park since 1973, this still-functioning eight-room frontier hotel receives dining and overnight guests. Its grounds prove a day-use oasis, with ancient-cottonwood- and white poplar–shaded lawns, picnic tables, drinking water, and an outhouse.

*Cormorants on a snag,
Malheur National
Wildlife Refuge*

79 STEENS MOUNTAIN RECREATION AREA

**22 tent/trailer units (Fish Lake
Campground)
Standard service fee campground
Nonflush toilets
Water
Open seasonally: July through
mid-October
For information: BLM, Burns
District**

**Map: Steens Mountain Recreation
Land
Access: From OR 205 at
Frenchglen, turn east onto Steens
Mountain Loop Road, a good to
fair two-lane gravel road, to reach
the campground in 16.0 miles.**

This campground provides access to an unusual land feature: Steens Mountain, a glacier-carved 30-mile-long fault-block mountain (elevation 9,733 feet) rising from the desert floor. As driving is the primary means of discovery, a high-clearance vehicle in good repair, with good tires and a full gas tank, helps ensure a pleasant visit. The camp's two halves straddle Fish Lake and are tied by a lakeside footpath. The facility holds both aspen-shaded and open sites, a boat ramp (no motors on the lake), and a day-use area, with public horse corrals across the road. Smaller lakes nearby offer additional recreation and relaxation. Jackman Park Campground (water and fee), to the east, holds six small sites in an open flat ringed by aspen and meadow.

SUMMIT TRAILS

1.5 miles round trip	Access: From the campground,
Elevation change: 400 feet	turn right and go 10.6 miles
(between the lake vista and Steens	southeast via the loop road and the
Mountain summit)	summit spur road. The final 2.5
Trail condition: rocky, former roads	miles is a bucking ride to the
Moderate	parking area and trailheads (at
Late spring to fall	gated roads).

A 0.5-mile trail wraps its way uphill to the radio facilities, the summit, and a 270-degree vista, offering overviews of Wildhorse Lake and its meandering creek along the way. On this wind-scoured site, only the sides of the radio facility offer shelter to visitors taking in the view of the sweeping desert expanse to the east.

A relatively steep old road leads downhill for 0.25 mile to a vista point overlooking Wildhorse Lake, a beautiful azure pool in a green-splashed cirque below the scree slope of a cliff. A steep, rocky, unmaintained route charges down the slope to the lake, inviting only the hardy to explore.

STEENS MOUNTAIN LOOP, NATIONAL BACK COUNTRY BYWAY

66.0-mile loop (plus side spurs)	Access: North entrance: Turn east
Road quality: gravel, with major	off OR 205 at Frenchglen. South
climb and descent; rough in places	entrance: Turn east off OR 205
Estimated speed: 15 to 30 mph	about 42.0 miles north of Fields
	and 10.0 miles south of Frenchglen.

The loop tour unveils the many faces and expansive views of this mountain "island" surrounded by semi-arid land. Continuing east from camp, the loop travels past moist meadows of false hellebore, aspen groves, and patches of mountain mahogany.

At 6.0 miles lies the 0.5-mile spur to Kiger Gorge Viewpoint, offering perhaps the route's best gorge vista. From atop the rim of the cliff that dams the gorge, the view features a classic U-shaped glacial valley, where the volcanic rim gives way to steep grassy slopes and an aspen-lined creek bottom. The Kiger herd of wild horses, believed to be descended from the mounts of the Spanish conquistadors, roams this canyon.

Within another 2.0 miles, the loop tour passes a memorial to the six Wilderness Review members who died in the Little Blitzen Gorge plane crash. Just beyond lies the Summit–East Rim junction. The East Rim View offers a spectacular look at the rugged, treeless escarpment that rises 5,000 feet above the Alvord Desert. This seemingly uninhabitable cliff is home to bighorn sheep. The view encompasses several dry lakes, Mann Lake, the desert floor, and irrigated fields. Hiking along the rim offers new perspectives. (For the summit spur offerings, see the above trail description.)

East Rim View, Steens Mountain

From the Summit–East Rim junction, the loop road gradually deteriorates but remains fine for high-clearance vehicles, traveling slowly. It serves up additional views, featuring Big Indian and Little Blitzen gorges, as it travels from summit grasslands (a wildflower showcase in July) past mountain mahogany–dotted slopes to reach the juniper–sage complex near the Donner und Blitzen River crossing. The road improves as it travels a semi-arid environment to OR 205. Going north to Frenchglen continues the loop for a return to camp.

Turnouts and stops lace the loop, allowing visitors to leave their vehicles and enjoy the surroundings. The openness of the terrain welcomes short cross-country hikes to rim views, snowfields, and wildflower patches.

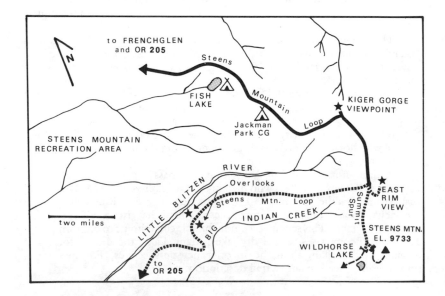

BLUE MOUNTAINS

Oregon's Blue Mountains are a range of quiet, understated beauty. The Blues lack the rugged terrain of the Siskiyous, the forest and floral exuberance of the Coast Range, the high peaks of the Cascades, and the newness and glacial splendor of the Wallowa Mountains. But they win over guests with mixed forests, rounded ridges, beautiful braided creeks and streams, extensive valley and smaller mountain meadows, quiet lakes, and some eye-catching free-standing stone pillars. The Strawberry Mountain Wilderness and the Elkhorn Range are the area's lone bids for status among the state's high-mountain attractions.

A U.S. Army directive prohibiting white settlement east of the Cascades delayed development of this region. Gold discoveries in Idaho and eastern Oregon finally tumbled the directive in 1858. Gold was then discovered in the Blues in the 1860s, with Baker City springing up as the center of commerce.

Trails and driving tours radiating outward from Baker City unfold the boom–bust story of this region. They string together a historic power station, the wooden pipe system carrying its water lifeline, ghost towns, shafts, ditches, tailings (mining rubble), cabins, and active and abandoned claims. The greatest concentration of ghost towns lies west of Baker City. In addition to prospecting, the region is also noted for its thunder eggs found at Ochoco Agate Beds, off FR 27 northeast of Prineville.

Wildflower meadows are a regional drawing card in spring and summer. Wet and dry meadows parade a kaleidoscope of color. The far-spreading valley meadows also attract varied wildlife, suggesting roadside stops en route to camp or trailhead. This region boasts some of the state's largest deer and elk populations; pronghorn antelope and wild horses also range the region. In autumn and spring, the Pacific Flyway hosts flocks of cranes and geese migrating to and from Malheur National Wildlife Refuge and other basin and range wetlands.

The Walton Lake fishing platform

Like much of the John Day River system, the North Fork of the John Day River holds spawning habitat critical to the restoration of the Columbia Basin fish runs. Special fishing regulations apply to its waters.

The area has year-round recreation, with skiing, snowshoeing, and ice fishing in winter. When the snow disappears, poison oak rears its head amid understory plants, so hikers should beware of it in off-trail explorations.   ■

80 WILDCAT CAMPGROUND

17 tent/trailer units
Standard service fee campground
Nonflush toilets
Water
Open seasonally: mid-May through mid-October
For information: Prineville Ranger District

Map: Ochoco National Forest
Access: From US 26 about 10.0 miles east of Prineville (at the east end of Ochoco Reservoir), turn north on Mill Creek Road/FR 33. Go 10.4 miles to the campground on the paved and gravel route.

Located alongside the East Fork of Mill Creek, the campsites and neighboring picnic area occupy a semi-open, fir-forested flat with a few ponderosa pine. The camp offers access to the Mill Creek Wilderness, meadows and old-growth groves, a wildflower showcase, creek and reservoir fishing, and exceptional trails with some exciting rock destinations.

TWIN PILLARS TRAIL

7.0 miles round trip (to the Twin Pillars vista)
Elevation change: 600 feet
Trail condition: good earthen path with multiple creek crossings, some on makeshift footbridges

Moderate; final leg to vista and pillars difficult
Spring through fall
Access: Find trailheads at the upstream end of the campground and at the day-use area.

The trail tours a slope forested in ponderosa pine and white and Douglas fir above the East Fork of Mill Creek, soon entering the Mill Creek Wilderness. Drawing deeper into the wilderness, it alternately tours the forested slope and the meadow floor alongside the scenic 5- to 7-foot-wide creek. Shooting star, lupine, larkspur, buttercup, and dandelion color the meadow. Heart-leafed arnica and Jacob's ladder add spring accents to the forest floor. Drier slopes sport mountain mahogany. Making its way, the trail slips easily back and forth across the creek in a whimsical game of tag.

Only a few gentle rises punctuate the hike's first 1.5 miles. Then the trail climbs to skirt a small gorge before dropping down to the Belknap Trail

Steins Pillar

junction (2.6 miles). At 2.8 miles, after the final creek crossing, the trail undergoes a character change, with a fast, steep uphill charge.

Don't let the first spurt of the climb intimidate you. The grade moderates from that initial intensity for a steady, serious climb to the vista site (3.5 miles); a strenuous climb completes the hike to Twin Pillars (5.5 miles). You may turn around at the base of the hill, but if you'd like to end the hike with at least a glimpse of the featured attraction, 0.7 mile of huffing and puffing finds a Twin Pillars vista where the trail draws over the ridge between Brogan Creek and the East Fork of Mill Creek. The branches of nearby ponderosa pine intrude on the view, but the vista adequately rewards the added expenditure. The saddle's grassy slope welcomes a supine appreciation of the rock.

STEINS PILLAR TRAIL

3.4 miles round trip
Elevation change: 400 feet
Trail condition: rolling, rocky in places
Moderate
Spring through fall

Access: From camp, go 3.7 miles south on FR 33, turning east onto FR 3300.500 (good, one-lane gravel road). Go 2.0 miles for the trailhead, parking, and a picnic site, on the left.

The trail tours a fir and ponderosa pine forest before taking switchbacks up an open slope dotted with balsam root, phlox, lupine, and bitterbrush. At 0.25 mile, it tops a small ridge with views to the south and west, including the Mill Creek drainage. Twisted juniper, mountain mahogany, and bunchgrass deck the ridge.

Contouring the southwest slope, the trail's northward journey unfolds nearly continuous views of the nearby drainages and distant Cascade peaks. At 0.8 mile, the trail descends into a dense forest of small-diameter trees, leaving the views behind. Crossing over a small ridge, the trail offers a brief early vista of Steins Pillar, its neighboring rock features, and Twin Pillars, far to the north.

At 1.5 miles, the trail passes a scenic lichen-etched rock. Steins Pillar, a massive, 350-foot free-standing pinkish stone with a black-streaked summit, awaits ahead. The imposing rock, shooting skyward, dwarfs all in its midst. Well below are the fields of Mill Creek Valley. Nearby forested ridges appear to recede in its presence. A steep 300-foot trail leads to the pillar base, offering a different perspective.

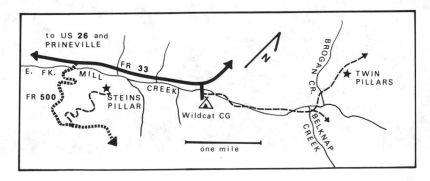

81 WALTON LAKE CAMPGROUND

30 tent/trailer units
Standard service fee campground
Nonflush toilets
Water
Open seasonally: mid-May through
mid-October
For information: Big Summit
Ranger District
Map: Ochoco National Forest

Access: Go 15.0 miles east of
Prineville on US 26, and bear
right onto paved County 123, at
the sign for Ochoco Ranger Station. In another 8.0 miles, County
123 becomes FR 22. Follow the
signs another 7.0 miles to reach
the campground.

A small earthen dam transformed this onetime meadow into a good-sized
mountain lake rimmed by low, semi-open, ponderosa pine–forested slopes.
Pull-in and roadside-parking sites occupy the north and south shores. A launch
for nonmotorized boats, a handicap-access fishing platform, and a day-use area
occupy the south shore. Alternative camping may be found at Ochoco
Campground, 7.0 miles west via FR 22. It holds six creekside camp units, a
picnic area, and the trailhead for the Lookout Mountain Trail.

SHORELINE TRAIL

0.75-mile loop
Elevation change: none
Trail condition: wide, fine gravel,
paved, or earthen trailbed

Easy
Spring through fall
Access: Begin at the campground.

While this short trail does not introduce a great variety of setting or habitat
changes, it does offer a peaceful appreciation of the lake as it tours the
ponderosa pine–dotted slopes; prairie grass meadow with false hellebore,
prairie smoke, and strawberry; and the grassy shoreline. Where cattails and
rushes invade the lake waters, red-winged blackbirds replace the stillness with
animation and song. The lake tour is a good wake-up hike before breakfast or
closing hike for day's end.

ROUND MOUNTAIN NATIONAL RECREATION TRAIL

10.0 miles round trip (from the
lake to the summit)
Elevation change: 1,500 feet
Trail condition: well maintained,
rocky in places
Moderate; final mile of ascent
difficult
Spring through fall

Access: Find the trailhead spur off
the Shoreline Trail. For a reduced
climb and 9.0-mile round-trip hike,
drive 0.5 mile east from the camp
entrance on FR 22 to where the
trail crosses the road. (Look for the
small sign for Bev's Ridge.)

The trail ascends the forest of the Walton Lake basin to the FR 22
trailhead. Crossing the road, it travels the fir–larch forest fringe along an open
grassy meadow. A jeep trail alternates with the footpath along the first mile of
the hike. Lupine, blue and yellow violets, lungswort, false hellebore, and other
wildflowers dot the meadow.

At 0.8 mile, the trail passes a snow station, climbs, and draws deeper into the forest. By 1.5 miles, it tops Bev's Ridge, with views to the northeast of the nearby rolling, recovering-cut slopes and the distant Mount Pisgah and a view to the south of Round Mountain. Juniper, sage, and pine deck the ridge.

Leaving the ridge, the trail descends slowly, gradually leveling out for a forest tour interspersed by meadow pockets. At 2.75 miles, the trail enters a more extensive meadow threaded by mature ponderosa pine. The meadow is an alternative destination, ideally suited for a lazy lunch before the return to camp. The summit awaits the hardy.

After swinging a wide loop skirting the meadow, the trail ascends the forested base of Round Mountain to arrive at the steep, open meadow slope just below the summit. Here, the heart-pumping switchbacks begin. As the trail climbs the west slope to the top, it gradually unfolds a 360-degree vista that includes Twin Pillars, Mounts Hood and Jefferson, the Three Sisters, Wildcat and Lookout mountains, the Ochoco Creek valley, and Big Summit Prairie.

MAYFLOWER MINING SETTLEMENT

Unmarked, public roadside stop, candidate for National Register of Historic Places
For information: see page 215

Access: Find the settlement alongside FR 22 3.5 miles west of the campground.

Resting against the hillside, the skewed, collapsing frame of a five-stamp mill, its scattered foundations, and a collapsed shaft all hint at the finer days of this 1873 Ochoco Mining District settlement. Look from a safe distance.

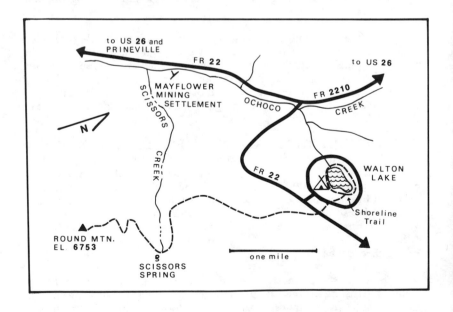

A mining cabin on the North Fork John Day River

---

82 NORTH FORK JOHN DAY CAMPGROUND

9 tent/trailer units
Standard service no fee
campground
Nonflush toilets
No water
Open seasonally: June through
October

For information: North Fork John
Day Ranger District
Map: Umatilla National Forest
Access: Find the campground at the
junction of FR 52 and FR 73, 39.0
miles southwest of Ukiah via FR
52 or 8.3 miles north of Granite
via FR 73.

The campground occupies a reclaimed meadow above a "wild" section of the North Fork of the John Day River. Small lodgepole pine intersperse and rim the sites but provide virtually no shade. The campground offers access to the foot and horse trails exploring the North Fork John Day Wilderness. The wilderness holds historic and present-day mining claims and cabins along with its natural boasts. The camp also lies along the route of the Elkhorn Drive, a 106.0-mile scenic loop (a car-tour booklet is available at the Baker Ranger District office). It, too, unfolds the mining tale of the region. Before doing any angling, consult the state fishing regulations booklet, as special conditions apply to the North Fork.

NORTH FORK JOHN DAY NATIONAL RECREATION TRAIL

5.2 miles round trip (to Trout Creek)
Elevation change: 400 feet
Trail condition: good, well graded, packed rocky soil

Moderate
Spring through fall
Access: Find the trailhead 0.1 mile north of camp, off FR 52.

A narrow path off the end of the trailhead road begins the hike, with a log side-creek crossing, a meadow passage, and a second log crossing over the larger Trail Creek. On the opposite shore begins the well-defined trail touring a homogeneous lodgepole pine forest with some beetle kill, many young trees, and no shade.

Along the way, the trail passes a river channel isolated from the main flow by a mining-rubble ridge of discarded rock and boulders. The volume of the dislodged rock is astounding. The river itself is mostly an even band of rushing water, with small riffles and deep pools, spilling over a rocky floor. The forest gradually introduces more variety, with ponderosa pine, larch, and spruce, and with huckleberry, grasses, lupine, wild geranium, columbine, and a host of other wildflowers.

Descending from an open slope marked by cliffs and rock outcrops, the trail begins passing the historic and present-day cabins and claims. The cabins show various sizes and styles of construction and the common household wares of the miner: makeshift seating; rusting cans, tins, and blades; frying pans and buckets; and crate shelving. Do not disturb the sites—they are either private or protected under the Antiquities Act.

Huge larch punctuate the forest near Trout Creek bridge, the hike's ending point. The 22.9-mile North Fork Trail continues, exploring the river

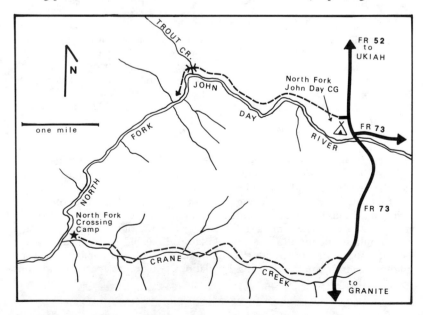

canyon, passing mining operations and claim markers, and touring fire zone and forest.

CRANE CREEK TRAIL

5.1 miles one way
Elevation change: 1,100 feet
Trail condition: wild, sometimes
faint, some fording; meadow
sections uneven and rolling from
horse and elk use
Difficult
Spring through fall

Access: Find the trailhead 2.2 miles
south of camp on FR 73.
The parking area is rough and
undeveloped, with a sharp bank off
FR 73. Forest Service plans call for
the construction of a new trailhead
facility with pull-through parking
and three campsites.

A hiker gate in the fence marks the beginning of this trail, which passes through a series of long, beautiful meadows threaded by Crane Creek and bridged by forest–meadow transition habitat. The flats prove a popular grazing area for deer and elk. An old "two-track" often guides the way through the knee-high grasses spangled with spring and summer wildflowers of purple, white, red, and yellow. In the stretches of lodgepole pine forest, downed trees weave across the floor, sometimes forming a steeple chase of step-overs.

Leaving the meadows, the trail skirts a charred standing forest, crisscrosses Crane Creek, draws deeper into a true canyon with steep rocky slopes and a more varied forest of mixed pine, aspen, larch, fir, and spruce. Downfalls, step-overs, and marshy drainages continue to burden the downstream trek. More evidence of fire lies ahead.

The trail halts at the North Fork of the John Day River, where placer tailings and mining ditches hint of the gold era. The North Fork Crossing Camp lies to the right on a bench above the Crane Creek–North Fork confluence, beside the river-fording site. With the trail's obstacles and no specific midway destination, hikers should personalize the hiking distance for their interests and abilities.

---

83 ANTHONY LAKES CAMPGROUND

38 tent/trailer units
Standard service fee campground
Nonflush toilets
Water
Open seasonally: July through
mid-September
For information: Baker Ranger
District

Map: Wallowa–Whitman National
Forest
Access: From I-84, take the North
Powder–Anthony Lakes exit. Go
west on North Powder River Lane
and FR 73, following the signs to
Anthony Lakes, to reach the camp-
ground in 19.8 miles.

The camp occupies a slope of small-diameter fir and lodgepole pine above Anthony Lake (elevation 7,100 feet). The Anthony Lakes area is a popular summertime destination for hiking, fishing, photography, self-propelled boat-

The Lakes Lookout and Lee's Peak above Hoffer Lake

ing, and car touring. (The 106.0-mile Elkhorn Loop Drive circles past the camp. Brochures are available at the ranger district.) Anthony Lakes is also a popular snow-sport area. Neighboring Forest Service campgrounds, alongside smaller, meadow-rimmed lakes, hold additional sites.

ELKHORN CREST TO BLACK LAKE LOOP

2.25-mile loop	Easy
Elevation change: 200 feet	Summer through fall
Trail condition: good, rock-studded or marshy in places	Access: Find the trailhead near campsite 12.

This trail of modest uphill grade meanders through a high-elevation forest of lodgepole pine, fir, and spruce, offers a glimpse of Gunsight Mountain, skirts a granite outcrop, and crosses a meadow. Mountain heather, shooting star, glacier lily, and dwarf huckleberry adorn the forest and meadow floor. Junctions along the way are well marked.

The outlet creek points the way to Black Lake, a dark shimmering mountain pool framed by forest, meadow, and rocky slope, with Van Patten Butte visible to the east. For a loop hike, retrace the Black Lake and Elkhorn Crest trails to the junction with the Anthony Lakeshore spur. From there, the loop travels the spur trail through meadow and forest to skirt shallow Lilypad Lake. Aptly named Gunsight Mountain looms overhead. The trail exits at the Anthony Lake boat launch. Turn right on the Lakeshore Trail to complete the loop and return to camp.

LAKESHORE AND HOFFER LAKES TRAILS TO LAKES LOOKOUT

5.6 miles round trip
Elevation change: 1,400 feet
Trail condition: sometimes steep,
some road travel

Difficult
Summer through fall
Access: Find the trailhead near campsite 3.

At the lakeshore, a left turn begins a clockwise tour of Anthony Lake, a mid-sized mountain lake with morning reflections of Gunsight Mountain, Lee's Peak, and Lakes Lookout. The route crosses over inlet creeks and passes the historic camp to reach the Hoffer Lakes trail, a steady uphill forest climb along stair-stepped Parker Creek. The trail grows steeper as it nears the lakes—two small pools with meadow rims at the base of Lee's Peak and Lakes Lookout. To the left, a marshy secondary trail ties together the lakes and a falls at the base of Lee's Peak. The main trail rounds the lake basin to the right, gaining views of Angell Peak and Gunsight Mountain before beginning a modest forest ascent to FR 185 (1.3 miles).

Go uphill on FR 185 and continue along FR 187 to find the trailhead to Lakes Lookout in another 0.8 mile. A saddle vista midway to the trailhead is alone worth the added walk. From the Lakes Lookout trailhead, a 0.7-mile, 700-foot climb leads to the 360-degree summit vista of the Crawfish and Anthony Lakes basins, the Blue Mountains, the Elkhorn Range, the distant

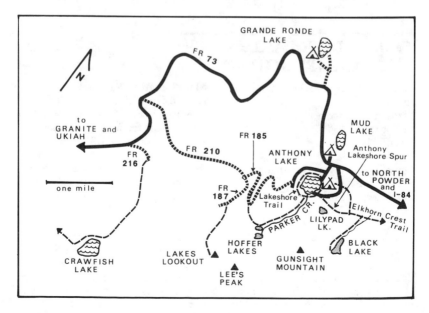

Wallowas, and the North Fork of the John Day valley. Low white-bark pine and twisted silver tree skeletons line this rocky summit trail.

Reaching the saddle vista and the Lakes Lookout trailhead via forest roads requires a high-clearance vehicle, as the dry-weather access roads off FR 73 are both narrow and winding, with some protruding rock and drainage cuts (estimated speed: 5 to 10 mph). From camp, go west 3.7 miles on FR 73, turn left onto FR 7300.210, and go 2.0 miles via FR 7300.210 and FR 187 to reach the trailhead.

CRAWFISH LAKE TRAIL

2.8 miles round trip
Elevation change: 500 feet
Trail condition: sometimes steep, rock-studded, or faint
Moderate
Summer through fall

Access: From camp, go 4.4 miles west on FR 73 and turn left onto FR 7300.216. Go 0.2 mile via foot or high-clearance vehicle along FR 7300.216 to find the trailhead.

This trail descends through habitats of dry meadow, open lodgepole pine–Engelmann spruce forest, a hit-and-miss fire-swept area, and a regenerating forest to cross a dirt road to a meadow boardwalk. Lupine, paintbrush, buttercup, and Jacob's ladder are among the ground-coloring wildflowers. With a creek crossing, the trail enters the undisturbed forest of the North Fork John Day Wilderness for its ascent to the lake. The open canopy of the forest provides only intermittent shade.

Crawfish Lake is a large, deep mountain lake rimmed by grassy bank and forest along three-fourths of its shore; a granite outcrop with trees rims the remainder. A tour of the footpath along the shore provides views of a side ridge off Elkhorn Crest, Lakes Lookout, and Lee's Peak.

---

84 OLIVE LAKE CAMPGROUND

15 tent/trailer units (better suited for tents)
Standard service no fee campground
Nonflush toilets
No water
Open seasonally: June through September
For information: North Fork John Day Ranger District

Map: Umatilla National Forest
Access: Go 12.0 miles west of Granite via FR 10 (wide, good gravel). Or, from US 395 north of Dale, take either FR 3900.100 or FR 55 east to follow FR 10 east, for about 27.0 miles total travel to the the campground turnoff. Find the campground off FR 480.

The campground occupies a forested hillside above the earthen dam–enlarged but scenic Olive Lake. Most sites have roadside parking with a short walk to tables, grills, and leveled tent areas; a few sites offer pull-in parking. A dock, boat launch, and angler paths provide access to the lake's offerings. Campers can also engage in hiking, photography, and history tracking. Area meadows burst with summer wildflowers.

SADDLE CAMP TRAIL

6.0 miles round trip (to Saddle
Camp)
Elevation change: 800 feet
Trail condition: path or abandoned
road, alternating rolling and steep
segments

Easy, becoming difficult
Late spring through fall
Access: Find the trailhead at the
end loop of the campground road.

The trail enters the Indian Rock–Vinegar Hill Scenic Area and turns right,
following the rolling grade of an abandoned road through a forest of larch,
subalpine fir, Engelmann spruce, and lodgepole pine. The patchy floor parades
dwarf huckleberry, heart-leafed arnica, prince's pine, Jacob's ladder, and
lupine. The trail bypasses small meadows and crosses Lake Creek, via a remnant
of the old bridge, to reach Upper Olive Lake (1.0 mile). This onetime reservoir
for the Fremont Powerhouse has returned to its meadow state. At the far end,
hikers gain easy access to the lush, extensive bowl of knee-high grasses cut by
Lake Creek and dotted by islands of boulders and trees.

The footpath begins upon entering the North Fork John Day Wilderness
and a deeper forest, for what becomes a hardy climb to the saddle. The saddle,
rimmed by trees, denies views. But by following the Blue Mountain Trail left
(south) along the ridge, toward Portland and Ben Harrison mines, a 5-minute
walk finds some dry meadow openings that afford views of Upper Olive
Meadow, the Blue Mountains to the east, and a limited Olive Lake view.
Another 30 to 45 minutes of walking delivers a prized 360-degree wilderness–
scenic area–Blue Mountain vista.

LOST CREEK TRAIL

2.0 miles round trip (to Lost
Meadow)
Elevation change: 200 feet
Trail condition: abandoned road or
meadow; the line of the path across
the meadow is not always apparent

Easy
Late spring through fall
Access: From camp, go 1.0 mile east
on FR 10 to the trailhead, which
has a single parking site in addition
to nearby roadside parking.

The hike begins away from Lost Creek, following the rolling grade of an
abandoned road into the North Fork John Day Wilderness. A lodgepole pine
forest with an understory of dwarf huckleberry and lupine frames the route.
The trail soon arrives at a connector on the wooden pipeline that drew water
from Olive Lake and Lost Creek for the historic Fremont Powerhouse.
Segments of this unusual pipeline in various states of repair now accompany
much of the route to Lost Meadow.

The hike enters the first meadow at the Indian Rock–Vinegar Hill Scenic
Area boundary. This meadow parades a wonderful array of wildflower color and
variety. Travel a straight line through the meadow and parallel to Lost Creek
to reach its bank at the opposite end.

Following the bank leads to a second, moister meadow just upstream.
Wild onions and elephant heads crowd its soggy reaches. Small drainage
channels riddle the thick knee-high grasses, requiring step-overs. A diagonal
course across the second meadow continues the Lost Creek trail, which travels
through meadow and forest to reach the trail junction for the Ben Harrison

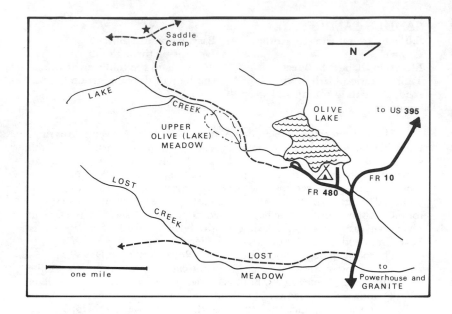

Mine (3.0 miles). Leaving Lost Meadow, the trail eventually grows steeper, and the meadow segments prove confusing, despite the occasional trail ribbons.

FREMONT POWERHOUSE HISTORIC DISTRICT

Public historic site; an on-site   **Access: Go 8.0 miles east of the**
caretaker offers tours   **campground on FR 10.**
For information: see page 222

This powerhouse, retired from service in 1967, holds the original 1908 machinery and blue Florentine marble instrument panel that were brought to the site by horse-drawn wagon. Built during the Eastern Oregon gold-boom days, the plant supplied electrical power to nearby claims at a time when steam power no longer proved efficient. The plant, much of its wooden pipeline, the historic town of Granite, and the area's many old mining sites preserve the tale of the days of gold.

The historic wooden pipeline below Olive Lake

Magone Lake

85 MAGONE LAKE CAMPGROUND

25 tent/trailer units
Standard service no fee
campground
Nonflush toilets
Water
Open seasonally: maintained
May 30 through October 15
For information: Long Creek
Ranger District
Map: Malheur National Forest

Access: Go 3.4 miles west of Prairie
City on US 26, and turn north
onto Bear Creek Road (County
18). Go another 13.0 miles, and
turn left onto FR 3620. After going 1.5 miles, turn right onto FR
3618 to find the campground in
another 1.5 miles. (Follow signs
along this paved and gravel route.)

These mostly fir-forested sites interspersed with some ponderosa pine,
lodgepole pine, and western larch rest just inland from this scenic mountain
lake formed by a landslide in the early 1800s. Snags pierce the water, and silver
logs bump the shore. The 50-acre lake is an ideal size for canoe, raft, or rowboat. It has a large day-use area, a boat launch, and a dock.

MAGONE LAKE TRAIL

1.5-mile loop	Easy
Elevation change: none	Spring through fall
Trail condition: pole-lined gravel path	Access: Find trailheads at camp, the day-use area, and the boat launch.

A counterclockwise tour from the campground begins skirting the developed end of Magone Lake, with forested campsites and well-spaced scenic picnic sites along the slope above shore. In 0.25 mile, the trail passes a section of cattails rimming the lake, with a beaver lodge just offshore. Along the tour, hikers can note pencil-point cuts of both long-ago and recent beaver harvests. Muskrats may be seen cutting wakes through the water, gnawing blades of grass atop silvered logs, or disappearing into their earthen mounds.

The trail crosses over the lake outlet, offering a look at the natural dam. In the downfall-cluttered, quiet waters of the outlet arm, mother ducks build the swimming confidence of their young. The trail alternately strings through an open, mature ponderosa pine forest with grassy floor and shows of strawberry, Oregon grape, kinnikinick, and avalanche lily and a multistory, predominantly fir forest with dwarf huckleberry, prince's pine, and yellow violet.

At 1.3 miles, the trail holds the finest view of the lake, looking down its length into the outlet arm. Crossing over the inlet, the trail arrives at the campground to conclude the hike. Despite its shortness, the trail reveals a wildlife and habitat diversity that welcomes repeat tours during a Magone Lake stay.

MAGONE SLIDE TRAIL

1.0 mile round trip	Easy
Elevation change: 200 feet	Spring through fall
Trail condition: earthen path, with meandering, gentle grade	Access: Find the marked trailhead on FR 3618 above the day-use area.

The trail begins with switchbacks up a slope, passing through a fir forest with some ponderosa and lodgepole pine. Dwarf huckleberry, kinnikinick, wild strawberry, and a treasury of cones add to the forest floor. Swaths of dry meadow interrupt the forest tour. In late May and early June, wildflowers dash the meadows with yellows, whites, and purples. The limited views of the lake quickly disappear.

At 0.3 mile, the trail arrives atop a ponderosa pine flat with many of the mature "yellow-bellies." Mountain mahogany threads through the forest. At the junction, a left leads to an overlook in a few hundred feet, with views to the south and east of the Magone Lake area and the forested valley to its west. In the background, the magnificent, often snowy Strawberry Mountain caps clear-day views.

Continuing the hike from the junction, follow the trail over a low ridge to arrive at the Magone Slide vista—a square-on view of the striking, long, eroded cliff with its steep rubble slope giving way to a rolling forested base. Trees and bushes tenuously cling to the edge of the cliff.

Strawberry Lake

86 STRAWBERRY CAMPGROUND

11 tent units (16-foot-maximum RV)
Standard service no fee campground
Nonflush toilets
Water
Open seasonally: June through October
For information: Prairie City Ranger District

Map: Malheur National Forest
Access: In Prairie City, turn south on Main Street. At the junction, bear left to take a quick right onto Bridge Street/FR 6001. The campground lies ahead in 11.0 miles. The final 2.0 miles of this paved and gravel route is a narrow, heavy-duty gravel road unsuitable for trailers.

Gateway to the Strawberry Mountain Wilderness, one of Oregon's most popular hiking areas, this campground quickly fills on summer weekends. Located next door to Strawberry Creek, the camp enjoys a mixed forest setting, with dwarf and true huckleberry rimming the sites. Trailer units find accommodations at two lower campgrounds along FR 6001: McNaughton and Slide. Both are small, semiprimitive camps along Strawberry Creek. They have wild-grass floors, mixed-forest shade, tables, grills, and pit toilets but no water.

STRAWBERRY BASIN TRAIL

5.4 miles round trip (to Little Strawberry Lake)
Elevation change: 1,200 feet
Trail condition: good, well-graded, some rock studding
Moderate

Late June through fall
Access: Find the trailhead at the entrance to Strawberry Campground, near a large hiker-designated parking area.

This wide trail switchbacks up the slope above camp and away from Strawberry Creek, soon entering the Strawberry Mountain Wilderness. In 0.6 mile, the Strawberry Basin and Slide Basin trails split, with the trail to the Strawberry lakes continuing straight. Strawberry Lake is a postcard-pretty, deep mountain basin pool. Its southeast skyline boasts an eye-catching dark, ragged ridge with a rockslide slope. A trail encircles the lake, traveling forested rim, skirting earthen beach areas, crossing grassy inlet-creek meadows, and traveling the rocky, open, south-facing slope with its aspen, purple penstemon, and currant.

Hiking left along the east shore quickly leads to the junction with the Little Strawberry Lake trail. It heads uphill through a dense mixed forest that chokes out any lake views. Yellow-flowering heart-leafed arnica colors the forest floor. At 1.9 miles, the trail offers a side-angle view from the base of 70-foot Strawberry Falls—a white lacy drop framed by moss-mantled cliffs. The trail then continues its ascent, crossing the creek above the falls to arrive at another trail junction.

The trail to Little Strawberry Lake climbs to the left, crossing Strawberry Creek, touring forest, and serving up cliff views before its descent to the lake.

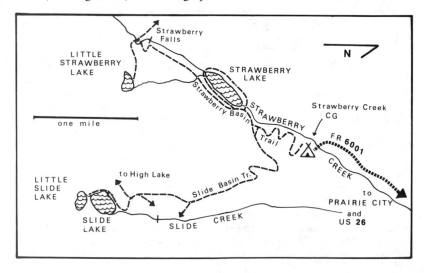

Little Strawberry Lake shines lime green at the foot of a slide. Planted trout weave through the clear waters; wind-snapped trees rim a portion of the lake. Yellow-green and orange lichen etch the dark cliff, while snow patches and islands of alpine trees further add to its rugged beauty.

SLIDE BASIN TRAIL

6.2 miles round trip (to Little Slide Lake)
Elevation change: 1,400 feet
Trail condition: good, well marked, narrow and rocky in places

Moderate to difficult
Late June through fall
Access: Begin at the trailhead for the Strawberry Basin trail.

At the 0.6-mile junction, the Slide Basin Trail breaks to the left, rounding and ascending the forested slope to cross the ridge. Atop the ridge, a detour from the trail to the open knob with scattered mountain mahogany offers a vista of Strawberry Canyon and the John Day valley.

Crossing the ridge, the now narrow trail slowly descends the open, steep west slope of Slide Canyon, with its wonderful array of summer wildflowers: lupine, heart-leafed arnica, balsam root, paintbrush, penstemon, wild geranium, forget-me-not, Jacob's ladder, phlox, and more. Patches of high-elevation firs break the open slope, and the crags and spires of the skyline slow one's stride. Down-canyon views of the John Day valley and the distant Blue Mountains and up-canyon views of Slide Basin add to the enjoyment of the hike.

Slide Lake is an oval lake at the base of a dark, layered cliff etched with lichen and mineral leaching. Snow patches linger on the cliff into July. The lake reflects the green of its forest rim. At the south end of the lake, a good secondary path just before the creek heads up the slope and over the low ridge to cloudy-green Little Slide Lake, at the foot of a slide.

---

87 CANYON MEADOWS CAMPGROUND

19 tent/trailer units
Standard service no fee campground
Nonflush toilets
Water
Open seasonally: mid-May through October
For information: Bear Valley Ranger District

Map: Malheur National Forest
Access: From John Day, go 9.5 miles south on US 395. Following the signs, turn east onto County 65/FR 15, and in 8.5 miles, turn left onto gravel FR 1520 to reach the campground, in another 5.0 miles.

A ponderosa pine, larch, and grand fir forest with patchy grasses and sticky laurel provides a pleasant backdrop for a camp stay. The main campground sports a more open canopy than the upper campground but has the advantage of being farther removed from FR 1520. Below camp, near the day-use area, Canyon Meadows has been dammed for a reservoir. While not scenic, it offers the angler a place to drop a hook and line and, when lake levels are sufficiently high, a place to launch a small raft or rowboat. The reservoir is at its most attractive in early spring, when the water level is high. Ospreys, muskrats, and mallards often capture the attention of shoreline visitors. The campground provides an ideal base for explorations into the southern portions of the Strawberry Mountain Wilderness.

BUCKHORN MEADOWS TRAIL

6.0 miles round trip (to the outcrop above Wildcat Basin camp)
Elevation change: 1,200 feet
Trail condition: steep stretches, with loose rock in places
Difficult
Spring through fall

Access: From camp, go 3.0 miles north on FR 1520, bearing left at the road fork. The road is narrow and rocky in places, but it is passable for conventional vehicles. The circular pad at road's end accommodates horse trailers; a hitching post and a corral are at the trailhead.

The trail immediately enters the Strawberry Mountain Wilderness, traveling the base of a long grassy meadow with columbine, wild geranium, heartleafed arnica, lupine, and forget-me-not. Beyond the meadow, the route briefly travels on an abandoned road. A moderate-grade trail replaces the road as the route climbs through a forest of ponderosa and lodgepole pine, mixed fir, and larch to round a rocky slope with patchy grasses, wildflowers, and mountain mahogany.

The hike then alternates between forest and open rocky slopes, crisscrossing over the ridge and mounting some steep climbs. Rewarding the effort, the trail assembles building-block vistas of the Canyon Creek drainage to the southeast, the valleys to the southwest, and Indian Creek Butte, Canyon and Pine Creek mountains, and the western crest of Strawberry Mountain, all to the northwest.

The demands of the trail ease as it travels through a forest of Douglas and high-elevation firs and some white pine. Just beyond (at about 2.0 miles), is a weather-chiseled conglomerate rock outcrop, which unfolds the finest vista yet—to the southeast, overlooking the Canyon Creek drainage. Beyond the outcrop, the trail again crosses the ridge for a descent to Wildcat Basin and camp, bypassing more of the badland-character rock. The camp has a fire pit,

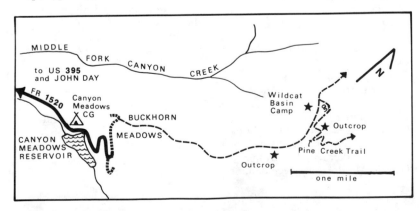

rustic benches, and a pulsing spring, with a pipe for easy access. A magnificently rugged skyline rises to the north.

At the trail junction near camp, going right for another 0.5-mile climb via Pine Creek Trail leads to a more extensive, dramatic bed of the beehive conglomerate. Its scalloped and terraced gray-white rock contrasts with the dark, jagged skyline above it. From this lofty post, hikers overlook Wildcat Basin, with Indian Creek Butte to the northwest and the valley and ridges to the southwest.

88 NORTH FORK MALHEUR CAMPGROUND

5 tent/trailer units
Standard service no fee campground
Nonflush toilets
No water
Open seasonally: maintained May 30 through October 15
For information: Prairie City Ranger District
Map: Malheur National Forest

Access: At Prairie City, turn south on Main Street and left on Bridge Street to follow County 62 due south to Summit Prairie (14.0 miles). From Summit Prairie, continue south and east on FR 16 for 15.0 miles. Turn south onto one-lane, improved-surface FR 1675 to reach the campground in 2.4 miles. The route is well marked.

This is an especially scenic river-flat campground along a braided stretch of the North Fork of the Malheur, where meadow and forest intermix. Western larch and ponderosa and lodgepole pine shade the well-spaced sites. A fence encloses the campground, protecting it from grazers. Gates at either end of the camp allow convenient passage to the upstream and downstream waters. The North Fork of the Malheur is a nationally designated Wild and Scenic River. Hiking, angling, wildlife viewing, and relaxing campside engage visitors. Those with larger trailer units may prefer campsites off the paved route: scenic, forested Little Crane Creek Campground, 4.7 miles south on FR 16, or Elk Creek Campground, which is forested but has more road frontage, 0.7 mile north on FR 16 (measurements are from the junction of FR 16 and FR 1675).

NORTH FORK MALHEUR TRAIL

5.0 miles round trip (to Crane Creek Campground)
Elevation change: 200 feet
Trail condition: well-maintained, earthen forest path
Easy
Spring through fall
Access: From camp, go 1.0 mile south on FR 1675 to the trailhead.

There is parking for only two or three passenger vehicles. Because of limited turnaround space, few parking sites, and worsening road conditions ahead, visitors with trailer or RV units should *not* go beyond North Fork Malheur Campground. Instead, park at the camp, and walk the road to the trailhead.

Hike across log footbridges and raised walkways over the braided waters and meadow islands of the North Fork Malheur to begin a downstream trek along the west bank. The trail tours the forest–meadow edge some 100 feet away from the stream. A multistory ponderosa and lodgepole pine forest mounts the slope and shades the trail. Throughout the hike, angler and daydreamer find easy North Fork Malheur access. Downfalls weave across the forest floor. Needle mat, heart-leafed arnica, lupine, yarrow, waterleaf, prairie smoke, and an abundance of cones comprise the understory.

At 1.0 mile, the trail affords an overlook of the river's crystalline, twisting watercourse. Some white fir and western larch gradually enter the forest mix, and more alders bump the shore. At 2.4 miles, the trail arrives at a log bridge over Crane Creek. Crane Creek Campground lies just downstream. At the camp, mature ponderosa pine, a sweeping meadow, and clear streaming water unite to create a beautiful setting for a relaxing picnic lunch. Steller's jays, Clark's nutcrackers, ducks, and kingfishers are among the passing visitors. The North Fork Malheur Trail continues downstream for almost another 10.0 miles, for those wishing to continue the river tour.

Another option is to explore the Crane Creek trail, which begins along the north bank of Crane Creek near the footbridge. It follows the two-track trail upstream from the primitive campsite for 500 yards. There, the path fords the 10- to 15-foot-wide Crane Creek to continue upstream along the south bank for some 4.0 miles. The early stretch follows a jeep track touring the creek flat of the forested canyon.

LOGAN VALLEY
Prairie Grassland Restoration Project, wildlife viewing area
For information: see page 231

Access: From camp, return to FR 16, and turn left to reach Logan Valley in about 21.0 miles.

Viewed from FR 16, Logan Valley is a postcard-pretty prairie grassland, thanks to the cooperative efforts of the USFS, private landowners, cattle grazers, and wildlife agencies. Wildlife attracted to this rich habitat setting include antelope, deer, coyote, Canada geese, and sandhill crane. Big Creek Campground and Picnic Area and the prairie immediately north of it are public, for those desiring a closer look at the grassland.

WALLOWAS
AND NORTHEAST
MOUNTAINS

The northeast corner of the state holds the land of greatest contrast. Dramatically placed side by side are the Hells Canyon National Recreation Area—home of the deepest gorge in North America, framed by arid steppes—and the Wallowas—a gallery of glacier-carved ridges and peaks, cirque basins, alpine meadows, hanging valleys, and chiseled canyons funneling clear-running waters. Together, they create a remarkable field of discovery for camper and hiker: the proposed Hells Canyon National Park and Preserve.

Upon first sighting Hells Canyon, in 1833, explorer Benjamin Bonneville remarked on its "wild majesty" and "impressive sternness"—descriptive tags that can be little improved upon. Reaching this magnificent bluff–canyon scenery via an overland route is a slow journey offering intimate canyon looks. While management plans call for improvement, roads are not yet accessible

Lupine

Jubilee Lake

to all vehicles— one with high clearance and a full gas tank is recommended. Riverboats offer the most popular, though limited, introduction to Hells Canyon country.

Wildlife, the Nez Perce Trail of Tears, Wild and Scenic River trails, and Snake River Canyon vistas draw the adventurous to this remote corner. Exploring the wildness of the area requires caution. Snakes, ticks, spiders, cactus, and poison ivy all occupy niches in this stern land. But the need for alertness should not deter anyone from the discovery of this unique treasure. The mild temperatures of spring and fall promise the greatest comfort for adventure.

The lower reaches of the Wallowas begin opening in June, with the high country becoming accessible in late June or July. The mountains know all four seasons, with temperature extremes and an accelerated passage from spring through fall.

The high lakes are the mountains' claim to fame. Day hiking, backpacking, and llama- or horse-pack trips are the means of entry. Mountain goats, deer, elk, and bighorn sheep range the Wallowas. Furry pikas whistle from rockslides, betraying their hideouts. In the valley bowl, Wallowa Lake attracts wintering geese and the occasional whistling swan. High, moist wildflower meadows blaze with color from late spring through the first snap of winter. July finds peak blooms, when mosquitoes prove the greatest nuisance. ■

89 JUBILEE LAKE CAMPGROUND

51 tent/trailer units
Standard service fee campground
Flush and nonflush toilets
Water
Open seasonally: mid-June through September
For information: Walla Walla (Washington) Ranger District

Map: Umatilla National Forest
Access: From OR 204 at Tollgate, go northeast 10.6 miles on FR 64 (a wide, improved surface road with heavily potholed sections). Turn right onto paved FR 6400.250 to reach the campground in another 0.5 mile.

These well-spaced campsites sit back from the shore of Jubilee Lake, a large mountain lake rimmed by low, forested hills. The lake retains a natural look, despite its dam. Day-use parking, lake accesses, and picnic areas intersperse the sites. Spire-shaped fir and spruce are dominant at the campground, with a few lodgepole pine and western larch dotting the more open areas. Dwarf huckleberry, prince's pine, twin flower, and low leafy bushes border the fine gravel floor of the sites. Fishing, calm-water rafting and canoeing (or electric-motor boating), birdwatching, hiking, and relaxing at camp are favorite pastimes. The trails of the Wenaha–Tucannon Wilderness lie just to the northeast.

JUBILEE LAKESHORE NATIONAL RECREATION TRAIL

2.6-mile all-ability loop   Easy
Elevation change: minimal   Late spring through fall
Trail condition: barrier-free, 30-inch- Access: Find the trailhead at the
wide, fine gravel pedestrian trail   campground boat launch.

A left at the boat launch begins a clockwise tour just in from the shore, skirting picnic and tent-camp sites and crossing an inlet to tour a forest mix and understory similar to that of the campground. Young, uniform-sized lodgepole pine crowd the lake edge, denying views. Where the trail enters a denser, richer forest, a bench overlooks the lake setting from the informally named Townsend's Point—a small jut of land. Fish ripple the lake surface. In late spring, mother ducks guide their young across the water. Gray jays await handouts and steal unattended snacks. After the trail passes the willow-lined second inlet, a spur trail enters the lake circuit from the left. At 1.0 mile, the trail travels a lakeside meadow to merge briefly with a dirt road. A pit toilet and a single walk-in-boat-to campsite rest just above the trail. At 1.3 miles is the crossing for Mottet Creek, a primary inlet on a quiet lake arm. Its scenic upstream meadow and more isolated location make it an ideal retreat.

Beyond the creek, the trail tours a more natural forest, with the lodgepole pine border distinctly absent. It again travels an abandoned road as it approaches the rock dam and spillway footbridge. Deeper waters near the dam attract shore anglers. The trail reenters the forest, bypassing campsites and a marshy area, for its return to the boat launch. Benches dot the route.

90 UMATILLA FORKS CAMPGROUND

11 trailer units; 7 tent units   Map: Umatilla National Forest
Standard service no fee   Access: At Mission Junction east of
campground   Pendleton, head east on Mission
Nonflush toilets   Road. Follow the signs for Gibbon,
Water   continuing northeast on FR 32
Open seasonally: June through   along the Umatilla River to reach
September   the campground. This 17.0-mile
For information: Walla Walla   route is mostly paved, becoming
(Washington) Ranger District   gravel.

Below bald-topped ridges, this long, narrow campground with separate tent and trailer sections lines the east bank of the South Fork Umatilla above the North Fork confluence. Fir and pine dot and fringe the camp meadow, while cottonwoods and alders hug the river bank. Sites offer access to creek and river fishing, nature study, and photography. Trails enter the North Fork Umatilla Wilderness and tour its neighborhood.

NINEMILE RIDGE TRAIL

8.0 miles round trip (to the summit knob)
Elevation change: 2,100 feet
Trail condition: good, steady-climbing, sometimes steep
Moderate to difficult

Spring through fall
Access: At the south end of camp, turn left off FR 32 for Buck Creek Trail. Find the trailhead for the ridge hike on the left side of the road, just before the parking area.

This trail steps uphill with a steep, steady incline. Ocean spray, thimble-berry, alder, and low leafy shrubs crowd its bed. At 0.3 mile lies a junction. To the left is the old trail, which has been closed to halt erosion and any further resource damage. The new trail journeys to the right, entering a long, comfortable switchback with brief sections of shade. Graves Butte, Bobsled Ridge, Buck Mountain, and the Buck Creek and South Fork Umatilla drainages combine for the vista.

Even the casual naturalist will note dozens of wildflower varieties along the trail; peak blooms occur in early to mid-June. Ponderosa pine, fir, and larch patch the mostly bald ridge.

As the hike progresses along the spine, conquering each new rise, it offers deeper looks into the heart of the North Fork Umatilla Wilderness. Just off the trail at 4.0 miles are two summit knobs that offer 360-degree viewing. Building upon previous views, the panorama from these points adds the lookout tower above Spout Springs, the High Ridge Lookout, and a greater expanse of the Umatilla River drainage.

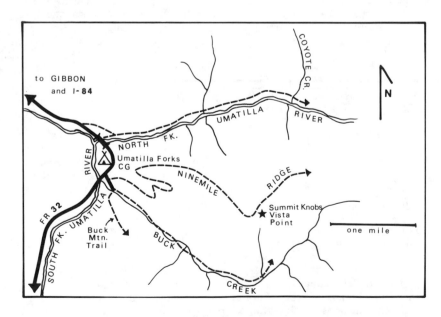

The North Fork Umatilla River

NORTH FORK UMATILLA TRAIL

5.4 miles round trip (to Coyote Creek)
Elevation change: 300 feet
Trail condition: well graded, with rock hops over side creeks

Moderate
Spring through fall
Access: Find the trailhead at the picnic area near the bridge, 0.2 mile north of the campground.

The trail quickly forks, with the left branch leading to the Lick Creek trailhead in 0.4 mile. The North Fork Trail bears right, entering the North Fork Umatilla Wilderness. The trail travels through a deciduous-tree and shrub corridor, with evergreens mounting the ridge. Columbine, orange honeysuckle, lady fern, maple, and alder frame the trail, with mature stands of fir briefly interrupting their claim.

From 0.5 to 1.0 mile, the path hugs and rounds the slope wall, traveling along a narrow terrace, which offers frequent unobstructed river views and looks at the forested north face of Ninemile Ridge. The open canopy of the trail promises a warm hike on cloud-free days. After 1.5 miles, the trail climbs farther above the river, offering only limited views upstream and across the North Fork canyon. The forest–meadow flat at the Coyote Creek–North Fork Umatilla confluence offers a pleasing destination for day hikers.

BUCK CREEK TRAIL

3.5 miles one way
Elevation change: 800 feet
Trail condition: numerous creek crossings, some wet
Moderate
Summer through fall

Access: At the south end of camp, turn left off FR 32 at the sign for the trailhead. At the road's end, park away from the gate to the Buck Creek Organizational Camp, and head upstream, hiking along an old, primitive road.

This trail was designed with hot summer days in mind. Its zigzag, upstream course along Buck Creek promises a refreshing adventure. Spring often finds high, fast, chilly waters—not recommended for the casual hiker. By summer, a dry 1.0-mile sampling of this multitextured, diversely vegetated creek canyon is usually possible, aided by log crossings. A right at the junction 100 feet from the trailhead leads to the footboard crossing for the 3.8-mile Buck Mountain Trail.

91 DUG BAR CAMP

3 tent units
Primitive no fee dispersed camp area
Nonflush toilet (beware of spiders in the outhouses)
No water
Open year-round
For information: Hells Canyon National Recreation Area
Map: Hells Canyon NRA
Access: From Imnaha, go 30.0 miles northeast on Lower Imnaha Road (FR 4260). (5.0 miles is pavement; the remainder is a climbing, snaking, 15-mph dirt road passing through some spectacular arid canyon scenery featuring grassland, plateau, basalt tiers, and rock temples.) The route is not recommended for trailers, RVs, or low-clearance vehicles. Start with a full gas tank. Management plans call for upgrading the road and providing a formal campground (tentative completion date 1998).

This remote, no-frills camp on a grassland bench above the Snake Wild and Scenic River offers solitude, spectacular canyon scenery, wildlife sightings, a boat launch (the river offers an alternate route to the site), and some fine trails to explore. Additional primitive sites (no facilities) are found near Cow Creek Bridge, on a bench above the Imnaha Wild and Scenic River, 12.0 miles southwest of Dug Bar via Lower Imnaha Road.

NEE ME POO NATIONAL HISTORIC TRAIL

6.0 miles round trip (to Lone Pine Saddle)

Elevation change: 1,600 feet

Trail condition: rugged grassland path, steep in places; early stretch not well defined

Moderate to difficult

Year-round

Access: Find the marked trailhead alongside the road 0.1 mile above the campground.

This hike preserves a segment of the Nez Perce "Trail of Tears." In 1877, in compliance with an army directive, Chief Joseph led his tribe across this rugged canyon country toward the Lapwai Reservation in Idaho, only to encounter settler problems along Idaho's Salmon River. These problems led to uprisings, and the tribe's attempted flight to Canada. A running battle spanned three months and 1,700 miles before the Nez Perce surrendered.

Tracing the route backward, this hike mounts the slope, passes through a fence opening, and follows some low rock cairns upward along the rock outcrops to find the defined footpath at 0.4 mile. The trail tours Hells Canyon Wilderness, traveling along grassland slopes dotted with prickly pear and colored with sunflowers. It dips into moist, tree-lined drainages, snakes over rises, and offers new perspectives on the canyon setting.

Atop the second saddle, the trail passes through a gate. A long-distance view of the road to Dug Bar illustrates the engineering challenge of canyon road building. Deer may be seen browsing the grasses of the higher slope; bighorn sheep and elk are less common sightings. Lone Pine Saddle, marked by an ancient lopped-top ponderosa and a few smaller pines, holds a spectacular vantage on the Imnaha River Canyon, Cactus Mountain, Cow and Lightning creek drainages, Corral Creek drainage, and Haas Ridge. The trail descends to

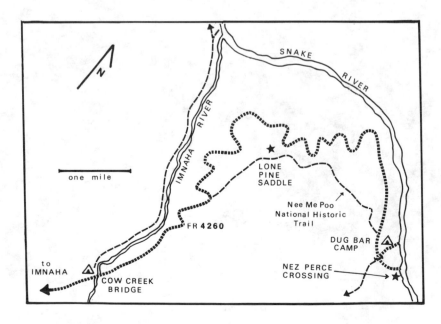

The Lower Imnaha River Road from Nee Me Poo Trail

Lower Imnaha Road, but the canyon road condition does not recommend a car shuttle.

The river-fording site for the "Trail of Tears," Nez Perce Crossing, lies upstream from camp. To reach it, continue along the road from camp, passing through the gate (USFS property, public right-of-way) to the boat launch. From there, a 0.1-mile hike along or just above the rocky bank leads to the riverside interpretive sign at the mouth of a gorge. During the forced exodus of 1877, the Nez Perce crossed a flooding Snake River. Women, children, and the elderly rode atop horsehide rafts pulled by swimming horses. Thousands of horses and cows swam the river; many were lost. Unbelievably, the tribe crossed without a single casualty.

IMNAHA RIVER TRAIL

7.0 miles round trip (to the Snake River confluence)
Elevation change: 300 feet
Trail condition: good but rocky, some encroaching poison ivy
Moderate

Year-round
Access: Find the trailhead on the northwest bank of the Imnaha River at Cow Creek Bridge, 12.0 miles southwest of Dug Bar.

The trail follows the river downstream through a scenic, narrow canyon, with reddish-gray metamorphic rock cliffs and a jagged skyline. The 40- to 50-foot-wide river holds a series of riffles and pristine dark pools. In early morning and pre-evening hours, bats patrol the canyon for insects. Bunchgrass and other graminoids, alder, abundant poison ivy, sumac, milkweed (food for

Hat Point Lookout view

monarch butterflies), wild rose, blackberry streamers, and prickly pear frame the path. A number of mine markers, test holes, shafts, and tailings dot both sides of the Imnaha River as the trail approaches the Snake River. The trail exits onto a gravel bar at the Snake–Imnaha confluence. Across the way is Idaho.

92 HAT POINT CAMPGROUND

6 tent/picnic units
Primitive no fee campground
Nonflush toilet
No water
Open seasonally: July through
October

For information: Hells Canyon
National Recreation Area
Map: Hells Canyon NRA
Access: From Imnaha, go 24.0
miles southeast on FR 4240, FR
4240.315, and FR 4240.332. (See
Hat Point Road Drive, below.)

Set amid the pine–fir fringe of an arid grass bluff overlooking the Snake River Canyon, these remote, little-developed sites offer escape from the cares and demands of civilization as well as easy access to Hat Point Lookout, trails, and vistas. The nearby Sacajawea Dispersed Camp Area has a few forested sites remaining. (A fire scoured this section of the Hells Canyon NRA in 1989.) Management plans call for the construction of an improved Hat Point Campground in the near future. It may be constructed at a new locale, with the present Hat Point Campground becoming a day-use-only facility.

HAT POINT TRAIL

4.0 miles round trip (to the vista
point)
Elevation change: 1,600 feet
Trail condition: well-graded,
utilizing switchbacks

Moderate to difficult
Summer through fall
Access: Begin at the campground.

The trail begins its winding descent, passing through dry, high-elevation meadows with peak wildflower blooms in early summer. By autumn, asters and Indian paintbrush alone add color to the russet-gold grassland gone to seed. Sweeping vistas of the canyon with its furrowed flanks and basalt terraces are found on the journey.

At 0.3 mile, the trail enters the Hells Canyon Wilderness. Thereafter, switchbacks alternate between forest and dry meadow habitats. Ponderosa pine, some firs, a few small maples, and mountain mahogany contribute to the tree cover. By 1.9 miles, the forest is fuller and wetter. Twisted stalk, thimbleberry, nettles, and bracken fern thrive beneath the evergreen canopy.

At 2.0 miles, the trail draws onto an open plateau, with one side steeply dropping away. A 50-foot detour from the trail leads to exceptional vistas of the river course and the canyon grasslands, bluffs, and orange spired cliffs. A few mountain mahogany cling to the plateau's edge. The site marks an ideal turnaround point for day hikers. The trail continues its descent, meeting the High Trail in another mile and the Snake River in another 4.0 miles, for long-distance hiking.

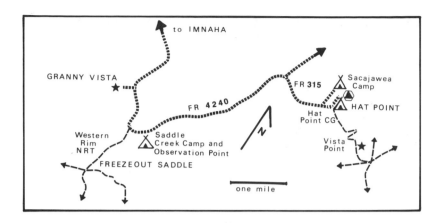

WESTERN RIM NATIONAL RECREATION TRAIL

4.0 miles round trip (to Freezeout
Saddle)
Elevation change: 900 feet
Trail condition: rugged, often
rocky
Moderate to difficult

Summer through fall
Access: Find the marked Summit
Ridge trailhead southwest of camp,
on FR 4240 between Granny Vista
and Saddle Creek Camp.

This trail begins wrapping around and down Summit Ridge, offering early views of the Imnaha River and Freezeout Creek drainages. It travels a mostly open, dry slope featuring western yarrow, buckwheat, bunchgrass, and fireweed interspersed by a myriad of summer wildflowers. A few fir and scenic snags dot the course.

By 0.4 mile, views of the Snake River Canyon expand the vista. At 0.8 mile, the trail angles back to descend the Snake River side of the slope. (Do not take the path ahead; a small rock-and-limb barrier indicates it is closed.) Views of Saddle Creek Canyon and silver snags from a long-ago fire add interest along this leg of the trek.

At 1.4 miles, the trail crosses back onto the Imnaha River side of the ridge, traveling a beautiful native bunchgrass meadow to Freezeout Saddle (the end of this hike). From the saddle, trails follow the ridge to McGraw Lookout or follow Saddle Creek to the Snake River. Both are long-distance hikes. Carry plenty of water, whether backpacking or day hiking.

HAT POINT ROAD DRIVE

24.0 miles one way
Road quality: winding, narrow,
dirt or rock surface, not suitable for
trailers or RVs. The road is
presently receiving improvement;
the finished road will be a single

gravel lane with turnouts.
Estimated speed: 15 to 25 mph
Access: From Imnaha, go southeast
on FR 4240, following signs to Hat
Point Lookout.

This necessarily slow road allows travelers to enjoy the scenery, vistas, and area wildlife (deer, elk, and grouse are commonly seen in the morning). At 14.0 miles, Granny Vista overlooks the Imnaha River Canyon's flat-topped bluffs, eroded slopes, and tree-lined side canyons, with the Wallowas in the distance.

At 16.0 miles is Saddle Creek Observation Point, with primitive walk-in camp and picnic sites on a forested rim overlooking Hells Canyon and Idaho's Seven Devils, a chain of high peaks.

The road continues to Hat Point Lookout and its nearby camp. The 90-foot fire lookout (elevation 7,000 feet) is open to the public (climb at your own risk, limiting groups to posted numbers). The tower vista includes the Snake River (elevation 1,250 feet) more than a mile below; the scarring from the 1989 fire, which burned up to the tower site; the usually golden slopes of Hells Canyon, with their deep finger drainages; and Idaho's Seven Devils. The multiple flights of narrow, steep stairs do not recommend a tower ascent for young children or anyone with vertigo, a heart or lung condition, or unsound legs.

93 SHADY CAMPGROUND

15 tent/trailer units
Standard service no fee campground
Nonflush toilets
No water
Open seasonally: June through October
For information: Eagle Cap Ranger District

Map: Wallowa–Whitman National Forest
Access: From Lostine (northwest of Enterprise on OR 82), go south 16.0 miles on paved and improved-surface Lostine Road (FR 8210).

Spaced for privacy, these conifer-shaded sites along the bank of the Lostine River welcome relaxation and recreation amid high-mountain splendor. Lake, meadow, and river trails, fishing, and nature and wildlife study engage visitors. Pack stations operate from bases along FR 8210, for those seeking true backcountry adventure. Other camps are also found along FR 8210.

HUNTER FALLS TRAIL

0.6 mile round trip
Elevation change: 200 feet
Trail condition: little-traveled path, steep in places
Easy

Spring through fall
Access: From camp, go north (left) on Lostine Road to find the trailhead on the east side of the road just north of the guard station.

The trail starts with a steep climb through a relatively open lodgepole pine forest to reach a small ridge above Lake Creek. There, it swings away from the creek. Rock cairns indicate the path as the trail enters a fir–western larch forest complex with lush grasses, snowberry, and yarrow.

At 0.25 mile, the trail splits. One branch goes 50 feet downhill to a view at the base of the broad, two-stage, 30- to 40-foot Hunter Falls. A steep, 100-foot uphill charge leads to a top view. The trail continues, but it grows more and more faint.

WEST FORK LOSTINE RIVER TRAIL

5.6 miles round trip (to the Copper Creek trail junction)	Moderate
	Summer through fall
Elevation change: 800 feet	**Access: From camp, go south to the**
Trail condition: steady-climbing earthen forest path	**end of FR 8210. Find the trailhead at the end of the lower parking area.**

Upon entering Eagle Cap Wilderness, turn right to begin the West Fork hike. This trail soon crosses the East Fork of the Lostine River, offers views of the West Fork, and then climbs away from the West Fork. A choked forest of thin, tall Engelmann spruce, alder, white fir, western larch, and lodgepole pine frames the path. Aster, thimbleberry, twisted stalk, and bride's bonnet color the forest floor.

Along the way, the trail passes granite outcrops, a boulder-littered slope threaded by huckleberry, and mature forest. It offers vistas of the West Fork and the Wallowas—rugged high peaks with snowfields, U-shaped valleys, and ribbony cascades.

At the 2.8-mile junction, bearing left continues the West Fork hike to Minam Lake, for a long-distance trek. A brief right along Copper Creek Trail leads to a tranquil day-hike destination—a beautiful, big meadow with mature spruce alongside the now creek-sized river fork, and below the talus slope of the dividing ridge of the Lostine River headwaters. Those seeking an alternative longer hike should ford the river to continue on the Copper Creek Trail.

EAST FORK LOSTINE RIVER TRAIL

6.4 miles round trip (to Lost Lake)	Moderate
Elevation change: 1,500 feet	**Summer through fall**
Trail condition: steady-climbing, with a few toe catchers	**Access: See the West Fork trail, above.**

Where the trail forks upon entering the wilderness, turn left for the East Fork Trail. Away from the river, this trail travels through a forest of spruce, white fir, larch, and lodgepole pine. Rocks, boulders, and outcrops litter the forest floor. Openings in the tree cover hold western views of the forested granite ridge dividing the Lostine River forks; Hurricane Divide rises to the east.

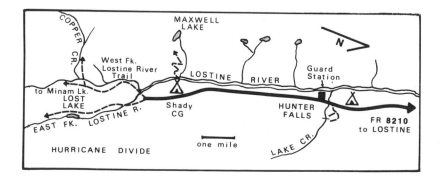

Hurricane Divide

At 1.0 mile, the trail crosses the East Fork via a log footbridge (children will require supervision). By 1.6 miles, high-elevation fir and spruce have begun to frame the trail as it switchbacks uphill. Aspen patches accent the boulder slopes. Forest openings unveil fine vistas of Hurricane Divide, with its furrowed flank, spired forests, snowfields, and seasonal waterfalls. A superior down-canyon view of the Lostine River drainage awaits ahead.

At 2.25 miles, the trail tops out, touring the forest fringe to a small high meadow threaded by the now slow, meandering East Fork. At 2.7 miles, the trail draws opposite a small falls on the river. Just ahead lies a pond—a preview of Lost Lake, still to come.

Lost Lake is actually a part of the East Fork, where the river broadens and slows, filling in a basin below Hurricane Divide and the west ridge. Small trees line its mirror waters. Although it is not one of the high basin lakes for which the Eagle Cap Wilderness is noted, it does provide the day hiker with a sense of the alpine country.

The Mount Howard Tramway

94 WALLOWA LAKE STATE PARK

210 tent/trailer units (summer reservations by mail)
Full service fee campground
Flush toilets; showers
Water
Open seasonally: mid-April through October

For information: State Parks, La Grande Regional Office
Map: Wallowa–Whitman National Forest
Access: Find the park off OR 82 about 6.0 miles south of Joseph.

At the foot of the Wallowa Mountains, these comfortable, close-set, forested sites on the Wallowa Lake shore offer access to water sport, alpine hiking, and sightseeing, as well as the steepest vertical-lift gondola in North America. Deer beg at camp, while wilder animals range the mountains. A marina, boat rental, small store, day-use facilities, and trailheads are all located nearby.

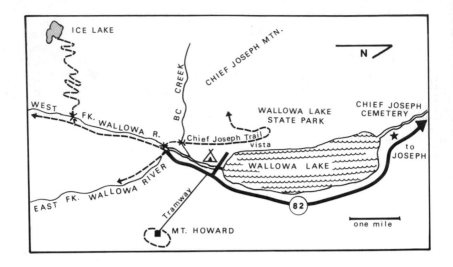

WEST FORK WALLOWA RIVER TRAIL

5.0 miles round trip (to a meadow
on the Ice Lake trail)
Elevation change: 900 feet
Trail condition: well-graded hiker
and horse path, with rock-hopping
crossings of small creeks

Moderate
Spring through fall
Access: Find the trailhead at the
south end of OR 82, opposite the
south picnic area at Wallowa Lake
State Park.

The trail tours a mixed conifer forest. At the 0.25-mile trail junction, it
continues straight, traveling parallel to but removed from the West Fork to
soon enter Eagle Cap Wilderness. Mountain goats may sometimes be seen on
the steep flanks of Hurwal Divide, which rises above the opposite shore. Where
the trail draws close to the river, informal side trails wiggle to its bank.

The scenery along the route is richly textured: rugged peaks and ridges,
talus slopes, rich forests, mountain streams, meadow clearings, and cloud
changes. At 2.0 miles is an overlook of a cascade on the river. Native red
raspberry and bride's bonnet speckle the forest floor.

At 2.2 miles is a trail junction. The West Fork trail continues straight up
the river canyon; the Ice Lake trail branches right for a scenic footbridge
crossing to an inviting forest-ringed meadow, with open views of Craig
Mountain's jagged skyline and steep rugged flank—a nice day-hike destination.

CHIEF JOSEPH TRAIL

4.4 miles round trip (to the
Wallowa Lake vista)
Elevation change: 600 feet
Trail condition: good, well-graded
earthen trail

Moderate
Spring through fall
Access: See the West Fork Trail,
above.

At the 0.25-mile junction, this 7.0-mile trail branches right to travel upstream, climbing the flank of Chief Joseph Mountain. Ponderosa pine, white fir, and Rocky Mountain maple frame the path as it briefly tours the east bank, 100 feet above the rock-bound river gorge.

Crossing the West Fork footbridge, the trail leaves the river behind as it climbs through a forest of lodgepole pine, larch, aspen, and mountain mahogany. Pikas whistle from their hiding places in the rocky slopes. After the footbridge crossing of cascading BC Creek, the trail arrives at a flat with views of an unnamed falls to the south, Wallowa Lake to the north, and Mount Howard to the east. It then enters Eagle Cap Wilderness.

At 2.0 miles, ten ponderosa pines cluster alongside the trail, marking the start of a series of vista clearings, which continues for the next 0.2 mile. Views feature the glacial moraine of Wallowa Lake, Mount Howard, and the patchwork fields stretching south. Thistle, pearly everlasting, and Indian paintbrush color the slope openings.

WALLOWA LAKE TRAMWAY

Private, fee; daily schedule: early June to September, 10:00 A.M. to 4:00 P.M.; deli, restrooms, and trails on top

For information: Wallowa Lake Tramway
Access: Find the tramway on OR 82 just south of the campground entrance road.

For 15 minutes, these enclosed four-passenger gondolas travel along 19,300 feet of cable to reach the top of Mount Howard (elevation 8,200 feet). The gondola ride offers sweeping vistas of Wallowa Lake, Joseph Valley, Chief Joseph Mountain, BC Basin, Hurwal Divide, and Mount Howard.

The 2.0-mile Mount Howard Summit Loop Trail showcases the area. A counterclockwise tour strings together alpine meadows of lupine, western yarrow, heather, bunchgrass, and dwarf huckleberry; fringes of wind-shaped white-bark pine; and outcrop vistas. Royal Purple Overlook offers views of the Wallowa peaks, Royal Purple Canyon, and the east and west forks of the Wallowa River drainage.

The Summit Overlook brings into focus Hells Canyon, Idaho's Seven Devils (a high peak chain), and Freezeout Saddle. Next comes Highlands Overlook, which reveals the McCulley Drainage Fire of 1989. Before returning to the tram, the loop tags Valley Overlook, featuring Wallowa Lake, the front range of the Wallowas, the Imnaha River drainage, and the patchwork of fields near Joseph.

CHIEF JOSEPH CEMETERY

Roadside historical site, open to the public

Access: Find the roadside pullout along OR 82 between the campground and Joseph, just above the Wallowa Lake outlet.

This small burial ground for the Nez Perce and Umatilla Indians houses the bones of the honored Nez Perce chief, Old Chief Joseph. A simple monument marks the gravesite. Elsewhere, the unmarked graves in this natural grassland setting reflect Indian values, showing a reverence for land and nature.

95 CATHERINE CREEK STATE PARK

18 tent/trailer units
Standard service fee campground
Flush toilets
Water
Open seasonally: mid-April to late
October

For information: State Parks, La
Grande Regional Office
Map: Oregon State, Wallowa-
Whitman National Forest
Access: Find the campground
alongside OR 203, about 8.0 miles
southeast of Union.

This campground and the park's upper and lower picnic areas rest alongside the 20-foot-wide pulsing green ribbon of Catherine Creek and one of Oregon's less traveled highways. Sites are landscaped with lawn and deciduous shade trees that blend well with the park's native ponderosa pine stand. Cottonwoods intermix with the mature pines near the creek.

The park borders 0.5 mile of shoreline, offering fishing access and an opportunity to cool the ankles on sultry summer days. Developed hot springs—Hot Lake and Cove Hot Springs—provide opportunities for excursions. Nearby, a hiking trail tours one of the creek's upstream forks into the Eagle Cap Wilderness. Primitive North Fork Catherine Creek Campground, located at the trailhead, may appeal to tenters seeking a wilder camp setting.

NORTH FORK CATHERINE CREEK TRAIL

5.0 miles round trip (to the creek-
side meadow just within the Eagle
Cap Wilderness)
Elevation change: 700 feet
Trail condition: climbing, rock-
studded, earthen foot and horse
trail, with rock-hopping crossings
of side creeks
Moderate
Spring through fall

Access: From camp, go south about
3.0 miles on OR 203, and turn east
(left) onto Catherine Creek Lane
(FR 7785). Stay on the one-lane
gravel road to reach the North Fork
Catherine Creek campground and
trailhead, in 5.7 miles. (Because of a
short dry-season-only dirt segment,
the road is not recommended for
trailers and large RVs, but it is passable for conventional vehicles.)

This trail climbs a mostly open slope punctuated by ponderosa pine, rock outcrops, and stumps. Trailside plants include currant, lupine, larkspur, strawberry, yellow composites, and grasses.

Throughout much of the journey, the trail travels within the sound of, but not within sight of, the creek. Where the trail does offer views, hikers discover that the creek has a face much altered from the broad, smooth-pulsing stream of the valley floor.

Fir and spruce fill in the forest, but enough light penetrates to allow meadow plant species to thrive. A foot and horse bridge over the North Fork of Catherine Creek (at 1.5 miles) signals a brief, more steeply climbing stretch of trail ahead. The forest here affords more shade. In autumn, the few trailside huckleberry patches slow the berry lover.

At 2.1 miles, the trail crosses Chop Creek, and at 2.4 miles, it enters the Eagle Cap Wilderness, with the Jim Creek crossing immediately following.

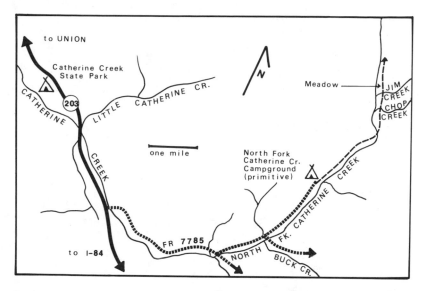

Both are rock-hopping or fording crossings. Above the Jim Creek confluence and just below the trail lies a long, scenic meadow, banking the clear-rippling North Fork of Catherine Creek—a pleasant day-hike ending. Side trails branch to the meadow, which parades some huge, shade-throwing cottonwoods, scattered fir, grasses, false helleborc, buttercup, waterleaf, and violets.

96 TWO COLOR CAMPGROUND

14 tent/trailer units
Standard service no fee campground
Nonflush toilets
Water
Open seasonally: mid-June through September
For information: La Grande Ranger District
Map: Wallowa–Whitman National Forest

Access: At Medical Springs on OR 203, turn southeast on Collins Road–Eagle Creek Drive and head toward Boulder Park. (The road soon becomes wide, good gravel surface.) In 1.6 miles, turn left onto FR 67. In another 13.5 miles, go north (left) on FR 77 to bear right on FR 7755 to reach the campground in 1.2 miles.

These informal pull-in sites occupy a forest–meadow bench above Eagle Creek—a wide, clear-rushing mountain stream with vegetated banks. Downfalls crisscross the creek. The campground serves as a gateway to the trails and stream fishing in the Eagle Cap Wilderness and the surrounding forest. The mountain lakes lie just out of reach for day hikers. Tamarack Campground, off FR 77, 0.6 mile east of the FR 67–FR 77 junction, offers 10 open-forest, formal pull-in sites above Eagle Creek.

Main Eagle Creek Trail

MAIN EAGLE CREEK TRAIL

5.7 miles round trip (to Copper Creek Falls)	Moderate
	Late spring through fall
Elevation change: 800 feet	Access: From Two Color Camp-
Trail condition: rock-studded;	ground, go 2.9 miles north on FR
slow, steady climbing	7755 to the trailhead.

This rerouted trail travels 0.25 mile along an abandoned road, skirting the landslide that scoured the wall of a nearby peak and altered the flow of Eagle Creek, broadening and slowing its stream and flooding the bases of living trees. A massive Engelmann spruce reigns trailside; forest and meadow interlock. From the valley floor, the trail provides wonderful views of the Wallowa ridges, including Hummingbird Mountain. Rugged granite peaks, evergreen spires, high-meadow shrubs, lingering snowfields, and seasonal falls contribute to the high-rise splendor.

Upstream from the first Eagle Creek bridge (at about 0.5 mile) lie two broad, fast-rushing cascades. From the bridge, the trail parallels the creek, alternately passing through forest and a deciduous shrub and tree corridor. Beware of nettles here. After entering the Eagle Cap Wilderness, the trail passes over several small side creeks to travel the length of two narrow meadows beside Eagle Creek. False hellebore and a myriad of wildflowers weave between the grasses.

Shortly after the second Eagle Creek bridge, ford Copper Creek (a broad waterway following snowmelt) to get a view of Copper Creek Falls. A short off-trail scramble upstream along Copper Creek via an informal path reveals an even better vista atop the rocks, below and alongside the unruly, tumbling torrent.

FAKE CREEK TRAIL

6.0 miles round trip (to the saddle)	Access: From camp, go 2.7 miles
Elevation change: 2,500 feet	north on FR 7755, and turn west
Trail condition: steep; rock-	onto FR 7755.090. Bear right to
studded, with some loose sand	reach the trailhead parking and a
Difficult	picnic area.
Late spring through fall	

This stamina tester begins by following narrow, rough FR 7755.090 uphill for 0.5 mile to the wilderness boundary. From there, a foot trail continues the ascent, traveling a mixed fir–ponderosa pine–larch forest and open meadow slopes, which afford early views of the landslide above Boulder Park. It then works its way toward and along the steep-flanked Little Boulder Creek Canyon. In places, streams of ponderosa pine cones spill along the trail. Grouse, deer, squirrels, grosbeaks, and bluebirds divert attention from the climb.

As the trail rounds the slope above Little Boulder Canyon, the vista broadens with each breath-stealing uphill spurt. The trail then contours and climbs the high-meadow headwater bowl to Little Boulder Creek. Aspen frame the feeding springs. Lupine, phlox, and Indian paintbrush dot the meadow.

Passing a false hellebore patch and a few white-bark pines, the trail tops a granite boulder knob, attaining views in all directions. The path grows faint in the meadow, requiring hikers to select their own uphill line to the saddle between Boulder and Little Boulder drainages. Attaining the remote saddle post—seemingly atop the world—visitors can look at the ridges disappearing into Idaho, rejoice in the Wallowa Mountain splendor, and measure the contrast between the snow- and ice-chiseled peaks nearby and the more arid slopes to the south and east. Winds lash the saddle, making eyes tear and adding to the wildness of the unspoiled view.

97 LAKE FORK CAMPGROUND

10 tent/trailer units
Standard service fee campground
Nonflush toilets
Water
Open seasonally: April through November
For information: Hells Canyon National Recreation Area
Map: Hells Canyon NRA

Access: From I-84 north of Baker City, take OR 86 east 52.0 miles to Halfway (where gas and services are available). From there, continue east on OR 86 toward Hells Canyon. In 9.7 miles, turn north on paved FR 39 and head toward Joseph to reach the campground in another 8.0 miles.

These well-spaced sites in a multistory fir–larch–pine forest along Lake Fork Creek invite shady rests at camp and provide a base for exploring the southwest end of the Hells Canyon NRA. Camper pastimes include hiking, fishing, swimming, and car touring of the Wallowa Mountain Scenic Loop (contact the Wallowa Mountains Visitor Center for tour highlights and information on road conditions). Continue east on OR 86 from the OR 86–FR 39 junction to reach an alternative campground, Copperfield Park, with seventy-two full-service, open sites along the Snake River.

LAKE FORK TRAIL

4.5 miles round trip (to Big Elk Creek)
Elevation change: 500 feet
Trail condition: good, gradually climbing path, sometimes dusty, with some protruding rocks

Moderate
Year-round
Access: Find the marked trailhead on the west side of FR 39 just north of the campground.

The trail begins with a quick climbing spurt to the bench above Lake Fork Creek. For the first third of the hike, it tours an open ponderosa pine–mixed fir forest with chest-high grasses interwoven with yarrow, salsify, bracken fern, and heart-leafed arnica. The area represents a transition zone between arid canyon grassland and mountain forest. Some magnificent yellow-bellied ponderosa pine intersperse the forest, while ancient cottonwoods reign creekside.

The trail travels above the creek, offering infrequent but exceptional views of the clear-coursing water spilling over rounded stones and forming deep pools. In late spring, hikers may flush families of grouse from the forest floor.

At 1.4 and 1.8 miles, the trail rounds exposed dry grassland slopes with balsam root and rainbow-colored wildflowers, rock outcrops, and scattered pines. These open sites offer views of Lake Fork and Big Elk creeks, respectively. From the slope at 1.8 miles, the trail briefly descends through shady forest to the Big Elk Creek fording. By fording the creek and staying to the left, hikers gain open vistas of the Lake Fork Creek canyon in another mile, for an alternative day-hike ending.

Copperfield Park Campground

HELLS CANYON TRAIL

4.0 miles round trip (to McGraw
Creek)
Elevation change: 200 feet
Trail condition: narrow, rolling,
sun-drenched, sometimes rocky, in
places overgrown
Easy to moderate
Year-round

Access: From the campground, return to OR 86, and go east to the
Snake River Canyon. At Copperfield Park, follow the narrow one-
lane gravel road north (downstream)
for 8.7 miles to the road's end and
the trailhead. The route is fine for
conventional vehicles, but there is
no formal parking or turnaround
site; park at the side of the road.

An easy fence crossing begins the hike, a tour of the arid west bank of the
Snake River between 5 and 70 feet above the waterway. Sumac, sage, wild rose,
bitterbrush, thistle, and poison ivy (in moister areas) are among the species
vegetating the slope. Wildflowers lend a spray of color. Deer may be seen
making their way to the water at the edges of day.

The Idaho side sports dry hillsides with rocky crags and summits and
green, shrub-filled drainages. In July, the fins of spawning carp slice the water's
surface; great splashes draw attention to the river. The Snake River is not free-
flowing here but part of Hells Canyon Reservoir, with boat traffic common.

The trail tags small Nelson Creek, proceeds through a gate (be sure to
resecure it after passing through), and rounds a slope of lichen-etched rocks en
route to McGraw Creek (2.0 miles). McGraw Creek boasts a more prominent
canyon with black cliffs, a jagged skyline, grassland, and crags. A delta forms
at the mouth, as McGraw Creek empties into a quiet reservoir arm. A canted
footbridge allows for a continuation of the hike, but a thick rush of vegetation,
including a bounty of poison ivy, may deny an approach to Spring Creek (3.0
miles). Spring Creek occupies the large canyon that has been in sight since the
hike began. A creek fording is required to continue the riverside tour from
there. A rock slide prohibits any river-trail hiking beyond Leep Creek.

SOUTHEAST CANYONLANDS

Oregon's southeast canyonlands promise to be a wilderness stronghold for the future. Their remoteness, the absence of population centers, the scarcity of improved roads, and the seasonally controlled access on most other routes—rather than legislative process—provide the region's present protection. But for any willing to bear the inconvenience that accompanies a visit to this remote land, a desert-canyon cache awaits: solitude, a humbling expanse, and a raw, quieting beauty.

A well-tuned vehicle, a full gas tank, water, and a shade source are the explorer's friends. Before striking out from tried routes, check with the BLM regarding road conditions, and purchase an area map to smooth the way to a fun outing. In this great expanse of public lands, signs remain few (although new budgets call for their installation), and service centers and passersby are far spread. Monitoring the weather report is also advisable, as sudden heavy rains can prolong a back-country visit.

The field of discovery is vast and varied, with lava flows, canyonlands, painted badlands, basalt rims, and scrubland. Only a few juniper dot the expanse. Coffeepot Crater, a wilderness proposal site northeast of Jordan, is a volcanic funland of lava flows, spatter cones, and tubes. Slicing through this forgotten corner of the state is the Owyhee Wild and Scenic River, which has a limited though prized rafting season in April and May.

Sandy washes form natural dry-season trails through this region's extraordinary canyonlands. Jeep trails and wagon roads of old provide other avenues of exploration. Golden eagles, wild horses, beaver, otter, mule deer, bighorn sheep, quail, chukar, bats, and coyotes are among the wildlife species.

Leslie Gulch

Petroglyphs and artifacts found in caves date early Indians in this area as far back as 12,000 years. The Oregon Trail crossed this corner, leaving an imprint on the land but leaving behind few pioneers. Prospectors found gold here in 1863.

Basque shepherds followed, to claim a share of the open range.

Spring and fall offer comfortable stays. Visitors should beware of and prepare for the hazards: springtime ticks, snakes, summer heat, and creekside poison ivy. Uncommonly fine stargazing caps a day in this isolated region. ■

Snively Hot Springs

98 LAKE OWYHEE STATE PARK

40 tent/trailer units (10 electrical)
Standard service fee campground
Flush toilets; showers
Water
Open seasonally: mid-April
through late October
For information: State Parks, La
Grande Regional Office

Map: Oregon State
Access: From Nyssa, go south on
OR 201 and turn west at Owyhee
Corners (or at the junction just
north of Adrian) to follow Owyhee
Reservoir Road south to the camp-
ground. Total distance is about
33.0 miles; signs mark the route.

V. W. McCormack Campground offers deciduous-shaded, lawn-separated sites above Lake Owyhee—Oregon's longest reservoir, stretching some 53.0 miles. Dramatic red-orange, multihued canyon walls embrace this artificial lake, with its varying widths of 1.0 to 7.0 miles. The fluted cliffs, imposing basalt rim, and irregular-shaped turrets and spires captivate artist and photographer. Below camp, a rocky shore grades to beach when the water level is low. Camp facilities include a fish-cleaning station, a boat launch, and a dock. South of the camp, on Owyhee Reservoir Road, lies a resort with a boat rental service.

SNIVELY HOT SPRINGS

Public access, primitive, no facilities
For information: BLM, Vale District
Access: From camp, go north on Owyhee Reservoir Road about

15.0 miles. The hot springs occupy a cottonwood grove on the east (right) side of the road. A short dirt side road provides access to the unmarked site.

Riverside hot springs feed these informal, rock-rimmed Owyhee River–edge pools, which blend the cool river current and the hot, steamy bath. Jagged pink volcanic cliffs tower above the setting. Aged cottonwood trees offer shady retreats. In early evening hours, nighthawks entertain with a swooping aerial display. Beware of poison ivy amid the understory plants.

KEENEY PASS–OREGON TRAIL REMNANT

Interpretive site, historic marker
For information: BLM, Vale District
Access: From camp, go north on Owyhee Reservoir Road, and

continue north on the indicated roads toward Vale. The marked site is located on the west (left) side of Lytle Boulevard.

Along the route to Keeney Pass, Oregon Trail markers (3-foot-tall white posts) dot the roadside of present-day Lytle Boulevard, which crisscrosses the historic overland route. Wagon-wheel impressions remain locked in the earth, still visible though overgrown by sagebrush and grass. Nearly 4.0 miles of the Oregon Trail remain detectable and walkable, south of the Keeney Pass Historic Site. Near the kiosk display, on the south side of the pass, the wagon ruts have eroded into a U-shaped gully.

North of Keeney Pass, signs indicating the route to Henderson Grave locate another historic site, where an Oregon pioneer tragically died of thirst, unaware that the Malheur River lay within easy striking distance. The original stone bearing the etched notice of Henderson's death rests amid the boulders on the east side of the gravel road, along with a modern-day marker.

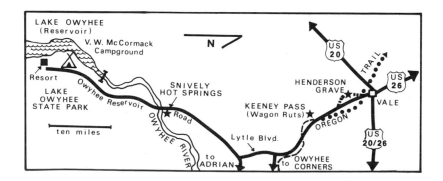

99 SUCCOR CREEK STATE PARK

19 tent units (camper or small trailer OK)
Standard service fee campground
Nonflush toilets
Water
Open seasonally: mid-April through late October
For information: State Parks, La Grande Regional Office

Map: Oregon State
Access: From OR 201 8.0 miles south of Adrian, go southwest 15.0 miles on Succor Creek Road to the campground. The route is on good two-lane, gravel surface, which becomes one lane.

The campsites with small planted trees for shade line both sides of Succor Creek, which flows through a beautiful, often dramatic canyonland with high rugged cliffs and spires. Dry grass and sagebrush spill between the canyon walls and climb the slopes. No formal hiking trails exist, but the natural playground of the canyon invites cross-country exploration. Jeep trails offer tried routes. As always, in desert-canyon country, be wary of hand placements and look where you plan to sit or stride. Such areas call for common sense, not alarm.

SUCCOR CREEK HIKE

1.5 miles round trip
Elevation change: minimal
Trail condition: old jeep and cow trails

Easy
Late spring through fall
Access: The hike begins across the bridge, amid the east-bank sites.

An easy 0.75-mile walk traces the east bank of gurgling Succor Creek upstream to the mouth of a gorge. From here, one may continue exploring the narrow passage, wading between the banks—a welcome hardship in this sun-baked canyon country. Deep, clear pools invite a refreshing dip but are not large enough for swimming. Vertical canyon walls provide shade. Golden eagles patrol overhead, quail rustle in the brush, and rock doves generate a continuous, echoing chorus of coos from their cliff-hollow roosts.

By following the east bank of Succor Creek downstream, hikers find a simple climb to the top of a low saddle with flowing grasses. The destination holds beckoning views of Succor Creek Canyon and the National Back Country Byway (at about 0.3 mile).

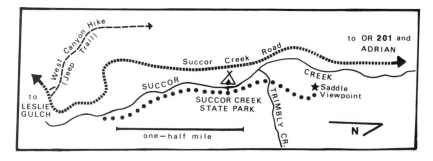

Succor Creek Canyon

WEST CANYON HIKE

2.5 miles round trip
Elevation change: 200 feet
Trail condition: old jeep trail or
cross-country
Moderate to difficult
Late spring through fall

Access: From camp, continue south (upstream) along Succor Creek Road for about 1.0 mile to where the road flattens out. Hike one of the jeep roads heading west, or select your own route up and over the grassy slope passing between the rock walls of the road's west side.

For the investment of a relatively short climb, hikers gain views of a second rugged canyon, with a broad grassland floor. The rock arches, windows, and jagged skyline spires, pinnacles, and shields invite closer inspection. Shadow-and-light play animates the rock. Deer may be seen at the edges of day as they thread their way to the refreshment of Succor Creek. Chukars sound from their low rock perches. Spring wildflowers bring splendor to the arid landscape.

SUCCOR CREEK–LESLIE GULCH NATIONAL BACK COUNTRY BYWAY

52.0 miles one way
Road quality: winding, good gravel or dirt, some washboard
Estimated speed: 15 to 25 mph (dictated by scenery as much as by road conditions).

Access: Go 8.0 miles south from Adrian on OR 201 and turn southwest onto Succor Creek Road.

The green ribbon of tree-lined Succor Creek offers eye-catching contrast to the dry grass and sage land at the beginning of this journey. A third of the way into the tour is the canyon country of the state parklands. Cliffs of red, orange, tan, buff, and black line the route. Each road bend brings wonder.

From Succor Creek Road, the byway tour turns west (right) onto Leslie Gulch Road, which succeeds in topping all that has passed before it in drama, hue, and surprises. Massive flows and dikes, fissures, and elemental sculpting create a canyon rich in character. Scanning the skyline with binoculars may bring the bonus of a bighorn sheep sighting. The byway tour ends at the Owyhee Reservoir boat launch.

100 LESLIE GULCH CAMPGROUND

6 to 8 informal tent/camper units
Primitive no fee campground
Nonflush toilets
No water
Open seasonally: dry-weather destination
For information: BLM, Vale District
Map: Oregon State

Access: This campground is about 45.0 miles southwest of Adrian via Succor Creek–Leslie Gulch National Back Country Byway (see trip 99). From OR 201 8.0 miles south of Adrian, go southwest on Succor Creek Road to Leslie Gulch Road. Then follow Leslie Gulch Road west to Owyhee Reservoir, the boat launch, and the campground.

Named for Silver City pioneer Hiram Leslie, who was struck by lightning here in 1882, Leslie Gulch unfolds the beauty of volcanic ash carved by erosion, offers one of the few accesses to Oregon's longest reservoir (some 53.0 miles), and captures the isolation and romance of the wilderness. The shadeless campground—virtually a large, open parking area—occupies the flat at the mouth of Slocum Gulch. Improvised shade sources and swimming in the reservoir ease the passage of midday. The canyon washes provide natural avenues to explore for morning and evening outings. At night, bats scour the canyons for insects, coyotes moan at the moon, and a sparkling showcase peppers the sky.

SLOCUM GULCH HIKE

3.5 miles round trip
Elevation change: 400 feet
Trail condition: sandy canyon wash
Easy

Spring through fall
Access: From camp, enter the
canyon mouth.

An artichoke-shaped rock with folded plates of red and orange hues guards the canyon entrance. The trail winds inland, passing multicolored slopes, bunchgrass hillsides, and isolated rock features to probe a rich amber-gold canyon with honeycomb walls. What first appears to be a unified wall later reveals itself to be a series of rock plates and shields separated by narrow gorges and channels. The best time to tour the canyon is early evening, when the soft lighting accents the golden hues. The turnaround point for this hike is at 1.75 miles, where the canyon splits. Golden eagles, jackrabbits, and chukars are common sightings. Bighorn sheep may also be seen by the keen observer.

JUNIPER GULCH HIKE

2.0 miles round trip
Elevation change: 400 feet
Trail condition: sandy canyon wash
Easy
Spring through fall

Access: From camp, go east about
3.0 miles on Leslie Gulch Road,
passing Timber and Dago gulches
to arrive at Juniper Gulch and its
trailhead, on the left (north) side of
the road.

Juniper Gulch is one of the area's four primary viewing sites for bighorn sheep (along with Spring Creek, Leslie, and Slocum gulches). Gold, red, and white cliffs immediately frame the trail; a desert varnish streaks their faces. This narrow canyon boasts windows, pockmarked walls, and rock ledges. Junipers punctuate the sagebrush slopes and wash edge.

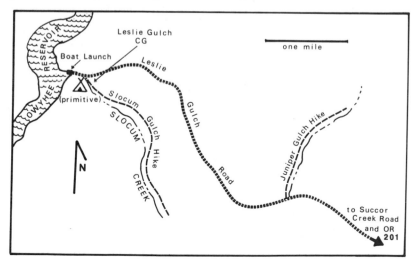

At 0.75 mile, a boulder jumble seemingly blocks the route, but by skirting around the right side, one can continue the wash hike. An intermittent, light trickle of water attracts canyon wildlife. At 1.0 mile, the canyon walls pinch together. From here, one can continue threading up Juniper Gulch or climb the slope for a canyon overview. Side canyons along the way hold additional adventure. Spring wildflowers adorn the rock niches.

101 THREE FORKS AREA

4 to 6 informal tent units
Primitive no fee camp area (four-wheel-drive destination)
No facilities
No water
Open seasonally: dry-weather destination
For information: BLM, Vale District
Map: Oregon State

Access: From US 95 about 14.0 miles west of Jordan Valley, go 35.0 miles south on Three Forks Road (a one-lane dirt road), following signs to the river destination. The final 2.0 miles recommend a four-wheel-drive or high-clearance vehicle. It's a steep rim descent via narrow road with rough sections of raised basalt.

The remoteness of this wild pocket of beauty and history calls to the adventurous. At the site of a former cabin, amid tall flowing grasses, are places to pitch a tent. Here, the Middle and North forks feed the main stem of the Owyhee River as it spills from the mouth of a narrow canyon. A sandy beach accesses a wide, deep pool at the convergence. The pool's sand and pebble bottom and unbelievable water clarity further recommend it as a swimming hole—one shared with the bass. Other wildlife sightings may include raptors, coyotes, and river otters. Old military wagon roads traverse the area. The overgrown foundation of the onetime fort occupies the grassy flat, but it is difficult to find.

MILITARY WAGON ROAD HIKE

4.0 miles round trip
Elevation change: minimal
Trail condition: in places overgrown, some wading required (old sneakers are recommended)

Moderate
Late spring through fall
Access: Below the cabin, ford the convergence of the Middle and North forks.

Time has reclaimed the first road fragment, so the hike begins by wading the tall river grasses to reach the foot of the sagebrush slope. Rounding the slope for the upstream trek reveals a weathered gate frame near the mouth of the canyon. Beyond the gate, along the left wall of the canyon, the rock-reinforced remnant of the old military wagon road presents itself.

This historic path is the guide to a spectacular river tour, enfolded by the steep red-brown cliffs. Still pools, reflections, shallow caves, sloping sandy beaches riddled with otter tracks, and the playful culprits themselves are among the highlights.

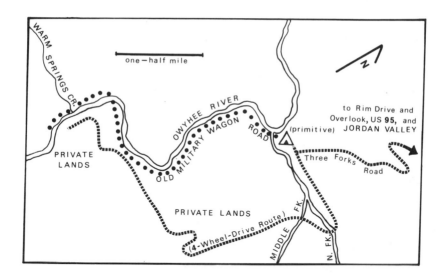

At 1.25 miles, the wagon road again dies, approaching the site of some driftwood rubble. Leaving the rubble site, cow trails lead the way to a large sandbar and the river's edge—the hike's end. The rock-reinforced wagon road resumes on the opposite shore, but it travels private property; return as you came.

OWYHEE CANYON OVERLOOK–RIM DRIVE

16.0 miles one way (from US 95 to the overlook)
Road quality: good, one-lane dirt road (passable for conventional vehicles)

Estimated speed: 20 to 30 mph
Access: Take the route described in the Military Wagon Road hike to the campground from US 95. The overlook lies 19.0 miles northwest of camp.

From US 95, the road to the overlook and camp area crosses an arid plain to travel the rim of the Owyhee River Canyon. Along the way, visitors may see wildlife near the small, scattered watering holes of the open expanse. Owyhee Canyon Overlook offers startling views of the imposing vertical black-basalt cliffs dropping some 1,000 feet to the canyon floor. The green ribbon of the Owyhee River threads the narrow canyon. This dark chasm commands awe. Atop the rim, the sage flat allows easy walking, but the heat rising from the canyon basalt can be intense. Carry plenty of water, and wear a hat.

ADDRESSES

Alsea Ranger District, 18591 Alsea Highway, Alsea, OR 97324; (503) 487-5811

Baker Ranger District, Route 1, Box 1, Pocahontas Road, Baker City, OR 97814; (503) 523-6391

Bear Valley Ranger District, 528 East Main Street, John Day, OR 97845; (503) 575-2110

Bend Ranger District, 1230 NE 3rd, Bend, OR 97701; (503) 388-5664

Big Summit Ranger District, 348855 Ochoco Ranger Station, Prineville, OR 97754; (503) 447-9645

Blue River Ranger District, Blue River, OR 97413; (503) 822-3317

Boardman Park, P.O. Box 8, Boardman, OR 97818; (503) 481-7217

Bonneville Dam, U.S. Army Corps of Engineers, Cascade Locks, OR 97014; (503) 374-8820

Burns District BLM, HC 74-12533 Highway 20 West, Hines, OR 97738; (503) 573-5241

Butte Falls Ranger District, P.O. Box 227, Butte Falls, OR 97522; (503) 865-3581

Cape Perpetua Visitor Center, P.O. Box 274, Yachats, OR 97498; (503) 547-3289

Chemult Ranger District, P.O. Box 150, Chemult, OR 97731; (503) 365-2229

Chetco Ranger District, 555 5th Street, Brookings, OR 97415; (503) 469-2196

Chiloquin Ranger District, P.O. Box 357, Chiloquin, OR 97624; (503) 783-2221

Clackamas Ranger District, 61431 East Highway 224, Estacada, OR 97023; (503) 630-4256

Clatsop County Parks, 1100 Olney Avenue, Astoria, OR 97103; (503) 325-8631

Columbia Gorge Ranger District, 31520 SE Woodard Road, Troutdale, OR 97060; (503) 695-2276

Cottage Grove Ranger District, 78405 Cedar Park Road, Cottage Grove, OR 97424; (503) 942-5591

Crater Lake Lodge Company, P.O. Box 128, Crater Lake, OR 97604; (503) 594-2511

Crater Lake National Park, P.O. Box 7, Crater Lake, OR 97604; (503) 594-2211

Detroit Ranger District, HC 73, Box 320, Mill City, OR 97360; (503) 854-3366

Diamond Lake Ranger District, HC 60, Box 101, Idleyld Park, OR 97447; (503) 498-2531

Eagle Cap Ranger District, P.O. Box 270A, Enterprise, OR 97828; (503) 426-4978

Eugene District BLM, 1255 Pearl Street, Eugene, OR 97401; (503) 683-6600

Fort Rock Ranger District, 1230 NE 3rd, Bend, OR 97701; (503) 388-5674

Galice Ranger District, 1465 NE 7th Street, Grants Pass, OR 97526; (503) 476-3830

Gold Beach Ranger District, 1225 South Ellensburg—Box 7, Gold Beach, OR 97444; (503) 247-6651

Hart Mountain National Antelope Refuge, P.O. Box 111, Lakeview, OR 97630; (503) 947-3315

Hebo Ranger District, Hebo, OR 97122; (503) 392-3161

Hells Canyon National Recreation Area, P.O. Box 270A, Enterprise, OR 97828;
(503) 426-4978

Hood River Ranger District, 6780 Highway 35 South, Mt. Hood–Parkdale, OR 97041;
(503) 352-6002

Illinois Valley Ranger District, 26568 Redwood Highway, Cave Junction, OR 97523;
(503) 592-2166

John Day Fossil Beds Headquarters, 420 West Main, John Day, OR 97845;
(503) 987-2333

Klamath Ranger District, 1936 California Avenue, Klamath Falls, OR 97601;
(503) 883-6824

La Grande Ranger District, Route 2, Box 2108, La Grande, OR 97850; (503) 963-7186

Lakeview District BLM, 1000 9th Street South, Lakeview, OR 97630;
(503) 947-2177

Lakeview Ranger District, HC 64, Box 60, Lakeview, OR 97630; (503) 947-3334

Long Creek Ranger District, 528 East Main Street, John Day, OR 97845;
(503) 575-2110

Lowell Ranger District, 60 South Pioneer, Lowell, OR 97452; (503) 937-2129

Malheur National Wildlife Refuge, HC 72, Box 245, Princeton, OR 97721;
(503) 493-2612

Mapleton Ranger District, Mapleton, OR 97453; (503) 268-4473

McKenzie Ranger District, McKenzie Bridge, OR 97413; (503) 822-3381

Medford District BLM, 3040 Biddle Road, Medford, OR 97504; (503) 770-2200

North Fork John Day Ranger District, P.O. Box 158, Ukiah, OR 97880;
(503) 427-3231

North Umpqua Ranger District, 18782 North Umpqua Highway, Glide, OR 97443,
(503) 496-3532

Oakridge Ranger District, 46375 Highway 58, Westfir, OR 97492; (503) 782-2291

Oregon Caves National Monument, 19000 Caves Highway, Cave Junction, OR 97523;
(503) 592-2100

Oregon Department of Fish and Wildlife, 2501 SW 1st Avenue, Portland, OR 97207;
(503) 229-5400

Oregon Department of Fish and Wildlife, Forest Grove, 801 Gales Creek Road,
Forest Grove, OR 97116; (503) 357-2191

Oregon Department of Forestry, Forest Grove, 801 Gales Creek Road,
Forest Grove, OR 97116; (503) 357-2191

Oregon Dunes National Recreation Area, 855 Highway Avenue, Reedsport, OR 97467;
(503) 271-3611

Oxbow Park, 3010 SE Oxbow Parkway, Gresham, OR 97080; (503) 663-4708

Paisley Ranger District, P.O. Box 67, Paisley, OR 97636; (503) 943-3114

Pine Ranger District, General Delivery, Halfway, OR 97834; (503) 742-7511

Powers Ranger District, Powers, OR 97466; (503) 439-3011

Prairie City Ranger District, 327 Southwest Front Street, Prairie City, OR 97869;
(503) 820-3311

Prineville District BLM, 185 East 4th Street, Prineville, OR 97754; (503) 447-4115

Prineville Ranger District, 2321 East 3rd, Prineville, OR 97754; (503) 447-9641

Prospect Ranger District, Prospect, OR 97536; (503) 560-3623

Refuge Headquarters, Umatilla National Wildlife Refuge, P.O. Box 239,
Umatilla, OR 97882; (503) 922-3232

Rigdon Ranger District, 49098 Salmon Creek Road, Oakridge, OR 97463; (503) 782-2283

Roseburg District BLM, 777 NW Garden Valley Blvd., Roseburg, OR 97470 (503) 672-4491

Salem District BLM, 1717 Fabry Road SE, Salem, OR 97306; (503) 375-5646

Sea Lion Caves, 91560 Highway 101, Florence, OR 97439; (503) 547-3111

Sisters Ranger District, P.O. Box 249, Sisters, OR 97759; (503) 549-2111

South Slough National Estuarine Reserve, P.O. Box 5417, Charleston, OR 97420; (503) 888-5558

Star Ranger Station, 6941 Upper Applegate Road, Jacksonville, OR 97530; (503) 899-1812

State Parks and Recreation Division, Salem, 525 Trade Street SE, Salem, OR 97310; (503) 378-6305

State Parks, Bend Regional Office, P.O. Box 5309, Bend, OR 97708; (503) 388-6211

State Parks, Coos Bay Regional Office, 365 North 4th Street, Ste. A, Coos Bay, OR 97420; (503) 269-9410

State Parks, La Grande Regional Office, P.O. Box 850, La Grande, OR 97850; (503) 963-3803

State Parks, Portland Regional Office, 3554 SE 82nd Avenue, Portland, OR 97266; (503) 238-7491

State Parks, Tillamook Regional Office, 416 Pacific, Tillamook, OR 97141; (503) 842-5501

Sweet Home Ranger District, 3225 Highway 20, Sweet Home, OR 97386; (503) 367-5168

U.S. Army Corps of Engineers, Walla Walla District, Walla Walla, WA 99362; (509) 522-6713

Vale District BLM, 100 Oregon Street, Vale, OR 97918; (503) 473-3144

Waldport Ranger District, Waldport, OR 97394; (503) 563-3211

Walla Walla (Washington) Ranger District, 1415 West Rose Avenue, Walla Walla, WA 99362; (509) 522-6290

Wallowa Lake Tramway, Route 1, Box 349, Joseph, OR 97846; (503) 432-5331

Wallowa Mountains Visitor Center, Route 1, Box 270A, Enterprise, OR 97828; (503) 426-4978

Zigzag Ranger District, 70220 East Highway 26, Zigzag, OR 97049; (503) 622-3191

INDEX

Salem, Oregon, residents Rhonda (author) and George (photographer)
Ostertag have spent more than a decade hiking extensively in the western states.
Rhonda is a free-lance writer specializing in travel, outdoor recreation, and
nature topics. George has participated in several environmental-impact studies,
including the California Desert Bill. The Ostertags have been published in *The
Los Angeles Times, Newsday, Backpacker,* and more. They are the author/
photographer team of *50 Hikes in Oregon's Coast Range and Siskiyous* (The
Mountaineers).